Critical Luxury Studies

Technicities

Series Editors: John Armitage, Ryan Bishop and Joanne Roberts, Winchester School of Art, University of Southampton

The philosophy of technicities: exploring how technology mediates art, frames design and augments the mediated collective perception of everyday life.
Technicities will publish the latest philosophical thinking about our increasingly immaterial technocultural conditions, with a unique focus on the context of art, design and media.

Editorial Advisory Board
Benjamin Bratton, Cheryl Buckley, Sean Cubitt, Clive Dilnot, Jin Huimin, Arthur Kroker, Geert Lovink, Scott McQuire, Gunalan Nadarajan, Elin O'Hara Slavick, Li Shqiao, Geoffrey Winthrop-Young

Titles available in the series
Lyotard and the Inhuman Condition: Reflections on Nihilism, Information and Art
    By Ashley Woodward

Critical Luxury Studies: Art, Design, Media
    Edited by John Armitage and Joanne Roberts

Forthcoming Titles
Cold War Legacies: Systems, Theory, Aesthetics
    Edited by John Beck and Ryan Bishop

Fashion and Materialism
    By Ulrich Lehmann

Critical Luxury Studies

Art, Design, Media

Edited by John Armitage and
Joanne Roberts

EDINBURGH
University Press

Edinburgh University Press is one of the leading university presses in the UK. We publish academic books and journals in our selected subject areas across the humanities and social sciences, combining cutting-edge scholarship with high editorial and production values to produce academic works of lasting importance. For more information visit our website: www.edinburghuniversitypress.com

Edinburgh University Press Ltd
The Tun – Holyrood Road, 12(2f) Jackson's Entry, Edinburgh EH8 8PJ

First published in hardback by Edinburgh University Press 2016

Typeset in Adode Sabon by
Servis Filmsetting Ltd, Stockport, Cheshire,
and printed and bound in Great Britain by
CPI Group (UK) Ltd, Croydon CR0 4YY

A CIP record for this book is available from the British Library

ISBN 978 1 4744 0261 3 (hardback)
ISBN 978 1 4744 2582 7 (paperback)
ISBN 978 1 4744 0262 0 (webready PDF)
ISBN 978 1 4744 0487 7 (epub)

Contents

List of Figures

List of Tables

Series Editors' Preface

Technological transformation has profound and frequently unforeseen influences on art, design and media. At times technology emancipates art and enriches the quality of design. Occasionally it causes acute individual and collective problems of mediated perception. Time after time technological change accomplishes both simultaneously. This new book series explores and reflects philosophically on what new and emerging *technicities* do to our everyday lives and increasingly immaterial technocultural conditions. Moving beyond traditional conceptions of the philosophy of technology and of techne, the series presents new philosophical thinking on how technology constantly alters the essential conditions of beauty, invention and communication. From novel understandings of the world of technicity to new interpretations of aesthetic value, graphics and information, *Technicities* focuses on the relationships between critical theory and representation, the arts, broadcasting, print, technological genealogics/histories, material culture and digital technologies, and our philosophical views of the world of art, design and media.

The series foregrounds contemporary work in art, design and media whilst remaining inclusive, both in terms of philosophical perspectives on technology and interdisciplinary contributions. For a philosophy of technicities is crucial to extant debates over the artistic, inventive and informational aspects of technology. The books in the *Technicities* series concentrate on present-day and evolving technological advances, but visual, design-led and mass-mediated questions are emphasised to further our knowledge of their often-combined means of digital transformation.

The editors of *Technicities* welcome proposals for monographs and well-considered edited collections that establish new paths of investigation.

Acknowledgements

We would like to acknowledge the help of all the people involved in the production of *Critical Luxury Studies: Art, Design, Media*, and, more specifically, our *Technicities* series co-editor Ryan Bishop and our editor at Edinburgh University Press, Carol MacDonald. We also gratefully appreciate the support that we received to complete this book from the Faculty of Business, Law and Art's Strategic Research Fund at the University of Southampton and from Winchester School of Art. Lastly, we would like to thank all the contributors to this volume for their hard work, good humour and sharing their expert knowledge of critical luxury studies.

John Armitage and Joanne Roberts

Notes on Contributors

John Armitage is Professor of Media Arts and Co-Director of the Winchester Luxury Research Group at Winchester School of Art, University of Southampton, United Kingdom. His research interests include luxury and visual culture, cultural and media theory, the work of Paul Virilio, new media art, continental philosophy and the critical theory of technology. John is the founder and co-editor, with Ryan Bishop and Douglas Kellner, of the Duke University Press journal *Cultural Politics* and has published articles in a variety of academic journals, including *Journal of Visual Culture, Theory, Culture & Society* and *CTheory*. He is the author, editor and co-editor of twelve books. His latest sole-authored book is *Virilio for Architects* (Routledge, 2015).

Christopher J. Berry is Professor (Emeritus) of Political Theory and Honorary Professorial Research Fellow at the University of Glasgow. A leading international scholar of the Scottish Enlightenment, he is the author of six books and recently co-edited *The Oxford Handbook of Adam Smith* (Oxford University Press, 2013). His *The Idea of Luxury* (Cambridge, 1994) has had widespread influence both outside and inside academia and has appeared in a Chinese translation (Century Press, 2005). He is an elected Fellow of the Royal Society of Edinburgh (Scotland's 'national academy').

Mary Breheny is a senior lecturer in the School of Public Health and researcher in the Health and Ageing Research Team at Massey University, New Zealand. Her research interests focus on understanding how social and economic issues intertwine to influence health and well-being across the life course. In particular, she is interested in the ways that inequalities throughout the lifespan accumulate in later life and constrain older people from ageing well. Mary has published articles in a wide range of international journals, including

Ageing & Society, *Journal of Aging Studies* and *Qualitative Research in Psychology*.

Jonathan Faiers is Reader in Fashion Theory, Winchester School of Art, University of Southampton, and his research examines the interface between popular culture, textiles and dress. His publications include *Tartan* (Berg, 2008) and *Dressing Dangerously: Dysfunctional Fashion in Film* (Yale University Press, 2013). Recently he has written essays for *Alexander McQueen* (V&A, 2015), *Developing Dress History: New Directions in Method and Practice* (Bloomsbury, 2015) and *London Couture 1923–1975: British Luxury* (V&A, 2015). In 2014 Jonathan launched *Luxury: History, Culture, Consumption* (Taylor & Francis Routledge), the first peer-reviewed, academic journal to investigate this globally contested term, and he is a founding member of the Winchester Luxury Research Group.

Mike Featherstone is Professor of Sociology at Goldsmiths, University of London. He is founding editor of the journal *Theory, Culture & Society* and the Theory, Culture & Society Book Series, and editor-in-chief of the journal *Body & Society*. His books include *Consumer Culture and Postmodernism* (Sage, 2nd edn 2007), *Undoing Culture: Globalization, Postmodernism and Identity* (Sage, 1995) and, as co-author, *Surviving Middle Age* (Blackwell, 1982). He is the editor of over a dozen books and author of numerous journal articles and book chapters on social and cultural theory, consumer and global culture, ageing and the body. His books and articles have been translated into sixteen languages.

Iain Hay is Matthew Flinders Distinguished Professor of Geography at Flinders University, South Australia. He is author or editor of ten books including *Qualitative Research Methods in Human Geography* (Oxford, 4th edition 2016) and *Handbook on Wealth and the Super-Rich* (Elgar, 2016, with Jonathan Beaverstock). He was recently editor-in-chief of *Geographical Research* and has had other editorial roles with journals including *Applied Geography, Ethics, Place and Environment* and *Social and Cultural Geography*. In 2006, Iain received the Prime Minister's Award for Australian University Teacher of the Year and in 2014 was admitted as a Fellow of the Academy of Social Sciences (UK).

Ulrich Lehmann, who studied philosophy, sociology, modern languages and the history of art in Frankfurt a.M., Paris and London, is

Associate Professor in Interdisciplinary Art and Design at The New School in New York and Honorary Research Fellow at the Victoria and Albert Museum, London. His research interests can be grouped into two areas: the histories of material culture in Europe from the 1780s to 1850, and the meaning and materiality of contemporary design.

Juliana Mansvelt is an associate professor in Human Geography in the School of People, Environment and Planning, Massey University. Her research interests centre on the geographies of everyday life, specifically the ways in which life-courses, mobilities, identity and well-being are shaped in relation to consumption practices and choices. Juliana is author of *Geographies of Consumption* (Sage, 2005), editor of *Green Consumerism: An A–Z Guide* (Sage, 2011) and co-editor of *Engaging Geographies: Landscapes, Lifecourses and Mobilities* (Cambridge Scholars Publishing, 2014). She has published in a variety of academic journals including *Area, Ageing & Society* and *Progress in Human Geography*.

Joanne Roberts is Professor in Arts and Cultural Management and Director of the Winchester Luxury Research Group at Winchester School of Art, University of Southampton, United Kingdom. Her research interests include knowledge management, innovation, creativity and luxury. Joanne has published articles in a wide range of international journals, including *Journal of Management Studies, Journal of Business Ethics* and *Research Policy*. Additionally, she has authored and edited a number of books. Her latest sole-authored book is *A Very Short, Fairly Interesting and Reasonably Cheap Book about Knowledge Management* (Sage, 2015).

Agnès Rocamora is a Reader in Social and Cultural Studies at the London College of Fashion, University of the Arts London. She is the author of *Fashioning the City: Paris, Fashion and the Media* (I. B. Tauris, 2009). Her writing on the field of fashion and on the fashion media has appeared in a broad range of international journals including *Fashion Theory, Journalism Practice* and *Sociology*. She is a co-editor of *Thinking Through Fashion: A Guide to Key Theorists, The Handbook of Fashion Studies* and *Fashion Media: Past and Present*. She is also a co-editor of the *International Journal of Fashion Studies*.

Thomaï Serdari is Adjunct Associate Professor of Marketing at the Leonard N. Stern School of Business, New York University, where she leads the Luxury Marketing specialisation in the MBA program. Her research interests include entrepreneurship, creativity, art and luxury as it applies to all fields of production. Thomaï is co-editor of the journal *Luxury: History, Culture, Consumption*.

Adam Sharr is the author or editor of six books on architecture including *Heidegger's Hut* (MIT Press, 2006), *Reading Architecture and Culture* (Routledge, 2012) and *Demolishing Whitehall: Leslie Martin, Harold Wilson and the Architecture of White Heat* (with Stephen Thornton, Ashgate, 2013). He is Professor of Architecture at Newcastle University, Principal of Adam Sharr Architects, editor-in-chief of *arq: Architectural Research Quarterly* (Cambridge) and series editor of Thinkers for Architects (Routledge).

Chapter 1

Critical Luxury Studies: Defining a Field

John Armitage and Joanne Roberts

In this opening chapter of *Critical Luxury Studies: Art, Design, Media*, our first task is to introduce and define the philosophical concept of luxury and the challenges of studying this seemingly ubiquitous idea. Using the example of the 'city of pigs', from Plato's *The Republic*, we delineate the key themes of luxury studies, including beliefs about necessity and morality.

Of course, there is an extant and contemporary literature concerning the investigation of luxury. Our second task is therefore to consider this literature. Beginning with a survey of the concept of luxury in Western thought, we then document its 'moralisation' and 'de-moralisation', before reflecting on luxury in its historical context from the eighteenth century onwards. Subsequently, we examine the contemporary literature on luxury, which is primarily concerned with luxury brand management.

Yet, as indicated in the title of *Critical Luxury Studies: Art, Design, Media*, ours is a critical view of luxury. Our third task, therefore, is to set out our own perspective on what we call 'critical luxury studies'. Indeed, our project is nothing less than an attempt to define an entirely new field of research. We begin by differentiating the idea of critique from ostensibly similar terms, such as criticism. This is important because, for us, critical luxury studies is not a static entity but a dynamic process. Moreover, critical luxury studies has a specific political and philosophical dimension that is crucially linked to the cultural politics of academic disciplinarity. For us, it matters a great deal that critical luxury studies is defined in relation to the important disciplines of art, design and media. For these reasons, we are concerned with luxury as 'cultural capital' and with the ever-shifting attitudes towards luxury as both a subject of study and a socio-cultural practice. These subjects and practices are especially important in a world of 'austerity' where food banks and Ferraris coexist in close proximity. None of this is meant to deny the pleasure we all feel with regard to the experiences associated with luxuries, such as viewing an Andy Warhol diamond dusted screen print, wearing a Chanel dress or owning an exceptionally well designed Patek Philippe timepiece. It is meant, however, to underscore the fact that luxury comes not only at a price but also at an environmental cost, as when animals are driven almost to extinction merely for luxury accessories such as handbags and shoes.

Taking a multidisciplinary philosophical approach, critical luxury studies thus draws on a variety of orthodox and radical perspectives within the arts, the humanities and the social sciences. Such a viewpoint enables new questions to be asked and old questions to be reframed and addressed anew. Critical luxury studies thus seeks to define and explore a new field that, while focused on the contemporary, nonetheless draws on the rich and developing field of historical luxury studies.

Hence, in what follows, we begin by defining luxury studies before discussing historical and contemporary approaches to luxury within philosophy, history and luxury brand management. We then advance the idea of critical luxury studies and define this new field of academic endeavour before concluding.

Luxury Studies

The term 'luxury studies' might be used to refer to all features of the study of luxury. 'Luxury', of course, is not easily defined, not least because it can have different meanings in different contexts. However, the concept that lies at the core of luxury studies, it may be suggested, is very much the concept that is found in the philosophy of luxury. As such, it avoids any exclusive concern with luxury as 'abundance' or 'excess' (the latter of which is found, for example, in the writings of Georges Bataille [1991], where excess is related to the unrestricted and elated expenditure or waste of energy in sex or acts of sacrifice). The philosophy of luxury entails recognition that all human beings live in a world that is created by human beings, and in which they find meaning in sumptuous enjoyment. Luxury is the complex everyday world we all encounter and, through our indulgences, we all traverse. Yet luxury truly begins at the point at which humans surpass necessity or whatever constraints determined by various external forces are simply given in their natural inheritance, inclusive of the limiting power of circumstances, conditions or states of things which force particular courses of action. Hence, the habitual use of, or indulgence in, what is choice or costly, whether food, dress, furniture or appliances of any sort, is thus as much a primary component of luxury as are the excesses of lasciviousness, of the world of lust, of lewdness and adultery, debauchery, brothels, shamelessness, fertility and superabundance. Consequently, the two most important elements of luxury may be the ability of human beings to construct concepts and practices such as flattery or jollity and to produce games, feasts and dance, and their capacity to luxuriate in choice tablecloths, expensive soft beds, opulent living rooms and even great inequalities of wealth.

Glaucon's use of the idea of 'the city of pigs' in Plato's *The Republic* is illuminating in this context (2007 [380 BC]: 53–66). In Part II, 'Preliminaries', Glaucon, Adeimantus and Socrates attempt to reach the 'First Principles of Social Organization'. They do not merely discuss the city, but, in order to enquire into questions of justice, individuality and injustice, they also examine the origins of society by way of a conversation concerning individual needs, which, argues Socrates, individuals cannot supply themselves. This story concerning the satisfaction of our many and varied needs can be seen as a description of the origin of the state. However, Glaucon, Adeimantus and Socrates take their conversation on individual needs further than a necessity for food, shelter and clothing. Indeed, they develop it into a narrative of leisure, of 'splendid cakes and loaves on rushes or fresh leaves', of feasting and wine, garlands, enjoyment and luxuries such as salt, olive oil, cheese, figs, myrtle berries and acorns (Plato 2007 [380 BC]: 59–60). Glaucon, Adeimantus and Socrates' discussion therefore pre-dates by some 2,000 years the key themes of luxury studies, including ideas concerning the civilised and 'the uncivilised community' (Glaucon's city of pigs), the conflict of diverse comforts, enjoyment, luxuries and civilisation, and how justice and injustice are bred in a community. It will be valuable to outline some of the themes here.

In response to Glaucon, Socrates' argument is that the city of pigs represents, not simply the true society, 'like a man in health', but also the possibility of studying a city, society and/or a man 'in a fever' (Plato 2007 [380 BC]: 61). Fevered cities, societies and individuals are a crucial luxurious watershed, for Socrates, for in the fevered city, diverse luxuries, including customs of 'satisfaction', beliefs about the 'standard' of living and 'values' concerning wants, whether lavish couches or plush chairs, come together. In a fevered city, people become intensely aware, perhaps not for the first time, that they are confronted with the question of luxury, for there is always some well-appointed table or delicacy, scent, perfume or confectionery, which, apparently, liberates them from all the confinements and bare necessities of food, shelter and clothing that, hitherto, they have always taken for granted. Our self-awareness as luxury-loving beings is grounded in this confrontation with the fine arts, embroidery, gold and ivory, and thus in the practice of 'unnecessary' enjoyment (as we struggle to sustain the values of 'necessary' hunters and farmers against an assault from 'unnecessary' artists and musicians, poets and actors). The point of the fevered city, and perhaps of all human luxury, is that in the productive achievement of the city beyond the pigs, humans gain various sorts of economic and cultural 'growth' (more manufacturers of women's dresses and make-up, more services such as private tutors, hospitals, personal shopping advisers and celebrity chefs). And while the individual may tire of foie gras, the building blocks of the fevered city continue to rise upwards in ever greater quantities and become part of the future of ever newer luxuries. A present-day exemplar of the fevered city is Las Vegas, where luxury in the form of excess and abundance flourishes. Indeed, in Chapter 8 Adam Sharr suggests that the very architecture of Las Vegas has been colonised by luxury, such that flagship stores, malls and hotels, including the Crystals at CityCenter mall designed by Daniel Libeskind, have become luxury commodities.

Luxuries endure even though the individuals who produce, distribute and consume them may very well tire of them long before they themselves expire. Therefore, at the very least, our understanding of 'growth' is transformed, and our understanding of enervation and cessation elevated. Yet this 'growth' entails the loss of what we might call a naïve conception of need. For the small numbers and history of the earlier, relatively isolated luxurious groups are today confronted and questioned by their encounter with a plurality of others seeking luxuries and making their own claims to the future of luxury. Paradoxically, at the very moment in which we become aware of ourselves as luxurious beings able to accomplish splendid new things, and, in principle, explore any extravagant territory we like, we lose forever our certainty about what is the right thing to do to 'support' ourselves. And so in doing anything luxurious, however small, we undeniably fall into conflict with others over what is 'enough' and what is 'excess', what 'necessity' and what the legitimate pursuit of unlimited material, and, increasingly, immaterial, magnificent possessions and modes of being.

Thus, luxury studies is necessarily concerned with morality, and the material and immaterial struggle to find and perhaps defend the meaning of the limitless. In this way, luxury studies might be taken to include the varied ways in which luxury is comprehended and examined, for instance, in philosophy and sociology, cultural studies, political economy, history, cultural geography, art theory, consumer culture, photography, architecture, fashion theory and new media.

Historical and Contemporary Luxury Studies: From Western Philosophy to Luxury Brand Management

In our usage, the historical origins of critical luxury studies can be traced back to the work of John Sekora (1977), Christopher J. Berry (1994) and Maxine Berg (2005; see also Berg and Eger 2003), and consequently to the foundations, and almost nascent formation, of a critical luxury studies academic community, under the sub-discipline of the history of luxury. Sekora's *Luxury: The Concept in Western Thought, Eden to Smollett*, for example, concentrates on the history of luxury from antiquity to the eighteenth century and, initially, on how luxury was viewed as the fundamental and general human vice from which all other vices sprung, inclusive of 'illegitimate' claims concerning political rights and human expressive needs. A slave desiring freedom was as 'guilty' of luxury as a poor woman in love with a prosperous man. Yet, conceived of as a 'crime' and indictable by sumptuary and other laws for thousands of years (Hunt 1996), luxury, Sekora argues, experienced a transformation during the eighteenth century. Describing these heightened social, political and intellectual changes, Sekora, a literary historian, dexterously analyses these changes through a contemplation of the writings of those who took part in the debate over luxury, such as the philosophers Bernard Mandeville (1989 [1732]), David Hume (2012 [1752]) and Adam Smith (1981 [1776]), as well as authors such as Jonathan Swift (2010 [1712]) and Henry Fielding (1988 [1751]). For Sekora, however, the key author is Tobias Smollett, and especially his novel *Humphry Clinker* (2008 [1771]), because, for Sekora, Smollett is the last, most obstinate and most persuasive defender of the classical position that involved an attack on both the concept and the shocking practice of luxury.

Berry's *The Idea of Luxury: A Conceptual and Historical Investigation*, on the other hand, explores the meanings and consequences of the concept of luxury from the perspectives of political theory (Plato, Aristotle), classical philosophy and theology (Cato, St Augustine), and the intellectual history of the transition to modernity (Mandeville, Hume, Smith). Utilising a sophisticated conceptual analysis of luxury that is complemented by a series of specific historical investigations, Berry (1994: 101–25) emphasises what he calls the gradual 'de-moralization of luxury' or the growth in the understanding of luxury in terms of economic prosperity rather than political morality. In a similar vein to Sekora, Berry also traces the eighteenth-century debates over luxury but, as a political theorist, diverges from Sekora through his focus on the history and politics of need and desire, necessity, and social identity. Berry's key contribution to the history of luxury is thus to show how the idea of luxury changed from being fundamentally a negative term, which described an endangered social virtue, to being essentially a positive term, which, today, describes a celebratory cultural form of branded consumption that we discuss below. Indeed, in Chapter 3, Berry revisits and extends his landmark contribution by considering the grounds upon which a re-moralisation of luxury might occur. In fact, he suggests that rising evidence of climate change could provide the 'objective' grounds for the adoption of constraints on the excesses of luxury consumption.

In her *Luxury and Pleasure in Eighteenth-Century Britain*, the economic historian Maxine Berg explores the eighteenth-century invention of making and buying new, semi-luxury, fashionable, quality and delightful consumer goods in Britain. Following the progress of luxury goods from the Far East (glass and Chinaware), Berg reflects on the luxury products of eighteenth-century Britain in terms of art, creativity and the luxurious production of everything from fine cutlery and silver shoe buckles to chic waistcoat buttons, brass and silver-plate candlesticks and ornate tea urns. Certainly, for Berg, eighteenth-century Britain was a 'nation of shoppers' made up primarily of 'self-respecting' and largely middle-class men and, especially, women, whose stylish acquisitions were subsequently displayed in the home. From Berg's perspective, then, luxury and pleasure in eighteenth-century Britain were crucially preoccupied with the introduction of new products and the appearance of new and seductive advertising campaigns. In fact, for her, such products and campaigns not only created new theatres of domestic display and new commodities but also new wants and new middle-class luxury consumers seeking the new idea of personal identity, of modern forms of social interaction beyond the cultural circles of the economic elite.

However, notwithstanding the existence of this body of work on the history of luxury, in this book we aspire to develop a multidisciplinary philosophical approach to *contemporary* critical studies of luxury. Yet this philosophical standpoint does not draw on the orthodox contemporary perspective derived from luxury brand management (see, for instance, Okonkwo 2007, 2010; Chevalier and Gutsatz 2012; Chevalier and Mazzalovo 2012; Kapferer and

Bastien 2012; Kapferer 2015; Som and Blanckaert 2015). This is because the theorists and practitioners of luxury brand management have little that is critical to voice about the study of luxury or, for example, about the domains of wealth driven by the fast expanding global market for luxury estimated to have exceeded €850 billion in 2014 (D'Arpizio et al. 2014).

Furthermore, luxury brand scholars or managers tend not to concern themselves with the ethics of the growing inequality upon which their business models depend, regardless of the negative social consequences of the increasing concentration of wealth in the hands of the 1 per cent, highlighted most recently by Thomas Picketty (2014), Danny Dorling (2014) and Joseph Stiglitz (2013). Rather, their attention is devoted to the activities of luxury brand companies, and to ensuring that, like those among the top luxury goods companies in Table 1.1, they deliver constantly improving profits. So, for instance, despite the subdued economic conditions in major markets (IMF 2015), Table 1.1 reveals that the top twenty luxury goods companies almost universally achieved profit growth rates in excess of the rate of global economic growth over the period from 2011 to 2013.

Thus, with their focus on luxury branded goods and services, luxury brand theorists generally avoid the type of social and spatial construction of life's little luxuries that are so important and effectively captured in Chapter 5 by Julia Mansvelt, Mary Breheny and Iain Hay. This is because the everyday luxuries that those of modest means indulge in occasionally, like a box of chocolates or a glass of wine, are of no interest to luxury brand managers who pursue the absolute conversion of consumers of means into an existence in which every aspect of their lives is imbued with branded luxuries.

Indeed, for luxury brand theorists and practitioners, the issues are not philosophical but pragmatic. They are concerned with questions such as how luxury brand value can be optimally marketed, capitalised upon, internationalised, licensed and extended into other market segments and into the future. One of the most influential texts in the growing discipline of luxury brand management, for instance, is Jean-Noël Kapferer and Vincent Bastien's *The Luxury Strategy: Break the Rules of Marketing to Build Luxury Brands* (2012). Wholly exemplifying the 'de-moralization of luxury', or the growth in the perception of luxury as a mere facet of economic prosperity as delineated by Berry, *The Luxury Strategy* is not so much preoccupied with the essence of luxury itself as with the essence of luxury as a marketing strategy. Accordingly, the important differences between 'premium', 'fashion' and 'luxury' are explained in *The Luxury*

Table 1.1 Top 20 luxury goods companies. (Source: compiled from Deloitte 2015)

Luxury goods sales rank FY13	Company name	Selection of luxury brands	FY13 total revenue (US$mil)	FY13 luxury goods sales growth	FY13 net profit margin[*]	FY11–13 luxury goods sales CAGR[†]
1.	LVMH Louis Vuitton Moët Hennessy SA	Louis Vuitton, Fendi, Bulgari, Loro Piana, Emilio Pucci, Acqua di Parma, Donna Karan, Loewe, Marc Jacobs, TAG Heuer, Benefit Cosmetics	38,717	0.0%	13.5%	8.7%
2.	Compagnie Financière Richemont SA	Cartier, Van Cleef & Arpels, Montblanc, Jaeger-LeCoultre, Vacheron Constantin, IWC, Piaget, Chloé	14,275	4.2%	19.4%	8.9%
3.	The Estée Lauder Companies Inc.	Estée Lauder, M.A.C., Aramis, Clinique, Aveda, Jo Malone; Licensed fragrance brands	10,969	7.7%	11.0%	6.3%
4.	Chow Tai Fook Jewellery Group Limited	Chow Tai Fook	9,979	34.8%	9.6%	17.0%
5.	Luxottica Group SpA	Ray-Ban, Oakley, Vogue Eyewear, Persol, Oliver Peoples; Licensed eyewear brands	9,713	3.2%	7.5%	8.4%

6.	The Swatch Group Ltd.	Breguet, Harry Winston, Blancpain, Longines, Omega, Rado; Licensed watch brands	9,128	8.8%	22.8%	9.9%
7.	Kering SA	Gucci, Bottega Veneta, Saint Laurent, Balenciaga, Brioni, Sergio Rossi. Pomellato, Girard-Perregaux	12,948	4.2%	0.4%e	14.7%
8.	L'Oréal Luxe	Lancôme, Biotherm, Helena Rubinstein, Urban Decay, Kiehl's; Licensed brands	7,791	5.3%	14.7%	10.5%
9.	Ralph Lauren Corporation	Ralph Lauren, Polo Ralph Lauren, Purple Label, Blue Label, Black Label, RLX Ralph Lauren	7,450	7.3%	10.4%	4.2%
10.	PVH Corp.	Calvin Klein, Tommy Hilfiger	8,186	42.0%	1.8%	22.7%
11.	Shiseido Company, Limited	SHISEIDO, clé de peau BEAUTÉ, bareMinerals, NARS, ISSEY MIYAKE, ELIXIR, Benefique	7,659e	17.8%e	3.8%	8.2%e
12.	Rolex SA	Rolex, Tudor	5,398	2.0%	n/a	3.1%
13.	Hermès International SCA	Hermès, John Lobb	4,975	7.5%	21.3%	14.8%

Table 1.1 (continued)

Luxury goods sales rank FY13	Company name	Selection of luxury brands	FY13 total revenue (US$mil)	FY13 luxury goods sales growth	FY13 net profit margin[*]	FY11–13 luxury goods sales CAGR[†]
14.	Coach, Inc.	Coach	4,806	−5.3%	16.3%	0.5%
15.	Prada Group	Prada, Church's, Car Shoe	4,776	8.8%	17.8%	18.5%
16.	Lao Feng Xiang Co., Ltd.	Lao Feng Xiang	5,329	17.6%	2.7%	15.1%
17.	Tiffany & Co.	Tiffany & Co., Tiffany	4,031	6.2%	4.5%	5.2%
18.	Burberry Group plc	Burberry, Burberry Brit, Burberry London, Burberry Prorsum	3,704	16.6%	14.3%	12.0%
19.	Michael Kors Holdings Limited	Michael Kors, MICHAEL Michael Kors	3,311	51.8%	20.0%	59.4%
20.	Hugo Boss AG	BOSS, HUGO, BOSS Green, BOSS Orange	3,231	3.7%	13.7%	8.7%

Notes: This list is limited to those luxury goods companies that publish their financial results. Consequently, *Chanel*, which is a privately owned company and not required to publish such data, is absent from the list, despite reported revenues of more than $7 billion in 2013, which would place it within the top 20 luxury goods companies (*Fashion avec Passion* 2013).

[*] Net Profit Margin based on Total Consolidated Revenue and Net Income; † Compound annual growth rate n/a = not available; e = estimate.

Strategy, alongside the 'social functions' of luxury and luxury industry best practices. Avoiding the idea of a critical approach, even in the terms advanced in the business and management field by critical management scholars (Adler, Forbes and Willmott 2007), Kapferer and Bastien evade the complexities of other academic disciplines and fields or the long and complex history of the concept of luxury in Western philosophy. Instead, they concentrate on setting out the 'rules' for success in the world of luxury brands. In fact, for Kapferer and Bastien, the diversity of meanings contained within the idea of luxury does not stretch across different disciplines; rather, their concerns reach across different markets and different marketised social media networks such as Twitter and Facebook. Consequently, they overlook the cultural, economic and socially mediated exclusion that globalisation and online luxury perpetuate, which is documented in Agnès Rocamora's insightful interrogation of Louis Vuitton's website in Chapter 10.

The Luxury Strategy thus restricts its concerns to those of the effective management of luxury brands and luxury companies, including issues of human resources, finance management, successful business models and the ongoing profitability or otherwise of automotive, jewellery, perfume and fashion luxury brands such as Ferrari and Cartier, Chanel, Armani, Gucci and Ralph Lauren. In short, *The Luxury Strategy*, as befits its envisioned readership, is intended to support aspirant luxury brand managers to achieve a detailed understanding of successful luxury brand management in luxury business organisations and their environment. Thus, common to the luxury brand management literature is a commercialised view of luxury that, as we argue in Chapter 2, promotes market valuations over socio-cultural practice-based ways of 'knowing luxury'. Moreover, as Ulrich Lehmann elaborates in Chapter 4, because 'aspects of *need* or *function* are secondary to luxury', the 'relational aspects within its social meaning' become ever more important. Yet, luxury brand theorists largely overlook this relational feature of the meaning of luxury.

Critical Luxury Studies: Defining a Field

In contrast to the field of luxury brand management and building upon historical antecedents, we seek, more specifically, to introduce, define, investigate and demonstrate the importance of the term 'critical luxury studies' in the sense of critique. Critical luxury studies, we suggest, is to be differentiated from 'criticism' of luxury studies.

While the latter presupposes a would-be 'unbiased' standpoint 'outside' the texts of luxury studies, critique adopts a view *within* the object of study, in our case luxury studies, and endeavours to draw out its inconsistent propensities and to focus on its valid elements. We emphasise the significance of critique in precisely this sense to the inauguration and development of critical luxury studies. Indeed, we mean critique in the broadest sense: not 'criticism' only, not even argument, but processes by which other traditions of luxury studies detailed in this chapter are considered both for what they may produce and for what they constrain. Critique entails taking the most valuable constituents and discarding the remainder. From this position, critical luxury studies is a process, a sort of experimentation for creating beneficial knowledge about the study of luxury. Indeed, as Berry (1994) and others have noted, because of its dependence on cultural, social and individual contexts and meanings, luxury defies objective definition. Hence, what is regarded as luxury varies through time and space, and across economic, social and cultural contexts. It is therefore essential that critical luxury studies reflects the need to follow the shifts and turns that the meaning of luxury takes through multiple and constantly evolving contexts.

We are interested in how critical luxury studies might appropriate the various methods of numerous academic disciplines, but critique here pertains equally and more generally to the study of luxury in relation to socio-cultural processes and extant texts concerned with luxury. Thus established, critical luxury studies is a radicalising, mostly political pursuit. It is not, though, at least for us, to be comprehended by that gesture as a research programme for specific political groupings. Its link with such political groupings is free and changeable but nevertheless an actual one, typified, we might say, by a productive wrangle with current methods of political discourse and modes of action. Critique is then a fundamental crucial feature of our engaged intellectual work concerning, among other things, the cultural politics of luxury (Armitage and Roberts 2016), which includes but also ranges beyond critical luxury studies to the numerous differently situated forms of the study of luxury.

Critical luxury studies is therefore to be taken, more precisely, to denote a new and distinctive field of academic investigation that we originally formulated in our (2014: 124) article entitled 'Luxury New Media: Euphoria in Unhappiness'. In the following paragraphs, we elaborate further on two core elements of our understanding of the field of critical luxury studies.

First, critical luxury studies is a new and distinctive field in the sense of being an academic discipline or branch of knowledge that should be taught and researched in higher education and recognised by university faculties, learned societies and more academic journals beyond *Luxury: History, Culture, Consumption* and *Cultural Politics*, in which we and other critical luxury studies scholars have already published our research findings. However, we readily acknowledge that there exist no formal criteria for defining academic disciplines, whether well-established ones such as philosophy that exist in almost all universities and have well-defined rosters of journals and conferences, or nascent ones supported by only a few publications and university faculty members, such as the contributors to *Critical Luxury Studies: Art, Design, Media*. Reference to art, design and media also reminds us that, as key ideas, they are equally explanatory phrases and evaluative concepts. For the purposes of this book, therefore, we take art to refer to the objects and procedures, aptitudes and effects involved in the creation of visual representations within a wide-ranging variety of media and materials (Danto 2014). Design, however, and particularly within the present context of our concern with art, history and visual culture, denotes both the conscious and methodical elaboration of a plan meant to fulfil a visible physical or structural project and a wider field of historical and contemporary material and visual practices such as silkscreen printing, architecture, fashion design and Internet communication graphics (Munari 2008). By media, we mean an agency, instrument or channel. Media employed within critical luxury studies and related discourses such as art and history, for instance, signifies both an assemblage of communicative forms and practices, such as painting and photography, and the mass media of TV and film as well as the physical materials that comprise artistic expression (McLuhan 2001 [1964]). Finally, like most disciplines, critical luxury studies has branches, such as the sub-disciplines of 'luxury art', 'luxury design' and 'luxury new media' (Armitage and Roberts 2014: 124). Fortunately, there is, as yet, no consensus on how an academic discipline such as critical luxury studies should be classified (e.g. whether it is a discipline belonging to the arts, the humanities or the social sciences), or on what the proper criteria for organising its contribution to knowledge are, all of which leaves the discipline of critical luxury studies open to debate and diverse contributions as it determines its own future. Indeed, this feature of the discipline is extremely valuable and offers wide-ranging possibilities. Moreover, this view of critical luxury studies as a process, evolving alongside the core focus of its attention, will, we hope, avoid the border policing characteristics common to many academic disciplines (Messer-Davidow, Schuway and Sylvan 1993).

Second, and much like the writings of the French sociologist of culture and education, Pierre Bourdieu (1984), but expressly not aligned with it, the new field of critical luxury studies is concerned with luxury as a network of relationships. Certainly, luxury is a place of struggle over various forms of indulgence. Yet it is also the context wherein particular individuals invest their 'cultural capital', to use a key term from Bourdieu (1984). Cultural capital can be defined here as the possession of knowledge about luxury, as luxurious achievements, as the formal and informal luxury qualifications by which an individual may secure admission to and obtain a standing in specific circles, such as luxury professions and organisations, wherein individuals employ their 'habitus' (Bourdieu 1990; Bourdieu and Wacquant 1992). Habitus can be defined here as the open set of attitudes and outlooks towards luxury by which individuals make their way in the domains of luxury and enjoyment. The role of cultural capital and habitus is usefully illustrated through the sartorial connoisseurship required to distinguish between an ordinary white T-shirt and the luxury Dior Homme plain white T-shirt costing $480 discussed by Jonathan Faiers in Chapter 9. The connoisseurship Faiers describes is also one that embraces so-called 'stealth luxury' and is therefore more likely to be underpinned by habitus embedded in luxury than habitus that supports conspicuous consumption.

The struggle between fields denoted by Bourdieu can be regarded as a struggle, for example, for exquisite food or surroundings or for luxury-as-dominance. Each such field of luxury might be perceived as encompassing a network of luxurious individuals, luxury institutions and luxurious influences, homologous with other rival fields, such as the field of 'austerity' (see, for example, Blyth 2015 and Mendoza 2015), but with its own luxurious logic and structure. The field of luxury thus contains a competition for power specific to itself, such as the cult field of Italian Aceto Balsamico vinegar, which, when regionally authenticated via a Denominazione di Origine Controllata label, indicating that the vinegar has been produced and aged a minimum of twelve years, costs $150 (£100) for a tiny bottle. Such bottles of vinegar are representative of those articles of luxury food removed by their powerful producers, character, consumers and costliness from the ordinary category of human food. But the field of luxury is also in conflict with other fields, such as the field of religious charities providing food banks in the United Kingdom and elsewhere on a non-profit basis to those who have difficulty purchasing enough food to avoid hunger (Woolford Barron 2015).

The number of fields that are conducive to enjoyment or comfort in addition to what are accounted the necessities of life is of course infinite, and individuals bring their characteristic habitus of desire and competing economic and cultural capital to them in varied and mismatched ways. Accordingly, producers and consumers in the luxury field are generally high in cultural *and* economic capital when contrasted with producers and consumers in the field of religious charities. These disparities then establish the terms of struggle for luxury-as-dominance. If the power of pleasure is realised in the luxury field, for instance, by a fashionable individual or group, then that individual or group may seek to transpose it to another field. Such is the case with the power of the visual pleasure in, for example, artworks by Alberto Giacometti and Nam June Paik, which have recently been transposed from museums around the world to the LVMH group's new Fondation Louis Vuitton in Paris: from the realm of the art museum to the realm of the luxury brand.

Mike Featherstone's analysis of the connection between art and luxury in Chapter 6 highlights the mutually beneficial outcomes of this field-spanning activity. Art employed as a source of cultural capital by luxury companies is elevated to the status of luxury consumption. Yet, this tendency for luxury companies to appropriate cultural capital from the fields of art, design and media can also entail the creation of new production-related knowledge. The collaboration between the Japanese photographer Hiroshi Sugimoto and the French luxury company Hermès, described by Thomaï Serdari in Chapter 7, provides an example of engagement that goes beyond the mere appropriation of cultural capital from art. In this case, Sugimoto and Hermès cooperated to capture the 'suchness' of colour in a limited edition of luxury silk scarves. But the benefits of this partnership reached beyond the association of art with luxury and involved valuable printing innovations that will have lasting value to Hermès. Importantly, such collaborative activity is far from new, nor is it always sought purposively, as evidenced by the 1981 chance in-flight encounter between the English singer and actress Jane Birkin and the then CEO of Hermès Jean-Louis Dumas, which led to the development of Hermès' Birkin bag (Leitch 2012).[1] Luxury companies exist in a network of social relations from which they are constantly seeking to absorb and leverage cultural capital, and which can, through appropriation and commodification in the form of goods and services, be converted to financial capital.

Unlike luxury brand management, then, critical luxury studies emerges from a multidisciplinary critical approach to luxury. It does not merely draw, for instance, on the orthodox perspectives on knowledge and society, cultural value and political economy derived from the social sciences (e.g. Veblen 2009 [1899]; Sombart 1967 [1913]; Frank 2001). It also employs more radical positions suggested by, for example, moral philosophy (Hume 2012 [1752]) and Marxism (Adorno and Horkheimer 1997 [1947]), cultural theories of time and place (Benjamin 2002), the object (Harman 2011), art, aesthetic meaning, signs, symbols, dress (Barthes 2010; Calefato 2014), and offline and online geographies of luxury production and consumption (Thomas 2008). This range of viewpoints enables the asking of new and, crucially, critical questions. Indeed, it facilitates a reconceptualisation of what, precisely, is entailed by the term 'luxury' in the present period. Above all, critical luxury studies can be seen to be setting itself against the preconceptions about luxury found in contemporary uncritical disciplines, exemplified by luxury brand management. For such disciplines predominantly treat luxury products and services as objects or services that can be legitimately, or even exhaustively, studied in isolation from the socio-cultural and historical contexts of their production, distribution and consumption. The exponents of critical luxury studies in this book, however, seek to situate luxury products and services explicitly in relation to other socio-cultural practices, and particularly concerning the politicised structures of luxury capital and labour, democracy, science, the city and other socio-cultural hierarchies, such as those advanced by haute couture fashion houses like Chanel, Dior and Versace. A significant implication of this approach is that the luxury products and services studied in this book are not merely those selected and celebrated by an intellectual and artistic elite or even the 'super-rich' (Irvin 2008; Freeland 2013; Hay 2013; McQuaig and Brooks 2013; Wilkin 2015), but include material and symbolic luxury products and services encountered in all strata and sections of society.

Critical luxury studies can thus be understood to be located between two philosophical views on luxury. The first is unambiguously against the celebration of the super-rich or the cult of 'meta-luxury' culture (Ricca and Robins 2012), as signified, for instance, in the classical philosophy of Plato (2007 [380 BC]), Cicero (2012 [44 BC]) and St Augustine (2003 [426 AD]). The second is a more positive stance descended from the history of modern moral philosophy (Hume 2012 [1752]), modern political economy (e.g. Smith 1981 [1776]; Marx 1990 [1867]; Veblen 2009 [1899]), and particularly from the modern and postmodern critical socio-cultural theories of Jean Baudrillard (2005), Pierre Bourdieu (1984), Theodor Adorno (2001 [1947]) and Herbert Marcuse (2002 [1964]).

Conclusion

Thus, in conclusion, the differences between the history of luxury, luxury brand management and critical luxury studies as forms of academic scholarship and teaching are clearly political and socio-cultural, as well as intellectual and analytical. We are seeking to develop critical luxury studies partly as a radical critique of the multiplying production, distribution and consumption of luxury goods and services developing in contemporary global capitalist society. Its academic roots, as we have outlined, lay in contemporary epistemology and moral philosophy, cultural and political studies, material culture, design and theoretical studies of commodity fetish-ism, fashion and media – and it will, we hope, migrate into university curriculums as an academic field over the coming years. It is our sincere desire that academics from other, even orthodox, established fields (e.g. fine art, graphic and industrial design, media and cultural studies) will join us, even critique our work, but, with any luck, for a healthy mixture of political, professional and, critically, intellectual reasons. In years ahead, it is our genuine wish that these debates, critical on occasion, will continue. The history of luxury and critical luxury studies in particular – as fields increasingly taught in universi-ties and as forms of still-evolving enquiry – in practice should feed off each other, and coexist, rather more than they should compete (Adams 2012). Kristin Ross's *Communal Luxury: The Political Imaginary of the Paris Commune* (2015), for instance, is just one apposite example of the history of luxury that is critical in spirit. The Paris Commune, of course, was the radical socialist and revolution-ary government that administered Paris from 18 March to 28 May 1871. However, the field of 'communal luxury', a term derived from the 1871 manifesto of the Paris Commune's Federation of Artists, which suggested that luxury was not the private accumula-tion of goods and services but the blossoming of beauty in all public areas, is not taught at any university today. Communal luxury, as a mode of embryonic investigation, was thus an aesthetic practice of freedom. Yet it was an aesthetic practice that not only fed *off* art, design and media but also – in the contemporary era of protests at migrant camps and the occupation of Wall Street – still feeds *into* all facets of our everyday life today, coevolving as a sort of collective possession, instead of as an individual possession acquired at the expense of others. That is to say, books such as Ross's *Communal Luxury* demonstrate that there is no necessary conflict between the history of luxury and critical luxury studies and that there is in fact great potential for them to cooperate in the development of historically informed yet critical approaches to the contemporary study of luxury.

Acknowledgement

We would like to thank Dr Jonathan Faiers for his helpful comments on a previous version of this chapter.

Note

1. In July 2015 Jane Birkin asked Hermès to rename the Birkin bag due to her concerns about cruelty to crocodiles in the farms supplying the company's leather (Bolton 2015).

References

Adams, William Howard (2012), *On Luxury*, Washington, DC: Potomac Books.

Adler, P. S., Forbes, L. C. and Willmott, H. (2007), 'Critical management studies', in J. P. Walsh and A. P. Brief (eds), *The Academy of Management Annals*, Vol. 1, Mahwah, NJ: Lawrence Erlbaum, pp. 119–79.

Adorno, Theodor (2001 [1947]), *The Culture Industry: Selected Essays on Mass Culture*, London: Routledge.

Adorno, Theodor and Horkheimer, Max (1997 [1947]), *Dialectic of Enlightenment*, London: Verso.

Armitage, John and Roberts, Joanne (2014), 'Luxury new media: euphoria in unhappiness', *Luxury: History, Culture, Consumption*, 1 (1): 111–32.

Armitage, John and Roberts, Joanne (2016), 'The spirit of luxury', *Cultural Politics*, 12 (1): 1–22.

Augustine, St (2003 [426 AD]), *City of God*, London: Penguin.

Barthes, Roland (2010), *The Fashion System*, London: Vintage Classics.

Bataille, Georges (1991), *The Accursed Share: Volume 1*, New York: Zone Books.

Baudrillard, Jean (2005), *The System of Objects*, London: Verso.

Benjamin, Walter (2002), *The Arcades Project*, Boston: Harvard University Press.

Berg, Maxine (2005), *Luxury and Pleasure in Eighteenth-Century Britain*, Oxford: Oxford University Press.

Berg, Maxine and Eger, Elizabeth (eds) (2003), *Luxury in the Eighteenth Century: Debates, Desires and Delectable Goods*, London: Palgrave Macmillan.

Berry, Christopher J. (1994), *The Idea of Luxury: A Conceptual and Historical Investigation*, Cambridge: Cambridge University Press.

Blyth, Mark (2015), *Austerity: The History of a Dangerous Idea*, Oxford: Oxford University Press.

Bolton, D. (2015), 'Jane Birkin asks Hermès fashion house to rename luxury Birkin bags after animal cruelty concerns', *The Independent*, 28 July. Available at: http://www.independent.co.uk/life-style/fashion/news/jane-birkin-asks-herms-fashion-house-to-rename-luxury-birkin-bags-due-to-animal-cruelty-concerns-10422738.html (accessed 31 August 2015).

Bourdieu, Pierre (1984), *Distinction: A Social Critique of the Judgement of Taste*, London: Routledge.

Bourdieu, Pierre (1990), *The Logic of Practice*, Cambridge: Polity.

Bourdieu, Pierre and Wacquant, J. D. Loic (1992), *An Invitation to Reflexive Sociology*, Cambridge: Polity.

Calefato, Patrizia (2014), *Luxury: Fashion, Lifestyle and Excess*, London: Bloomsbury.

Chevalier, Michel and Gutsatz, Michel (2012), *Luxury Retail Management: How the World's Top Brands Provide Quality Product and Service Support*, Singapore: Wiley.

Chevalier, Michel and Mazzalovo, Gérald (2012), *Luxury Brand Management: A World of Privilege*, Singapore: Wiley.

Cicero (2012 [44 BC]), *Three Books of Offices or Moral Duties*, London: Forgotten Books.

Danto, Arthur (2014), *What Art Is*, Princeton: Princeton University Press.

D'Arpizio, C., Levato, F., Zito, D. and de Montgolfier, J. (2014), *Luxury Goods Worldwide Market Study, Fall–Winter 2014: The rise of the borderless consumer*, Bain and Company, 2014. Available at http://www.bain.com/publications/articles/luxury-goods-worldwide-market-study-december-2014.aspx (accessed 15 May 2015).

Deloitte (2015), *Global Powers of Luxury Goods: Engaging the Future Luxury Consumer*. Available at: http://www2.deloitte.com/content/dam/Deloitte/global/Documents/Consumer-Business/gx-cb-global-power-of-luxury-web.pdf (accessed 23 August 2015).

Dorling, Danny (2014), *Inequality and the 1%*, London and New York: Verso.

Fashion avec Passion (2013), 'Top brands 2013, the most luxurious of luxury. Chanel. Coco, Karl, Marilyn', *Fashion avec Passion*, 10 December, Available at: http://www.fashionavecpassion.com/top-brands-2013-the-most-luxurious-of-luxury-chanel-coco-karl-marilyn/ (accessed 1 September 2015).

Fielding, Henry (1988 [1751]), *An Enquiry into the Causes of the Late Increase of Robbers, &c. with some Proposals for Remedying this Growing Evil*, Oxford: Clarendon Press.

Frank, H. Robert (2001), *Luxury Fever: Why Money Fails to Satisfy in an Era of Excess*, New York: Free Press.

Freeland, Chrystia (2013), *Plutocrats: The Rise of the New Global Super-Rich*, London: Penguin.

Harman, Graham (2011), *The Quadruple Object*, Winchester: Zero Books.

Hay, Iain (ed.) (2013), *Geographies of the Super-rich*, Cheltenham: Edward Elgar.

Hume, David (2012 [1752]), *Political Discourses*, London: Forgotten Books.

Hunt, Alan (1996), *Governance of the Consuming Passions: A History of Sumptuary Law*, New York: St Martin's Press.

International Monetary Fund (IMF) (2015), *World Economic Outlook Database*, April. Available at: http://www.imf.org/external/pubs/ft/weo/2015/01/weodata/download.aspx (accessed 27 August 2015).

Irvin, George (2008), *Super Rich: The Rise of Inequality in Britain and the United States*, Cambridge: Polity.

Kapferer, Jean-Noël (2015), *Kapferer on Luxury: How Luxury Brands Can Grow Yet Remain Rare*, London: Kogan Page.

Kapferer, Jean-Noël and Bastien, Vincent (2012), *The Luxury Strategy: Break the Rules of Marketing to Build Luxury Brands*, London: Kogan Page.

Leitch, L. (2012), 'How Jane's Birkin bag idea took off', *The Telegraph*, 6 March. Available at: http://fashion.telegraph.co.uk/news-features/TMG9126955/How-Janes-Birkin-bag-idea-took-off.html (accessed 31 August 2015).

McLuhan, Marshall (2001 [1964]), *Understanding Media: The Extensions of Man*, London: Routledge.

McQuaig, Linda and Brooks, Neil (2013), *The Trouble with Billionaires: How the Super-Rich Hijacked the World (and How We Can Take It Back)*, London: Oneworld Publications.

Mandeville, Bernard (1989 [1732]), *The Fable of the Bees: Or, Private Vices, Publick Benefits*, London: Penguin.

Marcuse, Herbert (2002 [1964]), *One-Dimensional Man: Studies in the Ideology of Advanced Industrial Society*, London: Routledge.

Marx, Karl (1990 [1867]), *Capital: Critique of Political Economy*, Vol. 1, London: Penguin.

Mendoza, Kerry-Ann (2015), *Austerity: The Demolition of the Welfare State and the Rise of the Zombie Economy*, Oxford: New Internationalist.

Messer-Davidow, E., Shumway, D. R. and Sylvan, D. J. (1993), 'Disciplinary ways of knowing', in Ellen Messer-Davidow, David R. Shumway and David J. Sylvan (eds), *Knowledges: Historical and Critical Studies in Disciplinarity*, Charlottesville: Virginia University Press, pp. 1–21.

Munari, Bruno (2008), *Design as Art*, Penguin: London.

Okonkwo, Uche (2007), *Luxury Fashion Branding*, London: Palgrave Macmillan.

Okonkwo, Uche (2010), *Luxury Online: Styles, Strategies, Systems*, London: Palgrave Macmillan.

Piketty, Thomas (2014), *Capital in the Twenty-First Century*, Cambridge, MA: Harvard University Press.

Plato (2007 [380 BC]), *The Republic*, London: Penguin.

Ricca, Manfredi and Robins, Rebecca (2012), *Meta-Luxury: Brands and the Culture of Excellence*, London: Palgrave Macmillan.

Ross, Kristin (2015), *Communal Luxury: The Political Imaginary of the Paris Commune*, London: Verso.

Sekora, John (1977), *Luxury: The Concept in Western Thought, Eden to Smollett*, Baltimore: Johns Hopkins Press.

Smith, Adam (1981 [1776]), *An Enquiry into the Nature and Causes of the Wealth of Nations*, Indianapolis: Liberty Classics.

Smollett, Tobias (2008 [1771]), *Humphry Clinker*, London: Penguin.

Som, Ashok and Blanckaert, Christian (2015), *The Road to Luxury: The Evolution, Markets and Strategies of Luxury Brand Management*, Singapore: Wiley.

Sombart, Werner (1967 [1913]), *Luxury and Capitalism*, Ann Arbor: University of Michigan Press.

Stiglitz, Joseph, E. (2013), *The Price of Inequality*, London: Penguin Books.

Swift, Jonathan (2010 [1712]), *A Proposal for Correcting, Improving and Ascertaining the English Tongue*, Whitefish, MT: Kessinger Publishing.

Thomas, Dana (2008), *DeLuxe: How Luxury Lost its Lustre*, London: Penguin.

Veblen, Thorstein (2009 [1899]), *The Theory of the Leisure Class*, Oxford: Oxford University Press.

Wilkin, Sam (2015), *Wealth Secrets of the 1%: How the Super Rich Made Their Way to the Top*, London: Sceptre.

Woolford Barron, Ray (2015), *Food Bank Britain*, Deptford: Deptford Heritage Publishing.

1 Critical Luxury Studies

Knowing Luxury: From Socio-Cultural Value to Market Price?

Joanne Roberts and John Armitage

The purpose of this chapter is to explore how luxury is known. Luxury has had an important role in society throughout the ages. For much of this history, luxury was aligned to the authority of political and social institutions. Since the eighteenth century, when the potential of luxury consumption to enhance social and economic development was advanced by David Hume (1987 [1742]) and Adam Smith (1982 [1776]), its diffusion through society has extended and its contribution to the economy has grown significantly. Indeed, in 2014, the value of the global luxury market exceeded €850 billion, having grown at a rate of 7 per cent on the previous year (D'Arpizio et al. 2014), well above the global rate of economic growth. In the twenty-first century, this luxury market growth is accounted for by increasing incomes in the advanced countries, especially among the wealthy, who have been less affected than most people by the global financial crisis of 2008, and the expanding middle classes in emerging countries. Today, the prevalence of luxury is such that we all have an idea of what it is, in the sense that we associate it with expensive goods and services supplied by well-known brands such as Louis Vuitton, Gucci and Hermès. Yet, the label of luxury is being attached to an increasing number of goods and services, giving producers the capacity to command a substantial price premium. The extended use of the term luxury begs an important question: how do we come to *know* luxury?

Much attention has been devoted to developing understandings of the place of expert knowledge in the production of luxury artefacts (Tungate 2009; Ricca and Robins 2012). Furthermore, knowledge of the management of luxury brands has grown rapidly in the past decade as the increasing number of books in the area attests (Chevalier and Mazzalovo 2012; Hoffmann and Coste-Maniere 2012, 2013; Kapferer and Bastien 2012; *inter alia*). In contrast, how luxury is known from a consumer, societal and philosophical perspective has been overlooked. Yet, luxury is often marketed through the promotion of mysterious and ambiguous references to undefined but somehow exclusive qualities. So much so, that it is possible to analyse the role that ignorance plays in the consumption of luxury (Roberts 2014).

Consequently, to advance a critical appreciation of luxury, it is useful to examine how luxury is known. Hence, this chapter engages in an examination of the epistemology of luxury. Epistemology is, of course, the branch of philosophy concerned with the nature and scope of knowledge. Thus, an epistemology of luxury is concerned with the nature and scope of knowledge about luxury. The purpose here is not merely to define luxury but, rather, to explore how luxury is known and, importantly, how this knowing is influenced by the rise to dominance of markets in the neoliberal era (Harvey 2005). Following an examination of the various meanings of luxury evident in current debates, the nature of knowledge and knowing is considered before knowing luxury goods and services is explored. Two distinct forms of knowing luxury are identified, the first based on socio-cultural practice-based understandings and the second on market valuations. We go on to argue that the privileging of the market under neoliberalism is leading to a shift in the nature of knowing luxury from the first to the second of these two forms. The implications of this shift for the way luxury is known in the contemporary world are considered before the chapter closes with a brief conclusion.

From the Socio-Cultural to the Economic Meaning of Luxury

Luxury is often associated with expensive, elegant and refined products and services of the highest quality as well as with a rich, comfortable and sumptuous lifestyle. Additionally, luxury is related to excessive quantity and frequently viewed as superfluous, unnecessary or an indulgence. While often seen as a divisive force in society, as suggested by the lifestyles of excess portrayed in Hollywood films – such as *The Wolf of Wall Street*, based on the true story of the multimillionaire financial broker Jordan Belfort – luxury can also be a unifying force. For example, in Ancient Greece, meat, which was one of the true luxuries of the time, was shared out among the whole community following the sacrifice of animals at the Acropolis (Scott, quoted in Ricca and Robins 2012: 33).[1] Even today, luxury is employed as a means of solidifying social relations, as in the consumption of champagne and elaborate feasts to celebrate significant social events like the marriage of loved ones or the arrival of newborns. In such circumstances, the consumption of luxury, in the sense of the extravagant and the out of the ordinary, confirms the importance of the event, elevating it from the everyday to something recognised as significant. Moreover, the celebration of such events and the communal consumption of luxurious food and drink facilitate the construction of individual and group identities as well as the renewal and extension of social relations (Bourdieu 1990; Putman 2000).

As Thorstein Veblen (1899) elaborated, the conspicuous consumption of expensive, elegant, yet superfluous luxury goods and services provides a means of displaying one's wealth and social status. For this reason, conspicuous consumption has been a common feature of the nouveau riche across history and geography (Skidelsky and Skidelsky 2013). Furthermore, such consumption includes the philanthropic use of one's wealth for the benefit of others (Nickel 2015). The display of wealth is also important for nations and national leaders as a means of demonstrating financial strength and political power. For instance, the French king, Louis XIV, was renowned for his deployment of luxury as a means of controlling the political classes in the seventeenth century (Elias 2000). Indeed, it was his promotion of luxury that earned France its premier position as the source of luxury, a position which it still holds today.

Despite luxury's role in society, its definition remains elusive. In his highly influential book, *The Idea of Luxury*, Christopher J. Berry (1994) provides a detailed historical exploration of luxury and defines it as the antonym of necessity. Luxury is thus distinct from basic needs, which are non-intentional and universal. For Berry, luxury occupies the realm of wants and desires. Yet, he goes on to argue that luxuries must be the object of socially recognised desire, and, as such, capable of giving pleasure rather than merely relieving pain. Additionally, Berry argues that goods and services, which may be regarded as socially non-necessary by some, may be 'needed' by others, either in a specific instrumental sense or because they are the object of intense desire (i.e. psychologically necessary) or intense identification (e.g. cherished objects). Consequently, not all unnecessary goods or services are luxuries to everyone. Thus, even conspicuous consumption can be interpreted as the instrumental consumption of luxury when signalling social status is essential to the maintenance of one's social position. For example, crucial to the achievements of an individual providing financial services to Ultra High Net Worth Individuals (UHNWI)[2] is the ability to signal their own success and high social status through the conspicuous consumption of luxury clothing, jewellery and transportation; for one could not expect an UHNWI to take financial advice from someone who is unable to display their own financial success.

Berry goes on to define luxuries as '*those goods that admit of easy and painless substitution because the desire for them lacks fervency*' (1994: 41, original emphasis). Contrary to this, in an earlier article, we offered an alternative definition of luxury goods and services inspired by Herbert Marcuse's (1964) critique of elites who follow their economic desires, or what Marcuse calls their 'false' social needs. Hence, we defined luxuries 'not as painless substitutes lacking fervent desire but as alienating surrogates saturated with the urgent sense of a life determined by external forces, and consequent lack of control or authenticity and oneness with ourselves' (Armitage and Roberts 2014: 118). In our view, the deployment of media, especially new media, including mobile phones, by luxury businesses plays a crucial role in promoting 'false' needs.

As an economic sector, luxury has also gained increasing importance as a driver for growth (ECCIA 2012). The economic potential of luxury has stimulated a burgeoning literature on the management of luxury brands produced by business and marketing scholars who often appear to display a high level of certitude in their definitions of luxury. For example, Chevalier and Mazzalova (2012) argue that a luxury product must meet three criteria. First, it must have a strong artistic content; second, it must be the result of craftsmanship; and, third, it must be international. The link between art, craftsmanship and luxury is not new. Works of art and the products of craftsmanship normally require high levels of skill, time and expensive materials. Therefore, their consumption has been the preserve of wealthy individuals and institutions. Nevertheless, changing income levels and techniques of production have made these products increasingly available to a wider range of individuals since the late twentieth century. Chevalier and Mazzalova's suggestion that, for something to be a luxury, it must also be international is very much a consequence of globalisation from the mid-1980s onwards. It is also a suggestion that is embedded in a business perspective on luxury, a perspective which is primarily concerned with market size and the expanding geographical reach of brands as a means to produce sustainable profits, especially among the large multinational luxury conglomerates, such as LVMH, Kering and Richemont.

Clearly, if goods and services must be international to be classed as luxuries, they must be recognised and known as such in various different locations and numerous diverse cultures. Yet, this definition of luxury is contrary to the fact that some goods and services have great social significance only in particular locations. For instance, barkcloth, known as *tapa*, holds a place of prominence in cultures across the Pacific, especially in Polynesia, where it is used for gifts on special occasions such as weddings (Neich and Pendergrast 2005). Such items, though luxuries in local contexts, thus fail to meet the definitions and classifications of luxuries by business scholars, yet they remain items of high significance in specific cultures.

Allérès (1990) classifies luxury in terms of three levels of accessibility, namely, inaccessible (exclusive unique items), intermediate (expensive replicas of unique items) and accessible (factory produced and in large production runs). In the contemporary era, increased accessibility and affordability is leading to a democratisation of luxury accompanied by a proliferation of terms such as new luxury or mass luxury. According to Kapferer and Bastien (2012), this increased accessibility is the result of, on the one hand, the efforts of traditional brands to trade up, and, on the other hand, the drive for profits among luxury businesses by offering products and services to a wider global market. Alongside the trading up of brands, Silverstein and Fiske (2008) also point to the trading down of other brands, such as Wal-Mart and Primark, which is leading to a greater polarisation between luxury and ordinary goods and services. Indeed, the ability to pay less for some things gives people more resources to indulge in occasional luxuries.

The development of so-called mass luxury also reflects the fragmentation of the production process, such that the design of luxury goods and services may involve significant artistic inputs and craftsmanship, but the final products and services can be mass produced in low-cost locations without any loss of quality (Thomas 2007). This shift to mass luxury has been accompanied by the emergence of the idea of meta-luxury (Ricca and Robins 2012) and über luxury (Quintavalle 2013) as counter-terms to the trend towards luxury for all and to make a distinction between mass produced luxuries and those luxuries that remain exclusive, often because they are the result of high levels of skill and craftsmanship, and their cost renders them accessible only to UHNWIs.

Yet, for all the efforts to define luxury from a business perspective, there has been a neglect of its local socially specific meaning. What is luxury for one group may not be so for another. However, sustained profits derive from the development of large markets not from catering to small, locally specific, markets.[3] Hence, there is a tendency among business and management scholars to focus on definitions of luxury that are shaped by the activities of the multinational luxury conglomerates, activities that have evolved significantly since the 1980s (Thomas 2007).

Despite the proliferation of terms to describe luxury in the business environment, as Berry's (1994) analysis reveals, due to its dependence on cultural, social and individual contexts and meanings, luxury cannot be objectively defined. The meaning of luxury varies through time and space, and across economic, social and cultural contexts. For example, in the 1960s, a holiday involving an aeroplane flight would have been a luxury for most people in the advanced countries, yet, today, such holidays have almost become the norm, although they remain a luxury in the least developed countries. Furthermore, luxury is relative. As Frank (1999) notes, if large houses are commonplace they do not qualify as luxury; rather, the house that is bigger than the norm is regarded as luxury.

Clearly, luxury is a complex idea, but it is also manifested in a very real form in the global marketplace where luxury goods and services may be defined by high price. According to economists, a wealth of distributed knowledge about the demand and supply of a good or a service is brought together in the marketplace where this knowledge is captured in the market price (Hayek 1945). The characteristics of demand for luxury goods and services differ from those of normal goods. They are often referred to as Veblen goods because they display high price elasticity of demand such that increases in price enhance rather than diminish their desirability (Kapferer and Bastien 2012). A Veblen good is not necessarily of a higher standard than a normal good; its status as a luxury depends on the perceptions of consumers as to its ability to indicate social standing through, for instance, recognisable luxury brand logos. While there is much anecdotal evidence to suggest that luxury goods and services do display the characteristics of Veblen goods (Bagwell and Bernheim 1996), it would be inappropriate to suggest that the price of all luxury goods and services is merely determined by consumer demand underpinned by the utility gained from signalling status. While the accessible luxury delineated by Alléres (1990) may be differentiated from normal goods largely by higher prices, with consumers willing to pay more to display their social rank, with regard to those luxuries that Alléres defines as inaccessible, in the sense of being exclusive unique items, their high price relative to normal goods is likely to be determined by the greater costs of production. Although the high price of such inaccessible luxuries will attract consumers who gain utility from signalling status, the price of such luxuries will primarily be based on the high costs of production rather than solely on demand derived from the desire of consumers to demonstrate their elevated social position. From a business perspective, goods and services acquire luxury status from the perceptions of consumers, or high production costs, or a combination of the two (Roberts and Armitage 2015).

In summary, then, the meaning of luxury is context specific and is constantly being defined and redefined according to individual and societal conditions. It is not possible here to explore luxury from the perspective of all these different times and locations or across all economic, social and cultural contexts. Consequently, luxury is viewed below from the perspective of an individual in an advanced country. Yet, in our exploration, we highlight two aspects of the individual: first, as an economic entity, namely, as a consumer and participant in the market place; and, second, as a social being, embedded in socio-cultural networks of meaning. Luxury has a role in both economic and socio-cultural environments. To develop a deeper appreciation of how luxury is known, we turn now to the meaning of knowledge and knowing before applying these understandings to luxury.

Knowledge and Knowing

As this chapter examines the epistemology of luxury, and specifically how we know luxury, it is necessary to begin by considering the nature of knowledge. According to the *Oxford Dictionary of English* (2003: 967), knowledge may be defined as 'facts, information, and skills acquired through experience or education; the theoretical or practical understanding of a subject . . . the sum of what is known'. As this definition indicates, there are several different types of knowledge, such as theoretical or practical knowledge.

In the Western philosophical tradition, knowledge is broadly defined as justified true belief. So, if we know something is luxury, our knowledge must be based not merely on a belief that something is luxury but also on a belief that we are justified in holding because it can be supported as truly so by evidence. Yet, truth depends on a given perspective or system of belief. In this sense, it is necessary to recognise that knowledge is socially constructed. Consequently, our knowledge of luxury is dependent on social context not merely on 'facts'.

In addition to recognising the socially constructed nature of knowledge, it is useful to consider the distinction drawn by philosophers between 'propositional knowledge' (know that), and 'prescriptive knowledge' (know how) (Ryle 2000 [1949]; Polanyi 1958). Propositional knowledge, in terms of 'know that', aligns with knowledge as an object to be captured, made explicit and possessed, while prescriptive knowledge, in terms of 'know how', is more concerned with tacit knowledge, which is developed and known through practice. We can think of tacit knowledge as knowing in action, whereas explicit knowledge is fixed at a particular point in time.

While explicit knowledge can be codified and shared through words, texts and images and embedded in tools and machinery, tacit knowledge is personal (Polanyi 1958). Although explicit knowledge may be acquired by, for instance, reading a book, tacit knowledge must be gained through practice and learning by doing (Arrow 1974). Tacit knowledge is embodied knowledge; it is used automatically and often held unconsciously. Our tacit understanding of our surroundings is developed through our experience over the course of our lives, in being and acting in the world. For instance, we are inculcated with particular beliefs and understandings from our earliest days. These come from our relationships with, for example, family members, friends, teachers and social groups as well as from culture and political organisations. Indeed, everything that we come into contact with leaves an impression on us, however slight or significant, and it is through a lens shaped by these experiences that we encounter and 'see' new artefacts, people, theories, ideologies and so on (Roberts 2000).

In his book on *The Tacit Dimension*, Michael Polanyi offers the valuable insight that 'we know more than we can tell' (1967: 4), in the sense that tacit knowing consists of knowledge that is indeterminate and its content cannot be explicitly stated. Polanyi (1966) demonstrates this in an earlier article in relation to the possession of a skill:

> If I know how to ride a bicycle or how to swim, this does not mean that I can tell how I manage to keep my balance on a bicycle, or keep afloat when swimming. I may not have the slightest idea of how I do this, or even an entirely wrong or grossly imperfect idea of it, and yet go on cycling or swimming merrily . . . I both know how to carry out these performances as a whole and also know how to carry out the elementary acts which constitute them, though I cannot tell what these acts are. (Polanyi 1966: 4)

Consequently, an important characteristic of tacit knowledge is that it cannot be articulated in codified form. Hence, it can only be transferred successfully through a process of demonstration, or show-how, facilitated largely though face-to-face contact between the transmitter and receiver (Roberts 2000).

The distinction between tacit and explicit knowledge is a significant one, as is the relationship between the two types of knowledge (Amin and Cohendet 2004). There is sometimes a tendency to see knowledge as *either* explicit *or* tacit. However, this is much too simplistic. Knowledge is rarely completely tacit or completely codified. For, as Polanyi argues, '[w]hile tacit knowledge can be possessed by itself, explicit knowledge must rely on being tacitly understood and applied. Hence all knowledge is *either tacit* or *rooted in tacit knowledge*. A *wholly* explicit knowledge is unthinkable' (1966: 7, original emphasis). Nevertheless, in the neoliberal market-dominated world of big data and digital media there are strong technological and commercial forces driving the codification of explicit knowledge and privileging this type of understanding over broader and more sophisticated forms of knowledge (Roberts 2001).

Knowing Luxury

Given the dynamic nature of luxury, how do we recognise luxury goods and services? How do we *know* luxury? How do we distinguish it from standard or premium goods and services? Does the addition of the label 'luxury' transform a product into a luxury? Visiting a high street coffee shop chain in the UK you may consume a 'luxury scone' with your coffee – but to what extent is the scone a luxury? Alternatively, is Andrex Touch of Luxury, the most luxurious product in the Andrex toilet tissue range, really a luxury? According to the marketing information, the 'Shea Butter . . . enriched sheets, scented inner core and luxurious dark brown packaging are designed to give you a fabulous feeling'.[4] What this product description captures is an important element of luxury – 'feeling' – which is much more than merely the feeling of the tissue on the skin. The feelings that luxury brands seek to evoke in their customers are emotional – in the sense of being 'deserved', or the desire to fulfil one's dreams (Silverstein and Fiske 2008; Kapferer and Bastien 2012). Given the high level of ambiguity and uncertainty in relation to what luxury is, knowing luxury is open to manipulation, especially through the appeal to our emotions.

Moreover, consumers need support in differentiating luxury from a whole host of premium and standard products and services. Thus, consumers generally and willingly absorb the codified knowledge delivered with authority from luxury companies and their retail staff – who 'really' know the 'authentic' luxurious qualities of the goods and services they offer. It is for this reason that luxury goods and services normally have a strong narrative that can impart to customers, through language, text and visual forms, the characteristics of their products and services, such as quality, rarity, heritage and timelessness. Of course, these heritage narratives are open to embellishment and multiple interpretations. They appeal to the emotions of consumers and feed the desire to possess the luxury good or service in order to be part of the story. Hence, luxury can provide a sense of belonging and identity. In the individualised society, people look to consumption for their sense of identity, but in the advanced societies choice can be a paralysing experience (Bauman 2001). Stories that are linked to a historical trajectory provide a promise of security; hence, luxury goods and services offer the ability to buy into well-established and long sought after ways of living.

Consumers therefore put their trust in luxury brands. Explicit knowledge about luxury branded goods and services, for instance, is easily accessible through a wide range of media from advertisements and brochures, newspaper and magazine articles, television programmes, websites and social media platforms such as Facebook, Twitter and Instagram. Furthermore, such brands are endorsed by market brand specialists, like Interbrand and MillwardBrown Optimor, who have developed highly sophisticated and proprietary methods to establish the validity, ranking and value of brands.

By way of illustration, the luxury brands included in Interbrand's 2014 brand value ranking are listed in Table 2.1. With a brand value estimated to be $22,552 million in 2014, Louis Vuitton is ranked as the top luxury brand while Burberry with an estimated brand value

Table 2.1 Best luxury global brands among Interbrand's* top 100 global brands of 2014. (Source: compiled from Interbrand 2014)

2014 Rank in Luxury Sector	Rank in Top 100 Best Global Brand 2014	Rank in Top 100 Best Global Brand 2013	Luxury Brand	2014 Brand Value (USD $ million)	% Change in Brand Value
1	19	17	Louis Vuitton	22,552	–9%
2	41	38	Gucci	10,385	2%
3	46	54	Hermes	8,977	18%
4	58	60	Cartier	7,449	8%
5	70	72	Prada	5,977	7%
6	71	75	Tiffany & Co	5,936	9%
7	73	77	Burberry	5,594	8%

Note: * Interbrand determines the top 100 most valuable brands each year by examining three key aspects that contribute to a brand's value: (1) the financial performance of the branded product and service; (2) the role the brand plays in influencing customer choice; (3) the strength the brand has to command a premium price or secure earnings for the company (Interbrand 2014).

of \$5,594 million is ranked seventh. However, even the top luxury brand only ranks in nineteenth position among all brands, down from seventeenth in 2013, compared to the technology company Apple, which, with an estimated brand valuation of \$118,863 million in 2014, took the top overall position in Interbrand's complete ranking of the top 100 best brands. Such rankings provide consumers and investors with valuable information about the health of luxury company brands and, by association, the quality of the goods and services they offer.

In addition to brand valuations, there are a many other sources of luxury company information, for instance, concerning sales revenue and profitability, including Deloitte's regular report on the *Global Powers of Luxury Goods* (Deloitte 2015). In the age of the Internet and social media, there is a growing capacity to measure or appoint value to goods and services through the mass of data that is collected and collated by market research companies and through automated systems such as the counting of 'visits', 'likes', 'followers' and 'retweets' on company websites, Facebook pages and Twitter accounts. Such information provides a codified means of evaluating the popularity of luxury brands. But, crucially, it does not tell us anything about knowing these luxuries in practice.

For knowing luxury through an appreciation of the expertise and craftsmanship that goes into the production of a luxury good or service (Ricca and Robins 2012) is simply not accessible to all consumers. This type of knowledge requires time to acquire an appreciation of the materials and techniques involved in the production process. Knowledge of luxury therefore takes different forms. Here, we seek to highlight a distinction between 'knowing that' something is luxury through the absorption of codified knowledge about it and, importantly, 'knowing how' something is a luxury through the development of a tacit appreciation of its qualities and significance gained through socio-cultural practices. First, we know that something is a luxury through the codified knowledge that is disseminated primarily through the promotional activities of luxury brand businesses conveying explicit knowledge as discussed above. Second, we know how something is luxury through a more tacit kind of socio-cultural knowledge that is embedded within and inculcated into us through social interaction gained in practice, as well as by having a deep knowledge of a good or service through an appreciation of, and engagement in, its production.

Bourdieu's notion of habitus, defined as 'systems of durable, transposable dispositions, structured structures predisposed to function as structuring structures' (1990: 53), is useful when considering an individual's tacit understandings of the world formed through the embedded schemes of perception, taste and action. For those individuals who are socialised in a world imbued with luxury, their habitus and the associated dispositions equips them with the socio-cultural knowledge of how something is a luxury. Yet this knowledge is developed over time and is drawn from the understandings held by the individual's social group. Of course, the development and dissemination of social and cultural understandings takes time, as Elias's (2000) account of the development of manners in Western Europe from the Middle Ages reveals. However, once established, individuals develop their appreciation of taste, manners and behaviour through their engagement initially with family members but also with the wider social community. One can only judge the appropriateness of someone else's taste, behaviour and manners if one already has knowledge of what is appropriate in a particular setting from the perspective of one's own social grouping. Importantly, over time, socio-cultural conditionings evolve in response to changes in the environment.

So, for instance, the rising consumption of luxury goods in eighteenth-century Britain traced by Berg (2007) was associated with increasing refinement in the home and social activity. The use of wooden eating utensils and earthenware crockery gave way to silver-plate cutlery and china tableware. As these patterns of consumption and behaviour emerged, they became embedded in the actions and expectations of middle-class members of society. People learned to recognise refinement and its opposite – coarseness. Hence, the middle classes of the industrialising countries of the eighteenth century came to tacitly appreciate the nature of luxury through their engagement with it in the household and through social interactions. The shifting cultures of consumption accompanied by rising levels of education enhanced both the demand for luxury products and the understandings of such luxuries through tacit appreciation. The growing availability of codified knowledge about luxury in the form of advertising bills and coverage in the press and journals supported this evolving understanding of luxury (Berg 2007). For instance, the German title *Journal des Luxus und der Moden* (*The Journal of Luxury and Fashion*) was established in 1786 and published until 1827 with the principal aim of disseminating information about luxury and fashion (Bertuch and Kraus 2016 [1786]). Clearly, such a resource provided readers with explicit knowledge of new luxury goods.

Today of course we have a wealth of information available to us about luxury. But, no matter what the quantity of information, codified knowledge only tells us *that* something is luxury rather than telling *how* it is luxury. Knowing that something is luxury does not ensure that we know how it is luxury. Let us take the example of a Patek Philippe wristwatch to illustrate this point. Here, the luxury brand name itself gives anyone who absorbs information from media sources an indication of the luxury status of the timepieces this particular company produces. If an individual is from a social grouping within which the purchase of luxury watches is a common practice, the brand name Patek Philippe will evoke a deeper socio-cultural appreciation. In October 2014, Patek Philippe launched what it claimed is the most complicated wristwatch in the world – the Grandmaster Chime – as part of its commemorations of the company's 175th year anniversary (Pulvirent 2014). Alongside the launch of the watch, a promotional video of over ten minutes shows the development and construction of the timepiece. The accompanying press release states:

> The effort invested by Patek Philippe in this unique anniversary timepiece is remarkable. More than 100,000 hours were logged for development, production, and assembly, of which 60,000 hours for the components of the movement. Each caliber consists of 1,366 parts and each case of 214 separate parts, bringing the total number of components for each Grandmaster Chime to 1,580. Thus, it took 11,060 meticulously hand-finished parts to assemble the seven limited-edition exemplars of Patek Philippe's commemorative Grandmaster Chime masterpiece. Seven watches that are making history reverberate. (Patek Philippe Geneva 2014: 2)

The press release goes on to provide details about the watch's components and qualities, including its 18 carat hand-engraved rose gold case, its twenty complications, and the seven patents and innovations that the production of the timepiece entailed. Priced at $2.63 million, the watch is beyond the reach of all but a small number of people, yet a book on the watch is available for only CHF140 from the Patek Philippe website. So, accessing knowledge about this extraordinary watch is actually within the reach of many interested individuals.

The knowledge that can be gained through the press release, the video and the book is explicit knowledge, in that it gives the reader or viewer the ability to *know that* the watch is luxurious. However, to truly *know how* the watch is luxurious in terms of an appreciation of the effort and expertise required to construct it, one must have the sort of deep knowledge and skill that is only available to an accomplished watchmaker following many years of apprenticeship and practice. Nevertheless, a certain tacit appreciation is gained by those who have the privilege of owning the timepiece through their regular physical engagement with it – although in the case of the Patek Grandmaster Chime it is most likely to be purchased as an investment rather than an object to be handled or used.

Interestingly, there are some luxuries for which our socio-cultural appreciation is so universal and so deeply embedded that they seem to be known innately, such that how we know them remains almost mysterious. For example, how do we know that the gold contained in the Patek Grandmaster Chime is actually luxurious? At over $1,000 an ounce in 2015, gold is expensive, but its price is sometimes exceeded by that of other precious metals like platinum and rhodium. Gold is in short supply, but rhodium is rarer still. Used in automobile pollution control devices (Davies 2014), rhodium is a mystery to many people. But that is because we do not yet have a cultural affinity with rhodium. All of which begs the question: why is it that we seem to naturally associate gold with luxury? We *know that* gold is luxurious through its high price and other codified means, but we also *know how* it is luxurious through our socio-cultural practices that revere golden objects. Yet, there also appears to be an innate understanding of gold which inspires awe – perhaps we cannot fully tell how we know gold. The comments of the British luxury jeweller Gary Wright concerning the production of gold objects go some way to capturing this point:

> with gold there is a particular part of the process that really is quite magical. It is the moment when the piece of gold is heated and then quenched, and then put into a pickling agent, like an acid, and the moment that the piece of gold comes out of that liquid is the magical moment.[5]

This magical quality no doubt accounts for the use of gold through the ages in religious artefacts and in symbols of sovereign authority. Gold expresses reverence, wealth and power. The attraction to gold is universal to such an extent that even when it is overused, and becomes gaudy or kitsch, it remains a source of fascination. Indeed, it is this almost global social value of gold that makes it a reserve store of wealth in times of economic and political instability and that fuels the investment market for the commodity.

Knowing luxury is thus much more complex than the mere provision of definitions and classifications. As this section has revealed, luxury can both be known through the absorption of codified knowledge, giving individuals the ability to *know that* something is luxury, or individuals can *know how* something is luxury through tacit knowledge deriving from a socio-cultural practice-based understanding. We now turn to consider how our understandings of luxury are influenced by the rise to dominance of the market in the contemporary neoliberal era.

Knowing Luxury: From Socio-Cultural Value to Market Price?

The neoliberal ideology, first adopted by President Ronald Reagan in the USA and Prime Minister Margaret Thatcher in the UK in the late 1970s, promotes free national and international markets with minimal state intervention (Harvey 2005). Supported by international institutions, such as the World Trade Organization, the International Monetary Fund and the World Bank, by the mid-1980s, this free market ideology had become widespread and an important driver, alongside new information and digital technologies, of the globalisation of markets (Held et al. 1999). Like all businesses, luxury companies have been exposed to increasing levels of competition, which has encouraged the consequent appropriation and commodification of knowledge through patents and trademarks, as well as through company-specific means of managing proprietary knowledge (Roberts 2015). It is against this backdrop that we must view the shift from knowing luxury through its socio-cultural value to knowing luxury through its market price.

Indeed, we argue that the prevalence of market valuation, supported by digital technologies and big data, is leading to the intensification of the codification and objectification of knowledge about luxury, to the detriment of the more subjective, socially constituted practice of what we term 'knowing luxury'. Consequently, luxury is, for instance, recognised and validated as such because it is produced by a company that is renowned and acclaimed for the production of luxury goods, ranked as a top luxury brand by Interbrand, and acknowledged as luxurious on popular social media platforms through the number of Facebook 'likes' or Twitter 'followers'. The market absorbs this multitude of information and reflects it in the price of the luxury branded good or service. Thus, we *know that* something is luxury because we can objectively measure its standing as 'verified' by its market price and other indicators of worth, but we still do not *know how* it is luxury.

Yet, proponents of the market as the most efficient means of collating knowledge tend to overlook its weaknesses. Markets, for instance, may fail to fully account for the social or environmental costs or benefits that are not wholly reflected in the conditions of demand or supply. Similarly, concentration among suppliers may give certain producers the ability to control the flow of knowledge to the market and thereby influence the market price. For instance, the luxury market is characterised by a degree of economic concentration, with the top ten companies accounting for 48.9 per cent of the top 100 luxury goods companies' sales in 2013 (Deloitte 2015: 22). This means that large luxury companies with strong brands, huge advertising budgets and loyal customers wield a degree of market power that can distort the efficiency of the market. Hence, the validity of the market price to truly represent the full range of knowledge about a luxury good or service is open to question.

Moreover, knowing how a good or service is a luxury within a certain context is based on knowing its socio-cultural value rather than merely its market price or brand ranking. Markets, as mechanisms for apportioning the worth of goods and services do, of course, incorporate socio-cultural values as factors determining price. However, as goods and services become disengaged from the socio-cultural contexts in which they originally gained value, through mass production and globalisation, for instance, the determinants of price become disassociated from socio-cultural values. Rather, price becomes a function of factors including the systems of international production, research and development, mass media marketing costs, and the need to ensure a good return on shareholder investments. Thus, through the intensified marketisation of luxury, price becomes dislocated from socio-cultural value and knowing that something is a luxury through the codified knowledge distributed by luxury brand companies and market prices becomes more prevalent than knowing how it is a luxury through socio-cultural practices.

Although the meaning of luxury rests on the relevant socio-cultural contexts, those concerned with the business of luxury seek to fix its meaning by providing various qualifiers and classifying different types of luxury. Only through this codification of luxury is it possible to develop universally accepted luxuries that can be marketed across the globe. Commerce seeks to untangle the inherent connection of luxury to specific socio-cultural contexts in order to ensure its universal acceptability in markets across the world. Yet, simultaneously, luxury companies exploit connections to socio-cultural values as a resource for promotional campaigns when and where they can. Dislocated from its socio-cultural roots in global markets, luxury therefore takes on alternative meanings in different contexts, but, importantly, it is also integrated into new environments as luxuries determined by high market price rather than emerging

Table 2.2 Knowing luxury: from socio-cultural to market-based understandings

Characteristics and context of knowing	Socio-cultural understandings of luxury	Market understandings of luxury
Type of knowledge	Know how – knowing	Know that – knowledge
Locus of the knowledge	Tacit socio-cultural understandings	Explicit, codified market mechanisms
Sources of such knowledge	Socially constituted through social groupings, e.g. communities/families/ national cultures etc.; learning by doing	Expressed by logos and other codified forms through websites, blogs, press and visual media, social media, promotional campaigns
Nature of the social context	Community-based, social grouping	Individualised
Spatial dimension	Local	Global
Nature of symbols	Symbols are a reified form of social identity	Logos are a marketing device to stimulate brand loyalty and 'signal' luxury
Valuation	Socio-cultural worth	Market price
Ownership of knowledge	Socio-cultural artefacts that are produced, owned and known by communities and social groups	Luxury brand value is reified in logos, which are commodified through registration and trade marking.
Relative positioning in the contemporary era	Diminishing/losing ground	Strengthening/becoming more dominant

from socio-cultural and practice-based valuations. This has implications for the way that we come to know luxury, as is summarised in Table 2.2, where a clear distinction is delineated between the various characteristics and contexts of knowing in relation to socio-cultural and market understandings of luxury. As Table 2.2 shows, these differences in understandings are far reaching, from, for instance, tacit to explicit, local to global, and community-based to individualised.

Hence, the market becomes the judge of luxury rather than any deeper socio-cultural imperative. Of course, there is to some extent a symbiotic process at work with socio-cultural valuations determining market price and market price influencing socio-cultural valuations in an ongoing and mutually reinforcing process. However, the growing pervasiveness of codified market-based evaluations of luxury promoted through new technologies, including social media and the collection and mining of big data, suggests that knowledge of luxury is becoming increasingly explicit rather than tacit. We *know that* something is luxury because we can interpret all the various forms of codified knowledge about it, but we do not *know how* it is luxury.

Luxury is thus gradually becoming disconnected from socio-cultural and practice-based understandings in order to maximise the global market for luxury goods and services. What were once objects and activities that were deeply entwined in socio-cultural valuations and practices become merely commercial goods and services gaining significance only from their market price and associated mediated valuations.

The drive for economic efficiency and profitability promoted by the rise of neoliberalism has led to a general intensification of the quantification and codification of knowledge stimulated by the desire to commodify and appropriate value from knowledge (Roberts 2001, 2015). In the case of luxury, the codification of knowledge about goods and services is driven by a commercial imperative to appropriate the maximum value from the idea of luxury in global markets. To do this, it is necessary to develop an understanding of luxury that can have relevance across the globe, no matter where it initially originated. Codified knowledge about luxury can be transferred across time and space more easily than tacit knowledge, which is derived from specific socio-cultural values and practices. Hence, the meanings of luxury embedded in socio-cultural understandings are gradually being superseded by market approaches in an era where price becomes the sole arbiter of the meaning of luxury in global markets.

Conclusion

With the aim of advancing a critical appreciation of luxury, this chapter has examined how luxury is known. Although much attention has been applied to defining the idea of luxury and the nature of luxury goods and services, little effort has been devoted to understanding how luxury is known. From the examination of luxury outlined in this chapter it is evident that how we come to know luxury is complex. We have elaborated on an important distinction between *knowing that* something is luxury based on market understandings and *knowing how* something is luxury based on socio-cultural understandings. Moreover, we have argued here that our appreciation of luxury is increasingly influenced by the rise to dominance of markets in the neoliberal era. Hence, tacit socio-cultural practice-based understandings of luxury progressively give way to market-driven codification and commodification of explicit understandings of luxury.

Notes

1. In 2014, Dr Michael Scott presented a two-part BBC television series on luxury entitled, *Guilty Pleasures: Luxury in* . . . The first episode focused on Ancient Greece and is available at https://www.youtube.com/watch?v=1b3JHO3KPkw (accessed 23 October 2015).
2. In their *World Ultra Wealth Report*, Wealth-X and UBS (2014) define Ultra High Net Worth Individuals (UHNWI) as those individuals that have a net worth of at least US$30 million.
3. Nevertheless, niche markets can be made profitable through the use of the Internet to reach sufficient customers to make a product or service commercially viable. However, such markets are not as likely to deliver the sustainable growth in profits available in global markets.
4. Description available at http://www.waitrose.com/shop/DisplayProduct Flyout?productId=61019 (accessed 23 October 2015).
5. Wright & Teague Jewelry: Workshop #1 Behind the Scenes https://www.youtube.com/watch?v=TL0AVbZ14Qs (accessed 23 October 2015).

References

Allérès, Danielle (1990), *Luxe, stratégies-marketing*, Paris: Economica.

Amin, Ash and Cohendet, Patrick (2004), *Architectures of Knowledge: Firms, Capabilities and Communities*, Oxford: Oxford University Press.

Armitage, J. and Roberts, J. (2014), 'Luxury new media: euphoria in unhappiness', *Luxury: History, Culture, Consumption*, 1 (1): 111–32.

Arrow Kenneth (1974), *The Limits of Organization*, New York: Norton.

Bagwell, L. S. and Bernheim, B. D. (1996), 'Veblen effects in a theory of conspicuous consumption', *The American Economic Review*, 86 (3): 349–73.

Bauman, Zygmunt (2001), *The Individualized Society*, Cambridge: Polity Press.

Berg, Maxine (2007), *Luxury and Pleasure in Eighteenth-Century Britain*, Oxford: Oxford University Press.

Bertuch, Friedrich Justin and Kraus, Georg Melchior (2016 [1786]), 'Introduction to the Journal of Luxury and Fashion', translated and with an introduction by Geoffrey Winthrop-Young, *Cultural Politics*, 12 (1): 23–31.

Berry, Christoper, J. (1994), *The Idea of Luxury: A Conceptual and Historical Investigation*, Cambridge: Cambridge University Press.

Bourdieu, Pierre (1990), *The Logic of Practice*, Stanford: Stanford University Press.

Chevalier, Michel and Mazzalovo, Gerald (2012), *Luxury Brand Management: A World of Privilege*, 2nd edn, Singapore: Wiley and Sons.

D'Arpizio, C., Levato, F., Zito, D. and de Montgolfier, J. (2014), *Luxury Goods Worldwide Market Study, Fall–Winter 2014: The rise of the borderless consumer*, Bain and Company, 2014. Available at http://

www.bain.com/publications/articles/luxury-goods-worldwide-market-study-december-2014.aspx (accessed 15 May 2015).

Davies, A. (2014), 'Rhodium rally pushes price past platinum, gold: chart of the day', Bloomberg Business, 24 August. Available at: http://www.bloomberg.com/news/articles/2014-08-24/rhodium-rally-pushes-price-past-platinum-gold-chart-of-the-day (accessed 20 August 2015).

Deloitte (2015), *Global Powers of Luxury Goods: Engaging the Future Luxury Consumer*. Available at: http://www2.deloitte.com/content/dam/Deloitte/global/Documents/Consumer-Business/gx-cb-global-power-of-luxury-web.pdf (accessed 23 August 2015).

Elias, Norbert (2000), *The Civilizing Process: Sociogenetic and Psychogenetic Investigations*, trans. Edmund Jephcott, revised edn, ed. Eric Dunning, Johan Goudsblom and Stephen Mennell, Oxford: Blackwell.

European Cultural and Creative Industries Alliance (ECCIA) (2012), *European Cultural and Creative Luxury Industries: Key Drivers for European Jobs and Growth*. Available at: http://www.eccia.eu/uploads/media/Key_drivers_02.pdf (accessed 27 August 2015).

Frank, H. Robert (1999), *Luxury Fever: Weighing the Cost of Excess*, Princeton and Oxford: Princeton University Press.

Harvey, David (2005), *A Brief History of Neoliberalism*, Oxford: Oxford University Press.

Hayek, F. A. von (1945), 'The use of knowledge in society', *The American Economic Review*, 35 (4): 519–30.

Held, David, McGrew, Anthony, Goldblatt, David and Perraton, Jonathan (1999), *Global Transformations: Politics, Economics and Culture*, Cambridge: Polity Press.

Hoffmann, Jonas and Coste-Maniere, Ivan (2012), *Luxury Strategy in Action*, London: Palgrave Macmillan.

Hoffmann, Jonas and Coste-Maniere, Ivan (2013), *Global Luxury Trends: Innovative Strategies for Emerging Markets*, London: Palgrave Macmillan.

Hume, David (1987 [1742]), *Essays Moral, Political and Literary*, Indianapolis: Liberty Fund.

Interbrand (2014), 'Interbrand's 15th annual Best Global Brands Report'. Available at: http://www.rankingthebrands.com/The-Brand-Rankings.aspx?rankingID=37&year=857 (accessed 23 October 2015).

Kapferer, Jean-Noël and Bastien, Vincent (2012), *The Luxury Strategy: Break the Rules of Marketing to Build Luxury Brands*, London: Kogan Page.

Marcuse, Herbert (1964), *One-Dimensional Man*, Boston: Beacon.

Neich, Roger and Pendergrast, Mick (2005), *Pacific Tapa*, Honolulu: University of Hawaii Press.

Nickel, P. M. (2015), 'Haute philanthropy: luxury, benevolence, and value', *Luxury: History, Culture, Consumption*, 2 (2) (forthcoming).

Oxford Dictionary of English (OED) (2003), Oxford: Oxford University Press.

Patek Philippe Geneva (2014), Press release: Patek Philippe Grandmaster Chime Ref. 5175: The sound of history, October. Available at: http://www. patek.com/press/en/2014_PatekPhilippe_GrandmasterChime_5175R. pdf (accessed 24 October 2014).

Polanyi, Michael (1958), *Personal Knowledge: Towards a Post Critical Philosophy*, London: Routledge and Kegan Paul.

Polanyi, Michael (1966), 'The logic of tacit inference', *Philosophy*, 41 (155): 1–18.

Polanyi, Michael (1967), *The Tacit Dimension*, London: Routledge.

Pulvirent, S. (2014), 'Patek Philippe unveils Grandmaster Chime: the world's most complicated wristwatch (ever)', *BloombergBusiness*, 13 October. Available at: http://www.bloomberg.com/news/2014-10-13/patek-philippe-unveils-grandmaster-chime-the-world-s-most-complicated-wristwatch-ever-.html (accessed 25 August 2015).

Putnam, Robert (2000), *Bowling Alone: The Collapse and Revival of American Community*, New York: Simon & Schuster.

Quintavalle, A. (2013), 'Uber luxury: for billionaires only', in J. Hoffmann and I. Coste-Maniere (eds), *Global Luxury Trends*, Houndsmill, Basingstoke: Palgrave Macmillan, pp. 51–76.

Ricca, Manfredi and Robins, Rebecca (2012), *Meta-luxury: Brand and the Culture of Excellence*, London: Palgrave Macmillan.

Roberts, Joanne (2000), 'From know-how to show-how? Questioning the role of information and communication technologies in knowledge transfer', *Technology Analysis and Strategic Management*, 12 (4): 429–43.

Roberts, Joanne (2001), 'The drive to codify: implications for the knowledge-based economy', *Prometheus: Critical Studies in Innovation*, 19 (2): 99–116.

Roberts, Joanne (2014), 'Luxury and ignorance', 19th DMI: Academic Design Management Conference 'Design Management in an Era of Disruption', London, 2–4 September.

Roberts, Joanne (2015), *A Very Short, Fairly Interesting and Reasonably Cheap Book About Knowledge Management*, London, Los Angeles, New Delhi, Singapore, Washington: Sage Publications.

Roberts, Joanne and Armitage, John (2015), 'Luxury and creativity: exploration, exploitation, or preservation?', *Technology Innovation Management Review*, 5 (7): 41–9.

Ryle, Gilbert (2000 [1949]), *The Concept of the Mind*, London: Penguin.

Silverstein, Michael, J. and Fiske, Neil (2008), *Trading Up: Why Consumers Want New Luxury Goods – and How Companies Create Them*, London: Penguin.

Skidelsky, Robert and Skidelsky, Edward (2013), *How Much is Enough? Money and the Good Life*, London: Penguin.

Smith, Adam (1982 [1776]), *The Wealth of Nations*, Books I–III, London: Penguin.

Thomas, Dana (2007), *Deluxe: How Luxury Lost its Lustre*, London: Penguin.

Tungate, Mark (2009), *Luxury World: The Past, Present and Future of Luxury Brands*, London: Kogan Page.
Veblen, Thorstein (1899), *The Theory of the Leisure Class: An Economic Study in the Evolution of Institutions*, New York and London: Macmillan.
Wealth-X and UBS (2014), *World Ultra Wealth Report 2014*. Available at http://www.worldultrawealthreport.com/home.php (accessed 23 August 2015).

Chapter 3

Luxury: A Dialectic of Desire?

Christopher J. Berry

I start at the beginning with a word about my title. I allude to the philosophy of Hegel. For Hegel, thought or reason has a dynamic tripartite structure: there is a posited affirmation, a negation or contradiction of that affirmation, then a negation of that negation or a reaffirmation. This reaffirmation, however, is not a return to the status quo ante but rather constitutes a preservative transcendence that is captured in Hegel's exploitation of the German term *Aufhebung*. I am not about to embark upon an investigation of Hegelian metaphysics but I do want to use this tripartite structure to frame this discussion. My title also ends with a question mark. It serves to signal the open-ended character of my argument, in particular whether there is a viable *Aufhebung*, a move beyond the second phase or Moment (in Hegel-ese).

More concretely, the three parts are as follows: Part I outlines the view that luxury as part of a moralised vocabulary was considered bad or dangerous; this view persists until about the seventeenth century. In Part II, I outline the rejection or negation of this, the process that I have labelled the 'de-moralisation' of luxury. In these first two parts I necessarily have to paint with a broad brush as I depict two and a half thousand years of speculation about luxury. In Part III, I examine what might be said about a 're-moralisation', that is, whether there is a viable or sustainable critique of luxury in the contemporary world. My triad is thus moralisation, de-moralisation, re-moralisation (question mark). A leitmotif through this is the role played by, and assessment of, human desire.

I. Moralisation

Classically luxury belongs generically in a moralised vocabulary. It takes its meaning from its role as a corruption of virtue. Hence poverty, frugality, simplicity and austerity are estimable practices that exhibit the virtues of temperance and continence. To be austere is to be in control of oneself and thus of one's actions. I have in mind here the Stoic sage who will drink but not get drunk or the Patristic prohibition of sex with, or by, a pregnant woman. One consequence of situating poverty in this lexicon is that it is not synonymous with 'necessity'; to be poor out of necessity has no place in *this* discourse. Indeed, it frequently and deliberately talked of 'voluntary poverty' (Seneca 1932: 111; Tierney 1959: 11). This has the further implication that the subjects of moral criticism were not the necessitous poor but either corrupt aristocrats (like Catiline who was the target of Sallust's polemic against the moral laxity of the age) or the upwardly mobile (who were the focus of the sumptuary laws of early modern Europe). The significance of this will become apparent.

The upshot of these initial schematic remarks is that when luxury is juxtaposed to poverty it is a vice. This manifested itself at both the individual and social level. To live luxuriously is to wallow in self-indulgence. Pointedly, men who live a life of luxury become effeminate. That is to say they become 'soft', unable to endure hardship and act in a 'manly' fashion, where that means acting in the public arena, including risking death and acting courageously. It is not mere coincidence that in both Greek and Latin the words for 'man' have the same root as those for 'courage'. Such a life has social consequences. A society where luxury is established will devote itself to private ends and men will be unwilling to act for the public good or fight for their *patria*. This society, it follows, will be militarily weak: a nation of cowards will easily succumb. The only way a luxurious, soft nation could meet its military commitments was by hiring others to play that role. Hence arose an important negative association between luxury, wealth (commerce) and mercenary armies.

It is this moralised picture that is de-moralised in the negative Moment of the dialectic. But before turning to that in Part II, I want to elaborate on this moralised picture. This elaboration focuses on the role of desire. The concept of desire can be aptly contrasted with that of need. Perhaps the crucial fact about needs is their non-privileged status. Whether or not you need something is not definitively answered by your beliefs about that something, whereas to desire or want something depends on a subjective state of mind. Hence (I simplify) you need a liver transplant without wanting surgery and, conversely, you desire another piece of pie without needing it to ensure your daily intake of calories. In the current context it is an implication of this latter example that is revealing. From the moralised perspective of frugality, taking that extra piece is a luxurious indulgence, a deleterious lack of resolve that by pandering to desire betrays a defect in character. An informative illustration comes from the late Stoic philosopher Epictetus. He is recorded as saying that the measure for a slipper is the foot, where 'measure' means not merely the correct size but, more significantly, that a slipper is needed for the purpose of foot protection. Once that appropriate or 'natural' measure of needfulness is forsaken then there are no limits and, as a result, there becomes nothing inappropriate about, successively, desiring a gilded, a purple and an embroidered slipper (Epictetus 1932: 525). It was this limitlessness associated with 'desire' that made it so threatening.

The classically virtuous life was a 'natural life'. Cicero (1927: 529) declares it to be self-evident that Nature's requirements are few and inexpensive. This 'natural life' is the 'simple', or Christian ascetic, life. Those who live simply will not be poor because poverty is only experienced by those who have exceeded the natural limits, that is, by those who desire more. Once the natural limit is passed then, as Epictetus' slippers illustrate, there is no resting place. And writ large, viewed from that perspective, life itself will always appear too short, so that those who 'wallow in luxury' become afraid of death (Seneca 1932: II, 197). Such fear is unmanly, hence the association between luxury, softness and effeminacy mentioned earlier. As Cicero (1913: 109) summarises it, this association exemplifies *turpe*, a corrupt way of life, in contrast to which a frugal life of temperance, sobriety and austerity is worthy or *honestum*.

There are two corollaries of this moralisation of luxury that I wish to mention briefly. The first is the somatic focus. It was held to be the definitive characteristic of desires that focus on the body that they are boundless (Seneca 1932: I, 109). For example, Seneca (1932: III, 373) disparages the enjoyment of fine food (bread made from inferior flour assuages hunger as effectively as that baked from better quality ingredients – the purpose of food is to fill the stomach not indulge it). From this perspective, what the desire for luxuries amounted to was investing inappropriate value in bodily satisfactions. My own conceptual analysis of 'luxury' emphasised this connection between luxury and the enjoyment of pleasing goods (Berry 1994: ch. 1). I still wish to affirm it. Of course, as with everything else, there is a semiotics of luxury that gives it a 'sign value in a world of signs' (Mortelmans 2005: 517). However, unless luxuries gave pleasure there would, pace Baudrillard (1988: 47) or Appadurai (1986: 144), be nothing to register or communicate; they are, as I termed them, 'refinements' of universal satisfactions, and some empirical investigations, making reference to my work, do provide some support for this (Kemp 1998; van der Veen 2003; Dubois, Czellar and Laurent 2005).

The second and related corollary is that those activities that serviced these bodily satisfactions should be contained within the household, the function of which was, in Aristotle's formative analysis, to meet limited needs. This literally 'economic' task may, within limits, go beyond the *oikos*, so tomatoes may be exchanged for some salt, as long as – and these are the limits – the recipient uses the tomatoes for their proper or natural purpose, that is, consumes them. But once the limitless desires for superfluous luxuries set in, then exchange itself or commerce becomes, in the form of traders or merchants, an occupation in its own right. In pursuing exchange these traders were seen as pursuing their private interest (Aristotle 1994: 35–49). This moralised perspective easily fed into the view that compared to a citizen in the full sense, that is, one who dedicated his life to the public good (including importantly military service), a merchant lived a less fulfilling, less humanly worthwhile, life.

The negation of this moralised context for luxury centrally concerns a re-valuation of the place of desire and the role played by commerce. To this I now turn.

II.   De-Moralisation

I employed the term 'de-moralisation' in my book and, while there have been some niggles with my chronology (e.g. Peck 2005: 6–8), which was anyway approximate, the term has been accepted. The process captured by this term is, of course, part of a broad shift. While I have been criticised for not going beyond the borders of intellectual debate into the wider fields of practice and consumer behaviour (Smith 2002: 64), I remain of the view that the debate over 'commerce' was a crucial component in the re-evaluation of luxury, which is not to say, of course, that it is the sole factor. We know that from about the early seventeenth century (certainly in England) consumption expanded and marketing structures, including credit networks, became more complex (Mulgrew 1998), to reach, as extensive scholarship has established, considerable sophistication in the eighteenth century (e.g. Brewer and Porter 1993; Berg and Clifford 1999). I picked out Nicholas Barbon as a key representative of this re-valuation, but here (drawing on Berry 1999) I focus for expository reasons on David Hume's essays 'Of Commerce' and 'Of Refinement of Arts', which on its first appearance in 1752 was titled 'Of Luxury'.

Hume opens 'Of Refinement' by stating that 'luxury' is a word of 'uncertain signification' (1987b [1752]: 268). He knows full well the position of those 'severe moralists' (as he calls them – Sallust is named as an example) that 'luxury' is a vice, and he also knows that Bernard Mandeville in the early eighteenth century was notorious for attacking this moralising line. Hume is also well aware that the critique had been taken up, more soberly, by contemporaries in France, like Jean-François Melon. Against this backcloth, and despite his declaration of uncertainty, Hume gives his own definition: luxury is 'great refinement in the gratification of senses' (1987b [1752]: 268). Any thought that this is intended to be read censoriously, as an endorsement of the moralised position, is displaced by his generalising remark that 'ages of refinement' are 'both the happiest and most virtuous' (1987b [1752]: 269). In a clear break from the moralist tradition, therefore, Hume is coupling, luxury/refinement with happiness/virtue *not* opposing them.

For Hume (1987b [1752]: 269–70) happiness comprises repose, pleasure and action. By 'action' he means the private endeavour of industry and not the Ciceronic *negotium*, with its preoccupation with public or political affairs. Where industry abounds then individuals will be both opulent and happy, as they 'reap the benefit of . . . commodities so far as they gratify the senses and appetite' (1987a [1752]: 263). Humans seek this gratification; they are motivated by 'avarice and industry, art and luxury' (1987a [1752]: 263). Since 'luxury' and 'avarice' were uniformly condemned by the severe moralists, this statement alone is a marker of de-moralisation, encapsulating as it does the switch in evaluations that has occurred. We can pursue what was involved in that switch by picking up on Hume's further remark that humans are roused to activity or industry (itself a source of happiness as we have seen) by a 'desire of a more splendid way of life than what their ancestors enjoyed' (1987a [1752]: 264).

It is the use of 'desire' here that is significant because it testifies to the presence of the premises of 'modern' psychology – to why, that is, somatic gratification is sought. The modern view rejects the classical teleological perspective, whereby food is eaten for the purpose of assuaging hunger or a slipper is worn for the purpose of foot protection. In rejecting this perspective, the 'modernist' also rejects the idea that desires can be limited to some fixed end. As Thomas Hobbes (1991 [1651]: Ch. 6) pointed out, the only way to be 'free' of desire is to be dead. Motion, or 'uneasiness of the mind', as John Locke (1854 [1690]: I, 377) had defined 'desire', is the correct description of how the world (not excluding humans) *is*. Humans move towards what they imagine pleases and away from what they imagine will occasion pain. For Aristotle, by contrast, mutability was characteristic of normative imperfection. This pre-modern conception set up a basic distinction between, on the one hand, the tranquil/ascetic life, devoted to the contemplation of the immutable First Cause or the eternal perfection of God, and, on the other, the mundane life which is unceasingly at the beck and call of the demands of bodily desires.

We can clarify the shift from the pre-modern to the modern as follows. The first sees meeting needs as part of some value-laden purposive order with definite limits, such that desire can be understood as transgressing them. This gives way to the second perspective, to the view that desires, far from transgressing some predetermined or naturally fixed boundary, are, rather, the definitive element in human motivation and are thus to be accepted for what they are – the motors and determiners of human values. The reference here to 'transgression' invokes the attendant idea of social discipline. The pre-modern moralists sought to police these desires in the light of a supposedly objectively valid account of the 'good life' or 'good and politic order'. I have principally in mind here sumptuary laws (the phrase 'good and politic order' comes from the preamble to the English Act of Apparel of 1533 [in Harte 1976: 139]). These laws were a persistent feature of early modern Europe (and beyond) and almost no one was excluded from their reach. This legislation gradually atrophied, even if at different rates, and was dismissed by modernists like Barbon and Hume. I see this decline as symptomatic of the new role played by 'desire'. That is, once desires are seen as the bearers of values then any individual self-discipline is a matter of calculation – the desire for the piece of pie against the desire to fit into that new dress. The social counterpart is a matter of weighing up the merits of freeing or restricting commerce. Hence the construction of a positive role for luxury goods; not only did they serve as aspirational incentives, leading to increase in employment and diffusion of pleasing/desirable goods, they also brought with them the crucial corollary that, as objects of universal desire, everyone is entitled to these aspirations and the free enjoyment of those goods. In contrast, the moralised world was in reality a world of slavery.

If we return to Hume, a significant move in his rebuttal of the moralised case was his claim that a commercial society that recognises the value of luxury is one that accords with basic human motivations or the 'natural bent of the mind', as he terms it (1987a [1752]: 263). Central to this 'bent' is the recognition of the motivational role of self-interest. The classical moralised disparagement of merchants, because they devoted themselves to private commercial pursuits, became modified, deflected and ultimately neutered by a succession of early writers on commerce like John Houghton (1677).

This vindication of commerce is intimately connected to a reformulation of what constitutes the common good. Instead of identifying this with some objective, rational doctrine of the 'good life', the appropriate question is: does this policy promote the material well-being of those individuals subject to it? The production, and enjoyment, of luxury goods meets this criterion, sumptuary legislation does not.

What we find emblematically in Hume, therefore, is a de-coupling of luxury from its role as the negative counterpart to the virtue of poverty. Thus detached luxury can be viewed positively because of its beneficial social effects; it promotes employment, industry, population and, significantly given its salience in the moralised indictment, military strength. If luxury is criticised it is on economic rather than moral grounds. The germs of this can be detected in seventeenth-century debates on 'trade' and, in the eighteenth century, it appears, for example, in the arguments of the Physiocrats that luxury was 'sterile', that is, was devoted to unproductive rather than productive ends (Mirabeau 1760). Of course, the evolution of ideas is not smooth, but once luxury was detached from a moralistic context, and 'economics' developed as a discipline, 'luxury' came to attain a technical neutral meaning as high income elasticity of demand.

The shift away from moralism that Hume's account exemplifies means that luxury can be understood as contingently not categorically differentiated from necessity, as a different point on a continuum. A life of necessity now signifies not the austere life of poverty but an impoverished one, a life of misery. There is nothing ennobling or redemptive about *this* poverty. As Adam Smith put it in the Introduction to the *Wealth of Nations*, those who are 'miserably poor' are 'frequently reduced' to infanticide and abandonment of the old and sick 'to perish with hunger or to be devoured by wild beasts'. While, in vivid and stark contrast, in a 'civilized and thriving country', 'universal opulence' extends itself to the 'lowest rank of people', who are supplied 'abundantly with what they have occasion for' (1981 [1776]: 10, 21). Not for nothing did Smith profess, in his lectures at Glasgow University, that 'opulence and freedom' were the 'two greatest blessings men can possess' (1982 [1763]: 185).

Once luxury is 'de-moralised' then with the rise of mass consumption it was easily pressed into service as a guileless description to make goods 'desirable'. And once seen in this light, its salience within the lexicon of 'ad speak' can be understood. Of course, as Epictetus asserts, no one *needs* a pair of embroidered slippers; their decorativeness is superfluous. But in the modern world there is such thing as superfluous value (Berry 2008). Embroidered slippers are more pleasing than plain ones, and where's the harm in that pleasure? Moreover, think of all the extra industry generated, and employment created, by the desire to have those exquisitely produced slippers and think, too, of the economic benefits that will flow from my now legitimised desire to own next year an even more fashionable and luxurious pair.

The dynamism of desire in this way fuels the engine of modern economies. One way of depicting this dynamism is to chart the seemingly never-ceasing transformation of luxuries into necessities as points on the continuum shift. However the rampant consumerism implicit in this luxury-to-necessity dynamic is not without its contemporary critics and it is to these that I turn in the final Part III.

III.   Re-Moralisation?

The language of 'luxury' is ubiquitous. Leaving aside the self-identified 'luxury goods sector', it is, seemingly without hesitation, tacked on adjectivally to almost any article of merchandise from bottled water to armoured vehicles and done so presumably to make them more desirable and thus more likely to be bought. Similarly reflecting this ubiquity, there exist consultancies like the 'Luxury Institute' as well as professional sectoral analysts employed by investment companies. Not surprisingly, contemporary discussion of luxury is extensive. Some of this is manifest in journalistic books like Dana Thomas's *DeLuxe* (2007) or Mark Tungate's *Luxury World* (2009), or popularising works like Stephen Twitchell's *Living it Up: Our Love Affair with Luxury* (2002), or historical surveys like William Adams's *On Luxury* (2012), or in management 'how to' books like Silverstein and Fiske's *Trading Up* (2003). There is also more academic work. This work cross-cuts a number of research interests such as, especially, marketing and consumer behaviour but also sociology, semiotics and history. What all this endeavour reflects is the growing interest in, and debate over, 'luxury', to the extent indeed of generating dedicated academic journals.

Consistent with my dialectic structure, the common thread of this part is whether the negative Moment of de-moralisation, allowing the pursuit of luxury to run unchecked, needs to be negated. I want, that is to say, to examine what grounds there might be for a 're-moralisation' of luxury. I acknowledge that often this is enmeshed within a more general critique of consumerism. My selective examination will cover three porous areas of critique before concluding with a very brief assessment of their plausibility. The three areas are the Ethical, the Social and the Green.

Ethical

Despite the sea change represented by de-moralisation, and the assumed innocence in consequence of using 'luxury' as a positive label to induce consumption, there has always been a substratum of moral disapproval to the effect that while we might be materially richer we are ethically poorer.

There are, of course, a number of ways to gauge this ethical impoverishment. From these I will pick up three. The first of these associates luxury with selfishness. As David Cloutier expresses it, 'luxury involves the securing of private pleasure at the expense of others and of the common good' (2012: 15). He deliberately juxtaposes this with Christian teaching, while a case more obviously echoing the classical moralisation of luxury is given by Robert and Edward Skidelsky. The Skidelskys openly commend the Aristotelian 'good life', where there is a 'natural limit' to acquisition and consumption, avowing that 'the just and temperate person accumulates just those things he needs for a good life and then stops' (2012: 74). It is a perversion to turn means (such as wealth) into an end. Recalling our reference to Epictetus' slippers, the Skidelskys make much of the distinction between needs and wants, indeed they plot the distinction between necessities and luxuries in those terms by defining the latter as 'things one wants but does not need' (2012: 25, 90). While claiming it is 'common sense' that 'needs should not be sacrificed to luxuries', they nonetheless recognise the classical provenance here and claim it offers a superior perspective to that now prevalent. They argue that at the heart of the current malaise is consumption, which modern capitalism induces and inflames (2012: 169, 203).

This fits the second strand of the ethical critique. Wolfgang Haug is unambiguous: capitalism generates 'the creation and control of a need for luxury' with the implication that this is 'not a good thing' (1986: 21). While Marx, despite his own fastidiousness about moral criticism, fairly obviously lies behind this proclamation, his followers have been forced to acknowledge the resilience of capitalism. They, nonetheless, reveal their basic allegiance when they treat 'ethical capitalism' as, in effect, an oxymoron (cf. Žižek 2010: 356) and when they argue that 'the creation and control of a need for luxury' is as true of late as it was of early capitalism (Holmstrom 1974: 431, 436).

'Late' capitalism is also the site (by and large) of cultural critique. One example will have to suffice. In her recent book on luxury, Patrizia Calefato makes but one passing reference to Marx but many to Georges Bataille. Perhaps reflecting that provenance the book combines the elliptical and the apodeictic. Yet an ethical critique is never too far away. Hence we are informed, as if the point was too obvious to require commentary, that luxury is a 'troubling presence' in the context of globalisation and that 'the ostentation of dress and manner all become occasions to portray implacably the obscenity that luxury and wealth reveal in their most frivolous and otiose manifestations' (Calefato 2012: 21; cf. 23, 67). Calefato makes ample use of advertising, film and media, since for her 'luxury is both myth and discourse. Its signs are visible and communicable and can be manipulated through visual images and words' (2012: 14). We will meet 'advertising' again, but it remains moot in Calefato how much this is to be censured. Although she includes in her title the term 'excess', which is redolent of the classical critique, this is seen as an ambivalence, as at once damagingly wasteful yet also as the space for exalted magnificence (2012: 3).

My final strand takes up the general charge that luxuries, as the acme of material prosperity, have not made us 'happier'. In contrast to Adam Smith's comments about opulence and freedom quoted above, Richard Layard, a leading exponent of what he calls the 'new science of happiness', declares that there is 'more to life than prosperity and freedom' (2006: 7). The basic finding of the research he surveys is that having more does not make you happier. At the heart of this lies the idea of a hedonic treadmill, which 'condemns' us 'to seek new levels of stimulation merely to maintain old levels of subjective pleasure, to never achieve any kind of permanent happiness or satisfaction' (Brickman and Campbell 1971: 289). The economist Richard Easterlin (2001) attributes this failure to the mismatch between income and aspiration; it is, in effect, a process of adaptation. Hence while subjective well-being rises directly with income, it varies inversely with material aspirations. It is accepted that the poorer are always unhappier than the wealthier within a country, but that is complicated when different countries are compared thus producing the 'happy peasant, miserable millionaire' phenomenon (Graham 2011).

It is the iterated finding from this multi-discipline research that the more goods you have then the more you aspire to which lends itself to the re-moralising of luxury. Robert Lane, for example, engages in an evaluative diagnostic. He too picks up the 'paradox' of the material-ist pursuit of wealth even though, beyond the poverty level, this has little effect on well-being. Like Layard, Lane invokes the notion of the hedonic treadmill and both authors also, in common with most 're-moralisers', criticise advertising for increasing dissatisfaction, by 'creating wants' and fostering illusions, so that with the purchase of this watch or this car or this technological gizmo, life will be better. This leads Lane to declare that there is an 'aching void' that neither materialism nor post-materialism can seemingly fill (Lane 2000: 158, 174, 79, 335; cf. Layard 2006: 48, 160).

Although there is evidence that 'self gift-giving' (or in Silverstein and Fiske's [2003: 35] less academic version, 'taking care of me') is a positive source of pleasure (Tsai 2005: 432–4), this fuels, rather than offsets, the case for re-moralisation in this body of literature. It is central to this ethical strand that it indicts luxury for encouraging self-indulgence and for undermining self-discipline, so 'self gift-giving' now looks like a symptom of a malaise ('affluenza' or 'luxury fever' if you will) not some innocent pleasure; it is a merely fleeting source of happiness, an elusiveness fuelled by the ease with which goods can now be purchased via electronic media. So when Brendan Sheehan identifies a 'morality of indulgence' as the consequence of 'the propaganda disseminated by the institution of marketing' (2010: 78–9), he is harking back to the strictures of a Seneca or an Epictetus. The recurrent finding that having more makes one dissatisfied which, in turn, stimulates the desire for more is a common refrain in classic moralism. It is, for example, captured exactly in the Roman poet Horace's (1961: 74) satirical jibe *semper avarus eget* (meaning, freely translated, the greedy are always needy) as well as being central to the whole moral philosophy of Stoicism. The fact that this philosophy provided the conceptual underpinnings for Roman sumptuary laws indicates that a social critique is never far removed from a moral one. It is to this social critique that I now turn as the second of the three areas of re-moralisation.

Social

Layard thinks (like Cloutier earlier) we will be happier if society could develop a concept of the 'common good' (Layard 2006: 5, 225, 234), while Lane places great stress on companionship as the key source for happier individuals and thence society (Lane 2000: 160, 187, 192, 321, 334). Implicit in these alternatives is the accusation that a society driven to consume instils to deleterious effect individualism, atomism, egocentrism and so on, while also at the same time fuelling a neglect of the public sphere. This is, furthermore, held to be self-fulfilling. One working paper purports to show an implicit link between exposure to luxury goods and self-interest (Chua and Zou 2009). And, here again, what Shu-pei Tsai (2005) calls a 'personal orientation' to the purchase of luxuries, of which self gift-giving is an arguable case, could be adduced in evidence.

The social critique literature is voluminous. It ranges across the spectrum. On the Left, critics like Herbert Marcuse (1964: 12, 88; cf. Tomlinson 1990) argue that consumers exist in a state of false consciousness such that the freedom to choose between umpteen brands of shampoo (say), each with their own luxury refinement, is a form of 'servitude'. While on the Right, critics like Daniel Bell (1979: 65) identify a baleful cultural transformation in the diffusion of luxuries. Out of this literature I can again merely select. Ben Barber, in his evocatively titled 2007 book *Consumed: How Markets Corrupt Children, Infantilize Adults and Swallow Citizens Whole*, encapsulates the central thread of this critique in his comment, '[in consumer capitalism] our selfishness is rationalized and excused, while the public goods after which we still yearn are construed as liberty-destroying and disempowering ... [as it] rationalizes corrosive private choosing as a surrogate for the public good'. He invokes what he calls 'obligatory consumerism' which mandates the stimulation of immediate wants for unnecessary products or, directly invoking Marx, the fabrication of 'imaginary needs'. For Barber, it is a travesty that the shopper has become the contemporary ideal citizen and in its stead he wants a reinvigoration of the classical republican ideal of citizenship, seeing, albeit dimly, in aspects of what has been called 'civic consumerism', a move to restore the sovereignty of citizens over consumption (Barber 2007: 143, 124, 9, 273, 134, 295).

This lament for the decline of the public, and concern at the rise of the private, is widespread. It fuels the communitarian critique of liberalism, to be understood here as privileging individual choice. Trust or social capital, the cohesive bond of society, is eroded as individuals concentrate on satisfying their own desires. While the moral critique in the guise of happiness studies, as we noted, queried the personal satisfactions derivable from the hedonic treadmill of seeking to acquire luxuries, this social critique focuses on the damaging external effects of that pursuit. The pursuit of luxury distorts the value-structure of society. Status and prestige are measured by the possession of the latest consumer good and the more luxurious, the more desirable, that good is then the more the signal of success is sent. But, so the allegation goes, this devalues the signals sent by public service. In contrast to the stability and principled commitment associated with a notion of public duty, luxury status is ephemeral, inherently unstable and transient. Not for nothing is there an affinity between luxury and fashion and both with women, with their proverbial prerogative to change their mind, as the embodiment of the fickleness of *Fortuna* (recall the moralised charge of effeminacy levelled at men who live luxuriously). Symptomatic of this transience is the web magazine of the luxury-good conglomerate LVMH titled, with absolute aptness, *Nowness*; a development, as John Armitage and Joanne Roberts (2014) urge, that is indicative of the social fact that contemporary 'luxury' is now at home in the frenetic immediacy of new media.

But for the critic, the social good of a vigorous public space has been crowded out by the rampant individualism associated with a desire for the personal enjoyment of luxuries. For these critics, this attenuation of a sense of common shared purpose has been effaced by a privatised consumerist lifestyle where the enjoyment of luxury trumps the values of civic virtue and responsibility. The broad thrust of this charge is evocative of the moralised classical view, as exemplified in Livy's influential identification of the importation of luxury as the cause of Rome's decline from republican rectitude (1919: 7). Whether the Roman measures to combat this are tenable in a de-moralised era I will turn to after I have considered my final component.

Green

There is nothing new in a deprecatory linkage between luxury and waste, but this has been given added zest by the rise of Green and ecological sensitivities. While several factors have contributed to this zestfulness, it is the emergence of the issue of 'climate change' that has seriously concentrated minds on lifestyles centred around consumption and a fortiori around luxury.

While there is a practice of 'green consumerism', I don't want to dwell on that save to remark that a number of 'luxury goods' manufacturers have tried to turn it to their advantage. A nice example of this an advertisement from a luxury watchmaker with its tag-line, 'You never actually own a Patek Philippe. You merely look after it for the next generation.' For all its archness, this taps into the key Green idea of stewardship and, more generally, illustrates a trend whereby these manufacturers tout themselves as purveyors of 'sustainable luxury'. According to one commentator this is 'refining the meaning of luxury' because in 'true contemporary luxury the best products need to be socially and environmentally responsible' (Giron 2014: 7, 20). The imperative here reflects an awareness of changing consumer perception and values that market success will have to heed. Hence to give another example, the web portal of *Positive Luxury* (www.positiveluxury.com/about) awards a 'butterfly mark' to luxury brands that are 'taking positive steps to better society and the environment – no animal cruelty, against sweatshops, caring for the planet and trying to conserve it'.

All that said, the Green critique of luxury consumption is more profound and would judge these as cynical manoeuvres that still sustain the unsustainable. The critique argues that by linking social success and esteem with the possession of consumption goods (even if these now come with the cachet of responsible sourcing and distribution), an acquisitive, environmentally destructive lifestyle is reinforced. The 'model' for this is Thorstein Veblen's 'law of conspicuous waste', understood as superfluous expenditure, which he equated with that spent on 'luxuries' (1970 [1899]: ch. 4). These luxury goods and services are enjoyed by those he labels the 'leisure class' who stand at the head of the social structure and whose standards establish the communal norm. While Veblen is very much of his time, his diagnosis resonates with that of the Greens, who would see in the diffusion of 'new luxury' the establishment of a new and more damaging norm.

In line with my theme of re-moralisation, the Greens (or at least some of them) reinvoke the classical advocacy of simplicity. The work of E. F. Schumacher was influential. We should, he argued, resist the 'temptation of letting our luxuries become needs' and should evolve a new lifestyle to replace that current which, by 'systematically cultivating greed and envy', has generated 'a vast array of totally unwarrantable wants' (1973: 34, 17, 32). At the heart of this new lifestyle will be what he called Buddhist economics, where material things are put in their legitimate, that is, secondary, place. More recent work has developed this mode of thinking. William Ophuls argues that the 'ecological crisis' necessarily requires a 'radical change in our basic values', and at the heart of this, in a clear echo of the original moralists, will be the achievement of a 'real freedom' as we 'govern our appetites' (1996: 34, 42). A second example is the work of Juliet Schor. She draws attention to, in her words, 'the ecological devastation created by the national [US] lifestyle' and, with a faint echo of Cicero and the advocates of voluntary poverty, evokes those she calls 'simple livers' who aspire to do what can and should be done more widely, that is, 'rein in desire' (1998: 146, xiii, 136). (Although this largely US based movement is more likely to be indebted to Thoreau, for whom luxuries are 'positive hindrances' to living a simple life [1973 [1854]: 14].)

The references here to a simple life and the governance of desire lead to one final aspect of the Green critique that I wish to mention. I earlier made the point that one dimension of de-moralisation was a re-conceptualisation of poverty-qua-simplicity from being a virtue, exemplifying principled resistance to bodily desires, to being a miserable condition of impoverishment. However, a re-moralised version of poverty or frugality has been put forward. At the heart of this is an imperative: 'we must rediscover how to live as our savage ancestors once lived' (Ophuls 1996: 42). This ties in with anthropologist Marshall Sahlins's argument that 'poverty' is a social status invented by bourgeois Economic Man, and pivotal to this invention was the fostering of infinite wants or desires, a phenomenon absent in hunter-gatherer economies. In terms that echo Schumacher (though he never cites him) Sahlins refers to the 'Zen road of affluence' (1974: 13, 2, 11), that is, one premised on human material wants being few and finite while the means to meet those is sufficient so that it is thus possible to be affluent without abundance. Sahlins himself does not press a 'green' agenda but the implicit argument that a different lifestyle is possible has been independently developed with a more overtly ecological slant. This is exhibited by advocates of 'voluntary simplicity', which is identified as a 'way of life [that] embraces frugality of consumption and a strong sense of environmental urgency' (Elgin and Mitchell 2003: 146). It is envisaged as functioning as a sustainable economy that meets 'what people actually need' rather than one premised on stimulating consumption (Johnson 2010: xix). As supporters of an 'ethic of sufficiency' recognise, this is an 'ideal' (Durning 1992: 145), but it is an easy and reasonable inference from this version of material simplicity that, like Epictetus' slippers, it has no room for luxury refinement.

Conclusion

I conclude with some very brief observations on these various endeavours at re-moralising 'luxury'. The question mark in my title indicates that the requisite dialectical transcendence is problematic. The nub issue is the 'policing' or weighing of desire. The classical moralist recourse to sumptuary legislation that the Skidelskys (2012: 204–5) openly advocate is a non-starter. This original recourse served to underwrite a hierarchical status quo because its overwhelming concern was to preserve the pecking order and thus to confine the incidence of a good and prevent its diffusion. Luxury, 'new' wealth, always threatened to overturn this. Those in the lower ranks of these societies may well have wanted some of those privileged goods, but that 'wanting' was a mark of their unworthiness, their failure to recognise the (often divinely) sanctioned values of rank and order. The decline of sumptuary laws is less a marker of greater economic equality than of what Werner Sombart (1913: 112) called *Versachlichung*, the wish to enjoy the tangible reality of magnificent clothes and comfortable homes. But central to de-moralisation is the conviction that this wish, the desire of the 'have-nots' for those goods currently possessed by the 'haves', is legitimate. It is this legitimisation that justifies the question mark. On what grounds can the warrantability of wants or the desirability of desires be contested so that in Barber's formulation 'our truly determinative public choices can be enhanced by restricting the domain of our trivial private choices' (2007: 142)? By definition, choosing to consume luxuries would seem to lie in the 'trivial box', but what benchmark is available to distinguish that choice from a non-trivial one and thus justify the restriction? The classical moralists, like many advocates of re-moralisation such as Armitage and Roberts (2014), invoke some valorised notion of need. This even includes Robert Frank's (2000: 211–16) advocacy of a progressive consumption tax and his ostensible disavowal of any moral judgement. However, though I cannot here elaborate, this invocation lacks potency. While it is defensible to say nobody needs footwear from Laboutin or Lobb, it is a further move to say, with Epictetus and his embroidered slipper, that this is pathological, a harmful attribution of value to what is without value. We might just think that the desire for a Jimmy Choo stiletto is foolish, representing a symptomatic mis-ordering of priorities, of the less necessary (luxury) being promoted ahead of the more necessary, but, even if in this case we baulk at 'restriction', the weight of this critical judgement is moot. It could well be the case that I postpone my liver transplant in order to fulfil my (in your eyes trivial/foolish) desire to go on a round-the-world cruise; that is my choice and my prioritisation trumps your evaluation; indeed, frustrating my desire here is not harmless.

A final speculative comment. Of the cases for re-moralisation, it is perhaps the last that has potentially the most purchase. If the evidence of climate change continues to mount, then the 'objectivity' of hard science could replace the purported philosophical objectivity attached to needs by classical moralists and their contemporary heirs. But precisely because it is a 'replacement', any subsequently authorised restriction of consumption does not constitute *in sensu stricto* a re-moralisation. Moreover, even in this scenario, rather than extirpate luxury, it is more likely to reinforce what advocates of so-called 'old-luxury' (Thomas 2007) or 'meta-luxury' (Ricca and Robins 2012) claim, namely, that 'quality' is the key, with the price incidental. On a more mundane, but, I think, conceptually more fundamental, level, it also seems eminently reasonable to believe that the desire for fresh over stale bread, for 'refinement' in my sense, will persist. Hence while Hegel's dialectic ultimately has a resolution in the Absolute, short of ice caps melting, the dialectic of desire for luxury seems likely to run and run.

Acknowledgement

This is an amended version of a keynote lecture delivered at 'In Pursuit of Luxury', a conference held in London in 2010. I am grateful to Steven Adams of the University of Hertfordshire for the invitation. Versions of the paper have subsequently benefited from discussions at universities in Italy, Japan, China, USA and UK.

References

Adams, W. (2012), *On Luxury*, Washington, DC: Potomac Books.
Appadurai, A. (1986), 'Commodities and the politics of value', in A. Appadurai (ed.), *The Social Life of Things*, Cambridge: Cambridge University Press, pp. 3–63.
Aristotle (1944), *The Politics*, London: Loeb Library.
Armitage, J. and Roberts, J. (2014), 'Luxury new media: euphoria in unhappiness', *Luxury: History, Culture, Consumption*, 1 (1): 113–32.
Barber, B. (2007), *Consumed: How Markets Corrupt Children, Infantilize Adults and Swallow Citizens Whole*, New York: Norton.
Bell, D. (1979), *Cultural Contradictions of Capitalism*, 2nd edn, London: Heinemann.
Baudrillard, J. (1988), *Selected Writings*, ed. M. Poster, Cambridge: Polity.
Berg, E. and Clifford, H. (eds) (1999), *Consumers and Luxury in Europe 1650–1850*, Manchester: Manchester University Press.
Berry, C. (1994), *The Idea of Luxury*, Cambridge: Cambridge University Press.
Berry, C. (1999), 'Austerity, luxury and necessity', in J. Hill and C. Lennon (eds), *Luxury and Austerity*, Dublin: University College Dublin Press, pp. 1–13.
Berry, C. (2008), 'Hume and superfluous value or what's wrong with Epictetus' slippers', in C. Wennerlind and M. Schabas (eds), *David Hume's Political Economy*, London: Routledge, pp. 49–64.

Brewer, J. and Porter, R. (1993), *Consumption and the World of Goods*, London: Routledge.

Brickman D. and Campbell, D. (1971), 'Hedonic relativism and planning the good society', in M. Appley (ed.), *Adaptation-Level Theory*, New York: Academic Press, pp. 287–302.

Calefato, P. (2012), *Luxury: Fashion, Lifestyle, Excess*, trans. L. Adams, London: Bloomsbury.

Chua, R. and Zou, X. (2009), 'The Devil wears Prada? Effects of exposure to luxury goods on cognition and decision-making', Working Paper 10-034, Harvard Business School.

Cicero (1913), *De Officiis*, London: Loeb Library.

Cicero (1927), *Disputationes Tusculanae*, London: Loeb Library.

Cloutier, D. (2012), 'The problem of luxury in the Christian life', *Journal of the Society of Christian Ethics*, 32: 3–20.

Dubois, B., Czellar, S. and Laurent, G. (2005), 'Consumer segments based on attitudes towards luxury', *Marketing Letters*, 16: 115–28.

Durning, A. (1992), *How Much is Enough? The Consumer Society and the Future of the Earth*, New York: Norton.

Easterlin, R. (2001), 'Income and happiness: toward a unified theory', *Economic Journal*, 111: 35–47.

Elgin, D. and Mitchell, A. (2003), 'Voluntary simplicity: a movement emerges', in D. Doherty and A. Etzioni (eds), *Voluntary Simplicity*, Lanham, MD: Rowman & Littlefield, pp. 145–71.

Epictetus (1932), *The Encheiridion*. London: Loeb Library.

Frank, R. (2000), *Luxury Fever: Money and Happiness in an Era of Excess*, Princeton: Princeton University Press.

Giron, M. (2014), 'Sustainable luxury', in M. Gardetti and M. Giron (eds), *Sustainable Luxury and Social Entrepreneurship*, Sheffield: Greenleaf, pp. 2–21.

Graham, C. (2011), *In Pursuit of Happiness*, Washington, DC: Brookings Institution Press.

Harte, N. (1976), 'State control of dress and social change in pre-industrial England', in D. C. Coleman and A. H. John (eds), *Trade, Government and Economy in Pre-Industrial England*, London: Weidenfeld & Nicolson, pp. 132–65.

Haug, W. (1986), *Critique of Commodity Aesthetics*, trans. R. Bock, Cambridge: Polity.

Hobbes, T. (1991 [1651]), *Leviathan*, ed. R. Tuck, Cambridge: Cambridge University Press.

Holmstrom, N. (1974), 'A Marxist concept of natural wants', *Philosophical Forum*, 6: 423–46.

Horace (1961), *Odes*, London: Everyman Library.

Houghton, J. (1677), *England's Great Happiness*, London.

Hume, D. (1987a [1752]), 'Of Commerce', in *Essays: Moral, Political and Literary*, ed. E. Miller, Indianapolis: Liberty Press, pp. 253–67.

Hume, D. (1987b [1752]), 'Of Refinement of Arts', in *Essays: Moral, Political and Literary*, ed. E. Miller, Indianapolis: Liberty Press, pp. 268–80.

Johnson, W. (2010), *Muddling Toward Frugality*, Westport, CT: Easton Studio Press.

Kemp, S. (1998), 'Perceiving luxury and necessity', *Journal of Economic Psychology*, 19: 591–606.

Lane, R. (2000), *The Loss of Happiness in Market Democracies*, New Haven, CT: Yale University Press.

Layard, R. (2006), *Happiness*, London: Penguin.

Livy (1919), *Ab Urbe Condita*, London: Loeb Library.

Locke, J. (1854 [1690]), *Essay Concerning Human Understanding*, ed. H. St John, 2 vols, London: Bohn Library.

Marcuse, H. (1964), *One-Dimensional Man*, Boston: Beacon Press.

Mirabeau, V. (1760), *Table Économique*, Amsterdam.

Mortelmans, D. (2005), 'Sign values in processes of distinction: the concept of luxury', *Semiotica*, 157: 497–520.

Mulgrew, C. (1998), *The Economy of Obligation*, London: Macmillan.

Ophuls, W. (1996), 'Unsustainable liberty, sustainable freedom', in D. Pirages (ed.), *Building Sustainable Societies*, New York: Sharpe, pp. 33–44.

Peck, L. (2005), *Consuming Splendor*, Cambridge: Cambridge University Press.

Ricca, M. and Robins, R. (2012), *Meta-luxury: Brands and the Culture of Excellence*, London: Palgrave.

Sahlins, M. (1974), *Stone Age Economics*, London: Tavistock Publications.

Schor, J. (1998), *The Overspent American: Why We Want What We Don't Need*, New York: Harper.

Schumacher, E. (1973), *Small is Beautiful*, London: Blond & Briggs.

Seneca (1932), *Epistulae Morales*, 3 vols, London: Loeb Library.

Sheehan, B. (2010), *The Economics of Abundance*, Cheltenham: Elgar.

Silverstein, M. and Fiske, N. (2003), *Trading Up*, New York: Penguin.

Skidelsky, R. and E. (2012), *How Much is Enough? Money and the Good Life*, London: Penguin.

Sombart, W. (1913), *Luxus und Capitalismus*, München: Duncker & Humbolt.

Smith, A. (1982 [1763]), *Lectures on Jurisprudence*, ed. R. Meek et al., Indianapolis: Liberty Press.

Smith, A. (1981 [1776]), *Inquiry into the Nature and Causes of the Wealth of Nations*, ed. R. Campbell and A. Skinner, Indianapolis: Liberty Press.

Smith, W. (2002), *Consumption and the Making of Respectability*, London: Routledge.

Thomas, D. (2007), *DeLuxe*, London: Penguin.

Thoreau, J. (1973 [1854]), *Walden*, Princeton: Princeton University Press.

Tierney, B. (1959), *Medieval Poor Law*, Berkeley: University of California Press.

Tomlinson, A. (1990), 'Consumer culture and the aura of the commodity', in A. Tomlinson (ed.), *Consumption, Identity and Style*, London: Routledge, pp. 1–38.

Tsai, S.-P. (2005), 'Impact of personal orientation on luxury-brand purchase', *International Journal of Market Research*, 47: 429–54.

Tungate, M. (2009), *Luxury World*, London: Kogan Page.

Twitchell, S. (2002), *Living it Up: Our Love Affair with Luxury*, New York: Columbia University Press.

van der Veen, M. (2003), 'When is food a luxury', *World Archaeology*, 34: 405–27.

Veblen, T. (1970 [1899]), *The Theory of the Leisure Class*, London: Unwin Books.

Žižek, S. (2010), *Living in the End of Times*, London: Verso.

Chapter 4

The Luxury Duality: From Economic Fact to Cultural Capital

Ulrich Lehmann

On Capital and Labour

Luxury has to be regarded simultaneously as an economic fact and as a medium to communicate social relationships. Like the physical definition of light as the duality of particle and waveform, the luxury duality manifests itself as material element and fluid phenomenon; it is a quantitative measure of capital (economic) as much as a qualitative measure of labour (social).

Capital is set within specific economic parameters; at any given time capital is the accumulated labour, in the form of materials, facilities, technologies, that serves as a means of (new) production. From this definition, Karl Marx – in 1847, at a time when the production of luxury commodities was set explicitly against industrialised manufacture – expanded the definition of capital thus:

> Capital consists not only of means of subsistence, instruments of labour, and raw materials, not only as material products; it consists just as much of *exchange values*. All products of which it consists are *commodities*. Capital, consequently, is not only a sum of material products, it is a sum of commodities, of exchange values, of *social magnitudes*. (Marx 1977: 212)

Since the relationship between commodities mirrors as well as produces social relationships, the above defines capital as the social relation of production. At the end of this (material) production comes the commodity that, in the present context of luxury, reflects at the same time the accumulated labour invested in its making as much as it transfers the social relationship of production into a social hierarchy where this relationship is demarcated through exclusive access and socio-economic dominance. Luxury goods serve as the reified and commodified expression of the social relationship of their production. In principle, this role is assumed by any object within a capitalist economy, but in luxury the role of capital as accumulation of exchange – as well as symbolic values and of the 'social magnitudes' that ratify dependencies – is particularly pronounced. Since aspects of *need* or *function* are secondary to luxury, the relational aspects within its social meaning are paramount.

The above quote from Marx on capital situates my discussion within the realm of a materialist political economy, where I consider a very fruitful debate on luxury to be situated. The synthetic analysis of economic and social facts encompasses subject (maker, consumer) as well as the object (commodity, media), production as well as consumption; it establishes relationships between individuals and society, the market and political institutions; it can be descriptive as well as prescriptive. Mapping an economic system onto a political power structure and social practice contextualises the above-mentioned relational aspect for luxury. When politics are determined by economics and the social effect of economic measures is sought to be commensurate with governmental decrees, the methods of political economy become the principal levers to prise apart the history and present of the industrial-political complex.

I want to introduce now the other part of the luxury duality: labour. Labour can be defined for the purpose of our present discussion in two ways: according to classical economists labour is simply equivalent to labour costs, i.e. the wage paid to a labourer; yet, as Marx demonstrated, the actual *value* of labour is always higher, as it contains both the wage paid to the labourer and the profit the owner of the means of production pockets from the sale of the commodity (its surplus value). For a luxury commodity like an expensive wrist-watch, this means that the craft necessary for its production, e.g. the expertise of the Swiss watchmaker, his training, his acquired skill set, is represented by the wage he receives for making the watch. But the actual value of the watchmaker's labour is much higher, because it resides in the very tradition of his craft, which is promoted through marketing and branding that necessitate further expenses for the manufacturer but all of which yield a higher commodity price than can be measured by the hourly wages of the labourer. We need to add here that such discussion of labour remains independent initially of the other costs in producing the commodity like raw material, energy, facilities and tools.

We will see in the following how the consummate value of labour, rather than the wage labour alone, becomes a principal constituent of the luxury commodity. This is partly because of the particular form of labour that is advertised for luxury, namely artisanal and 'independent' labour, where individual craft skills rather than mechanical manufacture elevate a commodity to its luxury status; and partly because the surplus value, the profit in the luxury commodity, is set higher than for other commodities, as its value resides in the social relationship it generates through dominance and exclusivity.

I want to describe briefly a material representation of this very aspect. In December 1994 the European Parliament issued a directive on packaging and packaging waste (94/62/EC), which stated that 'the weight and volume of any packaging shall be the minimum needed for safety, hygiene and acceptance for the packed product and for the consumer' (INCPEN 2014). A responsible relationship was to be established between the size of the commodity/good being packaged and the volume of its packaging. Luxury commodities (most prominently perfume and spirits) were exempt from this directive according to a so-called 'consumer acceptance clause'. This clause supposed that the consumers of luxury commodities willingly accept excessive and purely symbolic packaging that bears no concrete relation to the size, form and type of the commodity within it. Structurally speaking, EU law accepted luxury consumption as essentially symbolic, assessing the associated packaging that envelops the void around the form of the commodity as necessary to maintain the mirage of its exaggerated value. This acceptance of exceptional criteria for luxury commodities was termed polemically, by its own trade federation in France, as 'a "get out" clause for the industry. In this context, it is thought of as providing a reason to cease packaging source reduction' (CNE 2010: 1). In France, the 'Grenelle II' regulation on environmental protection (2010) unilaterally opposed the above EU directive by introducing a new packaging law that denied luxury commodities their symbolic and materially excessive shells (République Française 2010). France thus challenged directly its own luxury industry, most notably represented by politically influential conglomerates like LVMH, whose products include traditional brands of champagne, cognac and perfume bottles, as well as erecting trade barriers for luxury imports. The French government thus denied luxury commodities their symbolic value and aimed at reducing them outwardly to mere functional goods whose packaging has to comply with their material form and no longer design their socio-economic prestige.

The Value and Quality of Labour

Returning the discussion to the luxury duality, Marx regarded labour in relation to capital as distinguished by 'production' and 'labouring power'. The first is indeed the value of labour, as ascertained from combined wage and surplus value/profit, the second is defined as 'the temporary disposal . . . which he [the worker] makes over to the capitalist' (Marx 1985: 128). Labouring power is the sum of education, training and the development of skills. These are difficult to quantify in material terms – even when an apprentice remains with his employer to become a master craftsman in the same workshop – but they are telling for the production of luxury. The social function of labouring power combines productivity with cultural impact. The economic measure of labour might put forward a simple equation of man-hours spent making a particular good, yet in commodities that establish their relationship to the subject through non-functional, haptic aspects like surface texture and reflection, substance (weight of base materials) or size (in relation to the type of commodity), the quality of making is foregrounded. Luxury commodities are often bigger, heavier, more 'substantial' than other versions of their type and the consumer expects this material surplus to result from more elaborate and more individualised production processes.

One example here is the Bugatti Veyron, a (very weighty) production car that emphasises its luxury credentials not only through habitual elements like high sale price and limited production, but furthermore by transposing aspects of luxury production and consumption from more traditional commodities like leather goods or furnishings to modern car manufacture – all within a carefully designed context of the historical 'Bugatti' marque. The Veyron thus comes in signed 'special editions' (akin to artworks) dedicated to the past of the company, features hand-painted or engraved interior details, and affects a fusion with other luxury brands like Hermès, providing upholstery. The latter co-branding is detailed on the company's website as 'executed entirely by hand and requires a month of production time' (Bugatti 2011b). The car itself is hand-assembled, too, and even the pre-assembly of the engine block is spatially separated from the industrial surroundings of the parent company's huge engine plant in Germany. There, a single craftsman labours in a tiny room to complete the Veyron's engine block, which is then shipped with other components to the purpose-built workshop in the Alsace, denoted as the 'atelier'. Here, eight workers (mechanics, electricians, coachbuilders) complete each car by hand across a period of five weeks. This production narrative is relentlessly spread in the media and the story that each car costs five times more than its actual sale price is officially sanctioned.

In order to distinguish this automotive commodity as luxury, the environment, form and process of the labour involved in its production is constantly invoked. It happens not to highlight first technical expertise or progressive manufacture, as in other mechanical objects, but refers back to handmaking, to a tradition when the makers of commodities were supposedly identified as trained craftsmen instead of anonymous labour. For the Bugatti Veyron the discourse of engineering prowess – 'technical requirements [that] the exceptional serial production vehicle had to meet: a top speed above 400 km/h and 736 kW (1,000 HP)' (Bugatti 2011a) – becomes superseded by a luxury discourse: 'Bugatti has always been the epitome of exclusivity, luxury, elegance, style, extraordinary design, and a great passion for automobiles' (Bugatti 2011c).

For the Veyron, which is ostensibly produced at a loss, the surplus value/profit of the automotive commodity is denoted as deliberately subordinate to the labour costs. The acquisition of the most expensive production car in the world means buying into a narrative of luxury that is unconcerned with financial reward, and this is seen perhaps as the ultimate contemporary expression of luxury production. A global automotive company (VW) affords itself a (heavily) loss-making subsidiary, to be able to claim that it is preserving tradition, history and cultural significance for a particular brand of commodities.

Here, thus, the luxury duality of capital and labour assumes an odd form. Since the measurable 'particle' of luxury, its economic gain, is seen as less important than its 'fluid phenomenon' (waveform), its distinction of a form of production and, implicitly, a form of consumption occurs through the value of its labour. In this context, the materialism in luxury appears removed from an orthodox economic structure, and the fixed aspect of the commodity – its price – is positioned below its fluid aspect – its meaning. As Marx explained in his speech of 1865:

> As the *exchangeable values* of commodities are only *social functions* of those things, and have nothing at all to do with the *natural* qualities, we must first ask: What is the common *social substance* of all commodities? It is *Labour*. To produce a commodity a certain amount of labour must be bestowed upon it, or worked up in it. And I say not only *Labour*, but *social Labour*. A man who produces an article for his own immediate use, to consume it himself, creates a *product*, but not a *commodity*. As a self-sustaining producer he has nothing to do with society. But to produce a *commodity*, a man must not only produce an article satisfying some *social* want, but his labour itself must form part and parcel of the total sum of labour expended by society. It must be subordinate to the *Division of Labour within Society*. It is nothing without the other divisions of labour, and on its part is required to *integrate* them. (Marx 1985: 121–2)

When the social value of labour is positioned methodologically above its economic meaning, in that it encompasses want for the object of labour as much as the organisation that leads to it (the division of labour), rather than a simple equation with wages, the relational aspect within labour comes to the fore again. For the luxury commodities discussed here, like rare and expensive wristwatches or limousines, this social value appears anachronistic yet curiously prescient. There is no 'natural quality' to a luxury object, as another commodity of the same type would perform the same function, fulfil a similar need, at a much more equitable price. But certain, limited consumer groups prefer these luxury commodities above all others for their form, quality of make and material substance. The owning and handling of the commodity represents for them in an asocial way an intimate relationship to the labour contained therein.

Intimate Knowledge and Limits of Access

As suggested above, knowledge of the production process and a degree of intimacy with the maker distinguishes the acquisition of luxury commodities. The Veyrons, for instance, are 'picked up directly in Molsheim by their new owners. This is a pleasure that customers back in Ettore Bugatti's days also used to indulge in' (Bugatti 2011b). A similar adage applies to luxury products in the food sector, where the 'artisanal' production of, for example, coffee or chocolate is used at present to distinguish itself from the all-pervasive industrialisation of food production across the globe. Affluent consumers afford themselves the 'luxury' to select commodities through their degree of knowledge about the products' origins. Ostensibly, they do not condone anonymous production, as it might imply unsavoury labour practices or polluted raw materials, and they want to be reassured about the details of what they consume, even when the commodity is mass produced. These consumers aspire to get to know the artisan or craftsperson making their bread, dyeing their jeans or assembling their mode of private transport. For this 'privilege' – which can be part of a fictitious supply chain invented by the producer for marketing purposes – they are prepared to pay a premium, and familiarity with the background of the consumed object, which they are happy to discuss with other consumers from their social set, moves the product from an everyday context to the realm of luxury within its type and market. Obviously, this familiarity or intimacy is readily apparent in the individual interaction with clients in the service sector of the luxury market, from the 'concierge' service for select credit cards, via personal shoppers, to individual flight attendants in first class. For the present discussion I find it helpful, however, to remain with the manufacturing sector of luxury goods where the interpersonal relationship between producer and consumer has been introduced as a particularity.

The labour involved in luxury production needs to appear subjectified; it needs to be performed by an individual for an individual who can afford to pay an elevated price for a type and division of labour that is seen as deliberately anachronistic (handmade, elaborate) but perfectly fitting for post-industrial societies. When Marx spoke of a man's labour as being 'nothing without the other divisions of labour' in society and as 'required to integrate' within a political economy, he anticipated a very significant element in the positioning of contemporary luxury production, which refers back to conditions at the time of his writing. Labour for luxury is required to integrate itself into a system of global production where the distinction works not simply through diverse costing – outsourcing production to countries with low wages and reduced labour regulations – but through the substance of labour; its social and cultural value. More knowledge is expected from the labourers of luxury goods about their materials, traditional crafts and historical contexts. An awareness of the history of making and the history of the commodity is to be shared by maker as well as client so that a discursive link is established that can be added to the surplus value/profit of the product.

This link often works through the aforementioned elaborate packaging of luxury commodities and the narratives of their branding/advertising. An elaborate back story for the product is written into its promotion – on the box of the watch, in the brochure for the car, printed onto the garment label. The consumption of the luxury commodity is initiated by first consuming a discourse on its production, in which the maker or the making is described in detail, so that a fictional link is established to the consumer who can bask in the knowledge of paying directly for a labour process he deems himself familiar with. The description of painstaking handiwork, attention to detail and specialised tools and facilities all find their direct equivalent in the elevated price of the luxury commodity. The Italian brand of leather goods (and, more recently, garments) Bottega Veneta describes their heritage thus:

> Discretion, quality, and unsurpassed craftsmanship – Steeped in the traditions of Italy's master leather craftsmen and renowned for its extraordinary leather goods, Bottega Veneta has established a new standard of luxury since its founding in Vicenza in 1966

> ... [C]onstant is Bottega Veneta's commitment to its ateliers, where artisans of remarkable skill combine traditional mastery with breathtaking innovation. Indeed, there is an unusual and inspired collaboration between artisan and designer at the heart of Bottega Veneta's approach to luxury, a partnership perfectly symbolized by the house's signature intrecciato woven leather. (Bottega Veneta 2015)

The accompanying image on the company's website features the close-up of a hand holding down a garment label with the woven words 'Made in Italy' and a sewing needle inserted into the lining next to it. To put such hyperbole on subjectified production in context, one needs to understand the trademark 'Made in Italy' as a contentious construct, situated between existing EU legislation, which aspires to the free circulation of materials and components across the continent, and the protectionism of national lobbies for manufacturers, especially the Italian fashion industry.

On 8 April 2010 the 'legge Reguzzoni-Versace',[1] which regulates the labelling of products in the sector of 'high-quality'/'luxury' textiles, garments, shoes and leather goods, was passed through the Italian parliament (bill 55/2010). This law essentially covers two aspects: first, a system of labelling finished products in the above sector, detailing and tracing their production process and supply chain; second, the law permits the trademark 'Made in Italy' only for those textiles, garments, shoes and leather goods for which at least two major stages of production have taken place in Italy. The first aspect is an ostensible reaction to ensuring sustainable and responsible labour practices in outsourcing; the second is a more direct protectionist measure to equate domestic production in Italy with high quality, in particular denoting high-price, luxury goods made by identifiable, traceable and local labour.

This appears to be for the benefit of small and medium Italian-based producers and specialist manufacturers, using the skill base of craftspeople (especially) in the north of the country to produce 'substantial' labour of high *value* and *power*, as defined by Marx, namely the type of labour where a high exchange value and 'social magnitude' are evident. But here lies the crux of identifying particular types of labour and also the main problem with the Reguzzoni-Versace law. Because only two stages of the production have to be identified as 'Italian', these can be comparatively limited within the overall complexity of the global labour process and the commodity's supply chain. Two stages of, for example, finishing and packaging suffice for leather goods to be labelled 'Made in Italy', even when the raw material (hide), the tanning and dyeing stages, and the machine assembly have been outsourced to the Far East. These stages of adding, say, straps or clasps to a bag and putting it into an elaborate packaging is enough to sustain the local, traditional, craft-based narrative for labels competing within the luxury sector of the fashion industry. The notion of a localised, subjectified luxury product becomes a mirage of mainly outsourced labour that is given a final gloss through a relatively small and insubstantial labour input at home.

For Bottega Veneta, as part of François Pinault's Kering group of luxury brands, distinguishing the origins of their raw materials thus has become an important signifier within the contested semantic field of 'Made in Italy'. Prior to the second decade of this century Kering,[2] like its major competitor the Louis Vuitton Moët Henessy group (LVMH), was still relying on tanneries in Singapore, China, etc. Since 2010, however, Kering has embarked on a strategy to evidence its entire supply chain as 'domestic' or 'local', and has upgraded or acquired tanneries like Caravel Pelli Pregiate near Pisa, France Croco in Normandy and the Ruma Fabrika Koze plant northwest of Belgrade. While this says little about the origin of the raw hide itself, these tanneries process the majority of the leather that is used across the luxury group. Unlike the Milan-based conglomerate Prada, which continues to produce at least 20 per cent of its clothes and accessories in China, as well as manufacturing leather and textiles in Turkey and Romania (that is, countries with comparatively lax labour regulations and low wages),[3] Kering has very publicly 'domesticated' its labour within Western Europe.

The Reguzzoni-Versace law partly accounts for this explicit change in production but equally important is the required discourse on identifiable, subjectified luxury production, which prompted Bottega Veneta and others to detail their division of labour. Thomas Chauvet, Head of European Luxury Goods Research at the Citi Banking Company, stated in June 2013:

> Most Chinese and Japanese luxury consumers still associate the Made in Europe label with superior quality but increasingly feel the prices need to be justified not just on the basis of 200 years of history but also the transparency of the supply chain. (Sanderson 2013b: 4)

Bottega Veneta thus invested heavily in the facilities, tools and education of its labour force. In summer 2006 the company opened the Scuola della Pelletteria, a school for future leather artisans; in 2011 it agreed with the Veneto Region in Northern Italy to fund a cooperative employing women formerly working in Vicenza's gold industry and retraining them as leather 'weavers'; and in 2013 it restored the eighteenth-century Villa Schroeder-Da Porto in Montebello Vicentino as their atelier, complete with high-spec, glass-fronted workshops and material archives. The restoration project is very similar to Bugatti's architectural re-branding of the historic mansion in Molsheim as their atelier for handmaking the Veyron. These endeavours show a trend across the luxury sector to contemporise the historical roots of brands and to use particularised 'labouring power' (in a very un-Marxist fashion, of course) to distinguish their output. Marco Bizzari, chairman for Bottega Veneta stated last year:

> For us 'Made in Italy' is so important, the quality and the artisans and the material is so important, that if we feel any kind of pressure on our profitability we will put prices up. We've found that as long as our quality is maintained the customers are willing to pay a premium. (Sanderson 2013a: 19)[4]

This is reflected, too, in Bottega Veneta's operating margin. In the summer of 2013 the company listed the ratio of its profit divided by its net sales (revenue) as 31.8 per cent, 'one of the highest in the industry', and claimed it would indeed raise its sale prices to sustain this ratio (Sanderson 2013a: 19). It also stated that in 2012 alone it had invested €40 million in its infrastructure of boutiques and facilities, centring on educating artisans and developing production in northern Italy and the rest of Europe. Returning to our initial definition of the luxury duality as made up of a quantitative measure of capital (economic) and a qualitative measure of labour (social), we can see here how capital investment is linked to promoting a specific quality of labour in order to maintain profitability.

Cultural Capital

I would like to return once more to the definition of luxury duality. The physicist Niels Bohr called the debate about light as waveform and particle a 'duality paradox' and saw it as a metaphysical principle in nature that allows dual concepts to exist without the need for harmonising or unifying tropes. He observed that at times the wave aspect was apparent, at other times the particle aspect, with the same kind of quantic entity, but in respectively different physical settings (Bohr 1928: 580–1). This means that it is impossible to measure the full property of either wave or particle at any given moment (because they cannot exist at the same time), but that the measurement of each respective property has to be understood as complementary to the other. Bohr's use of the term 'metaphysical' refers back to the fundamental quality of the historical debate between phenomenon and matter, between, for example, Christiaan Huygens's theory of light as wave and Isaac Newton's atomistic definition of light as a particle.[5] A similar duality between the immaterial and the material animates the luxury duality. Luxury is at the same time an immaterial perception of social advantage and exclusivity and a material marker of economic value and material substance. While one 'quantic' entity of a luxury commodity, its material substance, weight, surface quality, etc., is maintained, the other, its social impact, fluctuates across time and space, depending on fashion, mores and modes of behaviour, but, equally, on the *cultural* and *social capital* that surrounds luxury.

In the context of luxury production, the action of the capitalist who accrues money in the form of a constant 'passionate chase after exchange value' (Marx 1996: 164) takes on a complex dimension. On the one hand, we have seen that holding companies like Kering foreground artisanal manufacture as evidence of a concrete, constructive connection to labour, most notably to a particular *quality* of labour, so one might surmise that capital in the simple form of money remains only as much its objective as increasing the measurable quality of the labour that it uses. Yet when commodities that are made through a particular quality of (social) labour are denoted as luxury, their use value is negated, as their price is obviously far in excess of what their simple function would merit: a woven leather bag by Bottega Veneta does not transport objects more efficiently or economically than an anonymous tote bag made from recycled cotton. Although making is communicated as being as significant as investing surplus or acquiring capital (for example machinery or property in the form of ateliers), the actual labour of the artisan or worker within the *accumulated* labour that manifests the capital is relatively small compared to the amount of surplus value (profit) of the labour that is contained within the luxury commodity in the form of brand value, or, to put it in less market-driven terminology, in the form of *social* or *cultural value*.

Kering invests money in a luxury brand in order to get a return on the sale of its commodities, and the profit margin, as detailed above by the chairman of Bottega Veneta, is a quantic value to be preserved at all costs. This means that whatever the factor of labouring power – and the specialised education/training of the worker and the elaborate hand-production processes greatly add to the sum total of this factor – it must stand in relation to the value of the commodity on the market. This value cannot be increased simply by ever more exclusive materials, more complex processes of making or the advanced expertise of the artisan; it needs to demonstrate additional social and cultural dimensions. The social and cultural value of labour is crucial for the success of the luxury commodity because its use value is so insignificant. Here, one might indeed employ Marx's definition of the exchange value as determinant, that is, the value of a commodity if it were traded or exchanged against other commodities, in contrast to its price and use value. The higher the exchange value of the luxury commodity, when posited vis-à-vis commodities that do not contain the same amount of labouring power, the more luxurious the commodity appears. As mentioned above, the material substance of the commodity remains important, but one particular cashmere coat or gold watch is seen as luxurious in contrast to another not only for their material origin or expense but for the expertise that becomes manifest in their designed and manufactured form. Once this value is obtained, the luxury commodity is distinguished by a factor that, in relation to the rest of (the division of) labour, generates further luxury consumption and production. Luxury becomes the supreme expression of a movement between money–commodity–money, which generates surplus: surplus as profit, surplus as capital and, most insidious, surplus as social value in the form of exclusivity and economic dominance.

> Capital is money: Capital is commodities. In truth, however, value is here the active factor in a process, in which, while constantly assuming the form in turn of money and commodities, it at the same time changes in magnitude, differentiates itself by throwing off surplus-value from itself; the original value, in other words, expands spontaneously. For the movement, in the course of which it adds surplus-value, is its own movement, its expansion, therefore, is automatic expansion. Because it is value, it has acquired the occult quality of being able to add value to itself. (Marx 1996: 165)

Marx's method of political economy leads to the understanding of capital as *social circulation*, as something that is intrinsically connected to political structures but appears equally as an independent, self-generating economic process. This process is embedded in a socio-cultural environment and, as we have seen in our definition of labour for luxury, such an environment provides the fertile ground for distinguishing one commodity as luxurious vis-à-vis another as everyday. Which brings us back to the notion of *cultural* capital, a more obscure and diffuse variant of *economic* capital, but intimately related to it.

In the 1940s Max Horkheimer and Theodor W. Adorno, under the double impact of living in an alien (US West Coast) culture of hyper-consumption and fascism in their home country, developed their neo-materialist, dialectical critique of the Enlightenment. Although largely unconcerned with the methods of political economy, they adopted a Marxist terminology for their critical theory of culture. In their critique, the spectre of bourgeois culture, rather than political repression or economic alienation, loomed large. Horkheimer and Adorno employed the term *Kulturindustrie* (culture industry) to demonstrate the nascent economisation of culture within the pervasive sphere of capitalism (Horkheimer and Adorno 1979 [1947]: xvi, 120–67).

The culture industry denotes two things: first, an industrial-political context wherein sets of manners and mores are propagated through mass media and industrialised, populist forms of entertainment; and, second, the advanced stages of a progressive elevation of culture as class distinction. In post-industrial cultures where labour has been redefined and where the manual expertise of the artisan is considered as a historic fact that requires preserving, terms like class or class consciousness are purged from the discourse of political economy as much as from other branches of the social sciences. Therefore the membership of a particular social stratum operates increasingly on cultural terms. Education, predetermined sets of knowledge, the ability to travel and access to global information networks now distinguish social groups instead of labour traditions or occupations that had situated workers in place and time. Information, in particular, now becomes a distinctive and highly priced commodity. The greater the amount of specific information – manifestly specific to a hegemonic culture still – is accessible to a member of society, the more elevated his or her status. Such access is highly selective in economic terms. The more capital can be mobilised to fly around the globe, to gain membership of exclusive clubs and sectors, or, in its most direct and banal form, to buy insider information about economic activity, the more a social position can be advanced. And a principal outward expression of such advancement is luxury consumption. Like the knowledge desired in obtaining luxury commodities by becoming familiar with individual makers, with specific techniques of making or exclusive points of sale, the *recognition* by others of such information about luxury is a distinguishing social marker.

It comes as little surprise then that holding companies for luxury brands and commodities are very interested in accruing cultural capital. This can be done in a number of ways, two of which I would like to note in the following: first, the more abstract discussion of contemporary art as an important variation of luxury consumption; and, second, the related capitalising on luxury through art institutions like galleries and museums. In order to understand why contemporary art in particular is significant in understanding the luxury duality of capital and labour, I want first to briefly mention the relationship between luxury and fashion.

Luxury stands in an ambiguous relation to fashion. Fashion in its abstract form is the materialisation of subjectivity within the socio-economic structure of capitalism and it repeatedly commodifies cultural expressions into a temporally accepted material language. Within capitalism, luxury has to succumb to fashion in order to attain the necessary amount of socio-cultural currency, and, like fashions in dress, luxury's cultural power dies away the moment it is communicated and consumed (too) widely. At this point, a new fashion or a new, more elevated manifestation or form of luxury has to emerge. A distinct lifespan and a temporal rhythm akin to fashion can be observed for luxury.

By the same token, however, luxury must negate fashion. As an original impulse, fashion aspires to 'democratisation'; it needs to be accepted by a group of people in order to turn an esoteric object or individual mannerism (for instance a sub-cultural style or artistic avant-garde) into a socially coveted commodity. Fashion needs to be agreed on socially, while luxury has to oppose such acquiescence on principle. As I have argued above, luxury has to remain esoteric to a certain degree in order to function as a cultural signifier; it has to distinguish itself through a particular materiality, surface quality and substance. The less exclusive in social terms a commodity or service is, the more difficult it becomes to perceive it as luxurious (even when it remains very expensive); or, inversely, the more a commodity or service becomes fashionable, the less it can be consumed as luxury.

In this context contemporary art bridges the ambiguity between luxury and fashion. Through the profusion of cultural institutions like museums, galleries, dedicated websites and more generic media outlets contemporary art has been democratised. The access to avant-garde trends in the visual arts, especially, has been opened up, and the artistic discourses of artists like Andy Warhol, Jeff Koons or Damien Hirst have been distributed widely and popularised as commentaries on socio-economic tendencies – in particular, as affirmative reactions to the pervasiveness of capitalism. Yet the actual acquisition of contemporary art, its consumption not as a cultural product to be viewed but as capital to be privately acquired, is prohibitively expensive. Even new artists with comparatively little exposure in the culture industry (without a monographic show in an established museum, for example) can command high prices, due to the speculative quality that the market for contemporary art has assumed, thus partly reflecting the profession of many of its collectors, namely managers of private equity and investment funds. Materially speaking, contemporary art as a commodity represents an absolute luxury, yet in cultural terms, as a medium that is exposed to more and more parts of the globe, contemporary art, like contemporary fashion, is becoming intellectually less exclusive and more visible to consumers.

A high degree of (often uncritical) self-reflexivity of the artistic avant-garde in regard to the culture industry they partake in has been a hallmark at least since the time of Horkheimer and Adorno, but today the structural alliance between trends in fashion and trends in contemporary art is very pronounced. Because of the increased information about cultural commodities and the spread of cultural tourism in post-industrial societies, the makers of luxury commodities in particular can exploit the kudos of well-known artistic movements. Conglomerates like Kering or LVMH can establish their own art museums and mine the reputation of featured or collected artists for the visual language of their commodities as well as their promotional strategies. Sometimes the references are obvious – using surface patterns in paintings for the decorative patterns on clothing, for instance – at other times the relationship is more coded – for example acquiring the site for a flagship store from a museum that had occupied it previously, so that the familiarity with its cultural capital is maintained from one usage of the site to another.[6]

The chairmen of both Kering and LVMH appear as avid collectors of contemporary art, and they cement this reputation by constructing museum spaces that place the brands of their holdings into considered institutional environments. In 2006 François Pinault transformed the venerable Venetian Palazzo Grassi into a space for art exhibitions, staging curated and thematic group shows as well as monographic exhibitions of artists from his own collection. The Palazzo has had an extended tradition as an art space, but the recent emphasis of Kering and its Gucci Group on their commodities 'Made in Italy' contextualises the refitting of the Grassi in Venice as a venue for contemporary art within a classical cultural tradition. The capital of the property is set in relation to the making of particularly coded cultural products – in the area of luxury fashion as much as in avant-garde art.

LVMH and its CEO Bernard Arnault have gone a step further in concretely linking cultural capital across retail and exhibition sites. The Foundation LVMH in Paris's Bois de Boulogne opened in the autumn/winter of 2014–15 within a building designed by Frank Gehry. A fleet of branded, electrically powered minibuses shuttles consumers back and forth between the museum in the park and LVMH's flagship store on the Champs Elysées to allow for an effortless segue from looking at expensive leather bags and other luxury commodities to looking at contemporary art that adheres to a similar dictate of fashion. In order to fill the museum space with the latest art and to substantially raise the capital – financial not cultural in this case – for his brands, Arnault also acquired the auction house Phillips de Pury in 1999. Thereby Arnault (and LVMH) wanted to effect a degree of control over the market for contemporary art in particular, for instance by expanding the resale values of major works and publicising auction results as a promotional measure for certain artists.

In 1998 Pinault acquired, through his holding company Artémis, a majority share of the auction house Christie and has since increased the exposure of the house to the contemporary art market. In 2014 Pinault transferred Patricia Barbizet from her role as vice chair of the board of directors at Kering, where she was responsible for supervising the finances of production in the luxury sector and for developing brands like Gucci and Alexander McQueen, to chief executive of Christie's. Hereby, the move from commodity production to producing surplus value for artworks is made explicit, ensuring that financial and cultural capital can be raised in tandem.

Due to the progressive economisation of culture, which today has become almost absolute and is allied with a thoroughly 'financialised' politics, luxury assumes a position within our culture industry that follows on from that of the erstwhile avant-garde. Luxury goods have approximated structurally the objects and manifestations in contemporary art whose consumption is no longer an 'ideological' choice, as in the erstwhile siding with the protest manifesto or the emancipatory appeal of an art movement. They are similarly structured now by (economic) advantages in information, time and movement. Consumers of luxury goods, like the collectors of contemporary art, are the extremely mobile recipients of insider knowledge; akin to financiers who manipulate stocks and bonds, these consumers create and dispel luxury through privileged information in order to maintain economic dominance.

Conclusion: Duality and Dominance

As stated at the beginning of this chapter, luxury is a medium to communicate social relationships. The method of political economy contextualises these relationships into a particular power structure where stratification is expressed in commodity forms. The *telos* of self-conscious individuality that animated critical discourses since the Enlightenment has turned throughout modernity into a political philosophy of freedom that is attained through economic dominance. The socio-cultural expression of this dominance is luxury. This is not to be confused with the idea of a 'conspicuous consumption' that concerned a rising bourgeoisie, who had to accommodate itself between a Protestant work ethic to create commodities and the desire to display their newly acquired wealth through them. Such positivist, sociological reflections have long been exposed as a self-reflexive justification of economic power structures, where inequalities and confined strata are seen as structural not ethical issues.[7]

For cultural objects or manifestations in modernity the refuting of fashion is necessary for staying desirable within a progressive socio-economic system. Exclusive, avant-garde manifestations in art, music or literature thus oscillate between rejection and affirmation. They require advanced information, leisure time and the potential for movement (travel) to be consumed, but simultaneously need to constitute a fashion. They need to be desired materially as signifiers of a perceived advantage in order to constitute capital that can be expressed through growing exchange value, while the labour involved in the production of artworks has – in stark contrast to the artisanal production of luxury commodities – been 'objectified'. After Warhol, Koons and Hirst, the artist's subjectivity has been regarded as old-fashioned. The consumer of contemporary art expects the works to be produced to a high material standard, often to evidence a material substance or quality of finish that is similar to luxury goods. Warhol's silk-screens dusted with diamonds, Koon's rendering of plastic toys as solid silver or coated aluminium and Hirst's gold-plated versions of his medicine cabinets attest to an expectation by visitors and art collectors that has been formed by their exposure to the materiality of luxury commodities.

Despite such quantifiable material exclusivity it remains problematic to express luxury's socio-cultural dominance in simple economic terms, as orthodox materialist studies might have it. It is not only greater financial means and extended disposable income that produce and permit luxury consumption. Luxury dominates more generally through the materialised desire to consume and display economic advantages, a desire that is circumscribed by the aforementioned factors of education, environment and access to information – as can be seen, too, in the specialist knowledge in the consumption of contemporary art. Although these factors change and are subject to fashion, they represent a set principle against which normative/mass consumption is posited. Time, movement (travel) and information are required to attain luxury, and the economic – and thus political/ cultural – freedom that certain strata enjoy within capitalist societies is the required basis for this concept of *luxury-as-dominance*.

I would like to conclude by integrating *luxury-as-dominance* into the duality of capital and labour. The structural understanding of such a duality allows for a general supposition that contradicting one phenomenon by another does not imply its negation or the establishing of a binary contrast. The wave-particle duality in physics demonstrates that a paradox does not need 'resolving' but can stand as a continuous conceptual challenge. I would argue that such continuity becomes significant for maintaining a critical perspective on luxury. We need to comprehend luxury as an economic fact to look at its concrete effect for systems of production and their interplay with modes of consumption. At the same time, we need to consider how luxury affects social relationships. The duality of capital and labour shows how much forms of production – in our example the affirmation of handmade, artisanal processes – are integral to understanding luxury. Such processes, whatever the ultimate aspiration of the owners of the means of production (and capital) like Kering or LVMH, reinstate the makers at the centre of production and advance once more their cultural significance.

Labour and capital can appear as antithetical, at times even paradoxical within political economies. Yet when, with Marx, we understand labour as the 'common social substance of the commodity' and capital as the 'sum of commodities, of exchange values, of social magnitudes' we begin to comprehend their relationship around the nexus of the commodity, which in turn informs social relationships in capitalism. Labour is a *substance*, capital a *sum*; one is a synthetic entity, the other the result of an additive process; one is a material foundation, the other is an end product. Historically, culturally and structurally speaking, labour exists first, capital comes later. For the production of the commodity this means that a particular process of exchange is taking place that is historically contingent but also grows more complex the further it is integrated into a political economy. Labour is not simply exchanged for capital in that a waged labourer produces value for the capitalist, but labour fundamentally imbues the commodity with a social value that can be expressed in relations between members of a society. The exchange of labouring power with capital also means that the surplus value is reflective of social organisation and the profit that its various members draw from it. For luxury the labouring power is creating a social exclusivity that is expressed through consumption, which in turn marks the type of social organisation that allows for such exclusivity. Luxury consumption must mirror the social relationships that dominate the society in which it is posited. Paradoxically, the more luxury is a dominant discourse, the more it appears 'democratised', the more, in reality, the society that espouses it has become *post-democratic*,[8] stratified, and its governance dominated by market forces.

When luxury was a discourse of the upper echelon of a society, as for instance in late eighteenth-century France or nineteenth-century North America, labour still had a pronounced social value, where relationships were defined by professions and occupations. In systems like the present post-industrialist Western societies, where capital has taken up the role of governing society and where it has declared luxury an attainable ideal of consumption for greater parts of society, labouring power has lost its relational and social aspect. It has become an artificial, historicised, even nostalgic discourse that can be evoked for promotional purposes but which hardly exists as a measurable economic substance – except for underscoring the symbolic value of luxury brands within capital holdings. Thus luxury has maintained across centuries its meaning of dominance, shifting it from labour to capital and in the process fully reifying our social system of consumption.

Notes

1. Co-signed by an entrepreneur/politician from the secessionist, right-wing *Lega Nord* and the president of the fashion company Gianni Versace SpA.
2. Founded in 1963, Kering was known for fifty years as PPR (Pinault-Printemps-Redoute), a conglomerate that was run like a private equity firm investing in luxury production, for example as shareholder of the Gucci Group of companies (in which they acquired a 60 per cent majority share in 2003). In 2013 Pinault decided to rebrand his holding company as 'Kering', based on the word 'ker', meaning *home* in the Breton language and a homophone of the English 'caring'. This ostensibly signalled the departure from anonymous financial holdings and investments towards responsibility and direct engagement with the diverse marques across the company.
3. For an overview, see Jones 2005, Thomas 2007, Passariello 2011 and Prada's own documentation for its launch at the Hong Kong Stock Market: Prada S.p.A. 2011, esp. pp. 124–9 on 'Production Stages'.
4. Incidentally, this issue of the *Financial Times* carried a full-page ad by Kering announcing the use of its new name from 18 June 2013 onward.

5. Bohr's observation gave rise to the recent notion of complementarity in physical phenomena (see also Kumar 2008: 47–54, 63, 146–53, 242).
6. One example would be the sale of the erstwhile Guggenheim Soho exhibition space in New York to Prada in 2001.
7. See the canonical text by Thorstein Veblen (1899), *Theory of the Leisure Class*, especially chapters 4, 6, 7 and 14. For a materialist critique of Veblen, see for instance Baran and Sweezy (1966: 29, 132–3, 209–10) and Reinert and Viano (2014: Part 4).
8. A term coined by Colin Crouch (2000, esp. ch. 2; expanded upon in Crouch 2007, esp. ch. 5).

References

Baran, Paul A. and Sweezy, Paul M. (1966), *Monopoly Capital: An Essay on the American Economic and Social Order*, New York and London: Monthly Review Press.

Bohr, Niels (1928), 'The quantum postulate and the recent development of atomic theory', *Nature*, 121 (3050): 580–90.

Bottega Veneta (2015), 'Our heritage'. Available at: http://www.bottegaveneta.com/gb/collection/women/our-heritage_grd14131 (last accessed 27 December 2014).

Bugatti (2011a), 'A harmony of design and technology'. Available at: http://www.bugatti.com/en/veyron/history-of-development.html (last accessed 21 December 2014).

Bugatti (2011b), 'A legendary brand is reborn'. Available at: http://www.bugatti.com/en/tradition/history/bugatti-today.html (last accessed 20 December 2014).

Bugatti (2011c), 'The pure fascination of a brand'. Available at: http://www.bugatti.com/en/tradition/the-bugatti-brand.html (last accessed 21 December 2014).

Conseil National d'Emballage (CNE) (2010), *Acceptance of Packaging for the Product, for the Consumer, for the User*, Paris: CNE.

Crouch, Colin (2000), *Coping With Post-Democracy*, London: Fabian Society.

Crouch, Colin (2007), *Post-Democracy*, Cambridge: Polity.

Horkheimer, Max and Adorno, Theodor W. (1979 [1947]), *Dialectic of Enlightenment*, London: Verso.

Kering (2014), *Sustainability Targets: Progress Report*, Paris: Kering S.A.

The Industry Council for Research on Packaging and the Environment (INCPEN) (2014), 'Packaging & environment legislation factsheet'. Available at: http://www.incpen.org/displayarticle.asp?a=11&c=2 (last accessed 19 December 2014).

Jones, Adam (2005), 'Prada ponders outsourcing to China', *Financial Times*, 20 May. Available at: http://www.ft.com/cms/s/0/ed8b45d

0-c8cc-11d9-87c9-00000e2511c8.html#axzz3TVL5Ud1Z (last accessed 5 March 2015).

Kumar, Manjit (2008), *Quantum: Einstein, Bohr, and the Great Debate about the Nature of Reality*, London: Icon.

Marx, Karl (1977), 'Wage labour and capital' [Lectures to the German Workingmen's Club of Brussels in December 1847], *Neue Rheinische Zeitung*, nos. 264–7 & 269 (5–8, 11 April 1849), in Karl Marx and Friedrich Engels, *Collected Works*, vol. 9, London: Lawrence & Wishart, pp. 197–228.

Marx, Karl (1985), 'Value, price and profit' [Speech at the First International Working Men's Association, June 1865], in Karl Marx and Friedrich Engels, *Collected Works*, vol. 20, London: Lawrence & Wishart, pp. 101–49.

Marx, Karl (1996), *Capital*, vol. 1, in Karl Marx and Friedrich Engels, *Collected Works*, vol. 35, London: Lawrence & Wishart.

Passariello, Christina (2011), 'Prada is making fashion in China', *Wall Street Journal*, 24 June. Available at: http://www.wsj.com/articles/SB10001424052702304231204576403680967866692 (last accessed 5 March 2015).

Prada S.p.A. (2011), 'Global offering', 13 June. Available at: http://www.pradagroup.com/documents/announcement/EWP101.pdf (last accessed 5 March 2015).

Reinert, Erik S. and Viano, Francesca Lidia (eds) (2014), *Thorstein Veblen: Economics for an Age of Crises*, London: Anthem.

République Française (2010), LOI n° 2010-788 du 12 juillet 2010 – Article 228. Available at: http://www.legifrance.gouv.fr/eli/loi/2010/7/12/DEVX0822225L/jo/article_228 (last accessed 19 December 2014).

Sanderson, Rachel (2013a), 'Bottega Veneta hits luxury sweet spot', *Financial Times*, 9 April, p. 19.

Sanderson, Rachel (2013b), 'Manufacturing: consumers push big luxury names to account for supply chains', *Financial Times*, 3 June, 'Business of Luxury' supplement, p. 4.

Thomas, Dan (2007), 'Made in China on the sly', *The New York Times*, 23 November. Available at: http://www.nytimes.com/2007/11/23/opinion/23thomas.html?_r=0 (last accessed 5 March 2015).

Veblen, Thorstein (1899), *Theory of the Leisure Class: An Economic Study of Institutions*, New York: Macmillan.

Chapter 5

'Life's Little Luxuries?' The Social and Spatial Construction of Luxury

Juliana Mansvelt, Mary Breheny and Iain Hay

While Berry (1994) and others identify the social and historical construction of luxury, little scholarly attention has been given to how luxury has been practised in particular places. Indeed, most contemporary literature on luxury focuses on the attributes of commodities (be they experiences, services or tangible goods) and those commodity practices favoured by wealthy consumers. Examining how luxury is understood beyond the realms of the wealthy is an important but neglected area of critical luxury studies. Consideration of how luxury is talked about and practised in the day-to-day lives of consumers, who range from the wealthy to those experiencing relative poverty, can provide insights into the kinds of contextual and moral factors which both produce and reinforce discourses and practices of luxury. Recognising the heterogeneity of luxury and the ways it is shaped by, and for, a range of consumers also enables us to understand how material contexts matter for what counts as luxury. Critical studies of luxury consumption must consider how temporal and geographical contexts are implicated in the construction of luxury.

In this chapter we consider how the concept of luxury is deployed in both talk and practice. Drawing on qualitative interviews with older New Zealanders from a range of socio-economic positions, ethnic groups and geographic locations across New Zealand, we demonstrate how understandings of luxury are materially grounded and morally constituted. This work provides some insights into how and why constructions of luxury are drawn upon to describe a range of consumption practices, and vary across people, place and time. By examining the heterogeneity and construction of luxury beyond the consumption practices of the wealthy, we demonstrate that a 'little bit of luxury' in everyday life matters and more critically reveals how the manifestations and moralities of luxury consumption vary greatly.

Situating Luxury in Time and Place

As already identified in this present volume (pp. 1–21), many studies of luxury centre on the price, quality, rarity, uniqueness, exclusivity, artisanship and aesthetic characteristics of luxury commodities, be they services or things (Hemetsberger, von Wallpach and Bauer 2012). For the individual, luxury is seen as a source of pleasure (Berg 2005), indulgence and desire (Kemp 1998). Traditionally, such understandings link the characteristics of commodity purchases to the pursuits of the wealthy and the upper classes, with luxury consumption connected to social status and distinction (Husic and Cicic 2009). This connection is visible in the work of Thorstein Veblen (1975 [1899]) in his *Theory of the Leisure Class*. Written in the 1890s, this work was produced at a time when economic prosperity in both industrialised Europe and America provided opportunities for the upper classes to exercise what Veblen termed 'conspicuous consumption', that is consumption directed towards the pursuit of pleasure and the fashioning of one's class and/or accomplishments through consumption. Veblen's writings highlighted the connection between wealth and the consumption of luxury commodities, yet a careful reading of his work also reveals how expressions of luxury change across time and place. Perhaps most obvious to the twenty-first century reader of his work is the way in which his theory draws upon particular moral framings of people and places, with women described as 'chattels' and particular peoples and cultures referred to as 'barbarian'. Veblen's work illustrates how the moral ascriptions of people, material cultures and their appropriate 'places' can be significant in framing discourses of value, value which is not only accorded to luxury commodities and practices, but to those who can and cannot gain access to them, and the places and positions those people inhabit.

Empirical expressions of luxury (consumption) and their exposition in academic discourse provide a rich vein for exploring ways in which people's moral ascriptions and place are connected, ascriptions which are themselves formulated in and across particular times and places. As Berry (1994) argues, the value attached to luxury matters, shaping both the ways in which society views itself and the way in which luxury itself is valued. Whether luxury is seen as socially useful, or a burden on a particular society, and whether it is seen as a legitimate or selfish pursuit, matters to those who are both subjects of and subject to such localised discourses. Robert Frank, writing in the context of US consumption, denotes luxury consumption there as a 'fever' based on emulation of the rich and practices of conscious consumption. He asserts that prevailing social and economic incentives assure 'that we will keep spending more and more money for nothing', resulting in greater wealth inequality and a system in which escalating luxury consumption standards provide levels of consumption that other Americans feel 'compelled' to meet (Frank 1999: 279).

While definitions of luxury have been based in both the relative scarcity of luxury commodities and their demand by wealthy consumers, Berry (1994) suggests it is the desirability of luxury commodities which is important to how luxury is understood. Bourdieu's (1986) concept of classed habitus allows us to understand how desires for luxury items are culturally constructed and therefore differ across living standards. What counts as luxury is in part influenced by, but also constitutive of, forms of economic, social, cultural and symbolic capital which place differing values on objects and practices of art, media and design. Values are central to the pursuit of luxury goods and services. In guiding or socialising luxury practices and thinking, the concept of habitus recognises that variations in the social ascription of value can influence why consumers of different social classes might choose and value different kinds of luxuries as a mark of distinction.

Desirability of luxury commodities is not only formed in classed habitus, but also by significant institutions in society, including the state, media, marketing, advertising and retailing industries. These industries – with their well-understood global and local dimensions (see, for example, de Mooij 2014) – both reflect and produce the social and economic values associated with luxury consumption. Goss (2005), drawing from Marx, notes that retailing and marketing directed towards the sale of commodities increasingly focuses on their imaginative rather than material qualities, associating them with 'magical' attributes, emphasising their identity and social functions. This commodity fetishism is perhaps most evident with high-end luxury items, whose presumed exclusivity, quality and excellence mark them as desirable and different from more ordinary (and less expensive) goods and services. Practices of connoisseurship, taste, display and distinction are embedded in this fetishism: it is the privileged and elite who possess, consume and fully appreciate these luxury items.

Luxury has long been associated with the exotic and the spectacular (Faiers 2014) and with exclusivity, wealth and privilege. However, democratising changes associated with globalisation, the resurgence of economic individualism, and new information and communication technologies (Trentmann 2006) are challenging such conceptualisations. Indeed, confronted with this barrage of forces it now seems plausible to argue that the concept of 'luxury' is imploding.

The Democratisation of Luxury

Ricca and Robins contend that the world of luxury has undergone such an incredible transformation in recent years that the term luxury has become 'virtually meaningless' (2012: ix). 'Luxury' is now affordable to the many, and many previously high-end products are available in forms or categories accessible to those on modest incomes. Commodities formerly considered luxuries and accessible only to the elite are now incorporated into the consumption practices of the middle classes (Dolan 2009). In response to the accelerating democratisation of luxury, many marketers and brand-based companies are endeavouring to put the 'Luxe' back into the concept (Danziger 2011). New terms like 'ultra-luxury', 'hyper-luxury', 'super-luxury', 'high luxury' and 'meta-luxury' are intended to recapture territory once associated with luxury goods and services and their consumption (Ricca and Robins 2012).

With an expanding sphere of consumer culture, and technological developments in production and distribution systems, access to goods regarded as luxury commodities has shifted, particularly over the course of the twentieth century (Featherstone 2014). The allure of luxury commodities, and the desirability of luxury lifestyles and pastimes – whether one lives in a context of plenty or lack – is seemingly inescapable, promoted and promulgated through advertising and marketing, in both traditional and new media contexts (see Featherstone, Ch. 6, this volume). The Internet and mobile devices, television, film and traditional paper-based media and even retail settings promote not only the desirability and identity qualities of such goods and services, but expose consumers to lifestyles and life-spaces in which luxury consumption is normalised, suggesting too that luxury consumption can and should be an 'everyday' phenomenon. As Featherstone observes so evocatively: 'luxury hovers over the surface of consumer culture goods, sites and people' (2014: 52).

The democratisation of luxury consumption (Yeoman 2011) is exemplified in so-called 'affordable luxury'. This has been expressed in such practices as the broadening of luxury brands like BMW, Swarovski and Louis Vuitton to provide products more accessible to consumers on moderate incomes. Variations in price, quality, quantity and brand importance and the rise of so-called 'masstige goods', where downward brand extension makes prestigious luxuries available to the masses at lower price ranges, clearly challenge traditional understandings of luxury (Silverstein and Fiske 2003; Ricca and Robins 2012: 3). Democratisation of luxury is fuelled further by growing opportunities to rent luxury experiences and commodities such as exotic cars, couture and designer clothing. The Internet and associated mobile technologies have facilitated a greater accessibility to 'luxury' with websites such as www.quintessentially.com offering members an international concierge service, including access to first-class airport lounges and premium concert bookings (Yeoman 2011). And in marketing, the notion of affordable luxury is now promoted heavily among everyday products, from foods to clothing to shower gels. Moreover, as we alluded to earlier, there is a continuing, if not growing, emphasis on enjoying the intangible 'magical' luxury qualities associated with goods and services, rather than on their specific material properties (Yeoman 2011).

Together with the democratisation of luxury, there has been a more-or-less simultaneous and paradoxical rise of the post-materialist consumer. Disillusioned with materialism and consumerism as aspirational goals, these consumers' lifestyles and values have shifted accordingly, and are characterised, for example, by voluntary frugality, simplicity, downshifting and downsizing, all elements of an alternative orientation, away from luxury consumption (Cherrier and Murray 2002). Notwithstanding sometimes ironic questions around the differing economic capabilities of individuals to engage in post-materialist consumer lifestyles, the framing of commodity values based on social and environmental conscience and sustainability widens further the scope and potential meaning of what constitutes 'luxury' in a changing world. The global economic recession of the late 2000s also resulted in some of the wealthy having to re-evaluate their consumption (Danziger 2011), with 'the new frugality' (Flatters and Wilmott 2009) evident in the search for bargains, even for high-end luxury goods.

Conjoined with democratisation of consumption is the argument that luxury consumption practices themselves have become demoralised, with luxury being less subject to negative ascription than previously (Berry 1994). Assessments that move away from viewing luxury as self-indulgent and a corrupting product of wicked or amoral desires detrimental to society (Featherstone 2014) also promote alternative considerations of the role, function and importance of luxury in everyday life.

Recognising the problematic nature of a more-or-less fixed categorisation of luxury, it is important to understand whether and how luxury's 'democratisation' and 'demoralisation' are experienced in place. Constructions and expressions of luxury do not only change over time, but also in and across place. Place is simultaneously a geographical location and an expression of meaning (Cresswell 2014). According to Agnew (1987), place encompasses not just elements of location in relation to other spaces but also 'locale'; that is, the broader, situated social, economic and material contexts in which people form relationships with one another and with things. The concept also includes one's *sense* of place. Thus, place is a spatially located amalgam of material things and environments, the practices through which people engage with other people and things, and the sense and meaning they make of these relationships (Cresswell 2009). While scholars have recognised that access to and expressions of luxury differ between places, it is important to consider how the role, status and meaning of luxury consumption might be understood in and between places. For example, Berg (2005) discusses the emergence of the new consumer society in Britain in the eighteenth century as illustrative of how the urban and middle classes began to delight in particular forms of luxury, and Wilson (2014) discusses how luxury might be defined in different contexts. Understanding place, with its constituents of local and subjective meaning, compels researchers to recognise how political, economic, cultural and environmental practices, flows and relations influence the particular ways luxury is constructed and the moralities attached to it. Place-based meanings also arise out of a *relational* view of place whereby places are understood in relation to their cultural, economic, environmental and political connections to other places – rather than as discrete containers. Critical perspectives on luxury consumption must acknowledge how luxury is experienced, valued and moralised in specific temporal and geographical contexts. It is to such experiences that we now turn.

Luxury as Talked About and Practised by Older New Zealanders

The remainder of this chapter examines how luxury is talked about and practised by older New Zealanders of varying living standards. The research involved in-depth interviews with 143 people between sixty-three and ninety-five years old in private households in a range of urban and rural areas around New Zealand between March 2010 and May 2011. The research aimed to understand how everyday practices and aspirations for consumption and social relationships were influenced by economic well-being. In total, fifty-two men, eighty-five women and eight male/female heterosexual couples were interviewed. Participants were recruited to represent a range of living standards. Using each participant's address a tentative level of deprivation according to residence was assigned. This geographically based assessment of deprivation was combined with the interviewer's on-site assessment of economic well-being, and together these categorisations were used to classify participants into low (36 per cent), moderate (42 per cent) and high living standards (22 per cent). Participants represented a range of ethnicities including Pakeha (44.1 per cent), Māori (23.4 per cent), Pasifika (7.5 per cent), Chinese (4.1 per cent), non NZ European (13.8 per cent) and Indian (6.9 per cent). None of the participants were in residential care, but some lived with adult children and grandchildren.

The interviews explored numerous aspects of managing choices and decisions in everyday life, focusing on the role of economic resources and the practices they enable. Interview topics included purchasing of food, household commodities and services and the ability to manage financially. Participants were asked about the role of luxuries in their lives, and to provide examples of things they wanted and needed to have and do, and to consider what they would change if they had more or fewer resources. In analysing the interview data, we were not concerned with just the thematic content of conversation, but also with *how* people talked about their economic decisions. This allowed us to understand better the structural and moral imperatives in which narratives were framed and the performative work that such talk achieved for the individual (Stephens and Breheny 2013).

The ability to have a little luxury in everyday life was discussed by participants across the range of living standards. In light of the trends discussed earlier in this chapter, it is not surprising that those things which participants viewed as luxuries varied greatly – from a box of chocolates to world trips and expensive cars. What was of critical significance was that, regardless of whether participants were wealthy or struggling financially, the *ability to choose* and purchase commodities or services that interviewees regarded as luxuries was valued as a part of subjective well-being. The purchase of luxuries provided pleasure and reward, and a sense of power through choice. For those with lower living standards, commodities purchased on a regular basis, but over and above normal everyday purchases, were constructed as luxuries. Examples included subscribing to pay-television services, playing 'pokies' (i.e. electronic gaming machines), buying alcohol or a lottery ticket, or purchasing 'treat' food. Those interviewees in relative poverty described any such purchases, beyond necessity, as 'luxuries'. Purchases of 'little luxuries' or engaging in activities regarded as luxuries in the context of their everyday lives provided relief from both tedium (and, for some, the daily struggle of life) and a sense of enjoyment. Siatu (Interview 137) explains: 'Sometimes I go to the pokie machines and even go to do some horse betting. Not that I spend a lot of money there but just to get out of the house and enjoy something else.' Siatu alludes to a valued quality that luxury purchases and experiences enable – a sense of being in, and participating in, the world. For many participants with lower living standards, luxury goods and services provide a connection to the world outside home and a sense of inclusion in economies and spaces from which they might normally be excluded.

Beyond the recognition that greater economic resources enable wider access to luxuries, we were also interested in how the concept of luxury was deployed in talk, and the effects this has. Interviewees were aware of the ways in which modest luxury purchases might be viewed as wasteful or extravagant in the context of their restricted income. Talking of these purchases frequently involved moral justification. George (Interview 48) recognised that having pay-TV services was an indulgence but defended this purchase on the basis of an absence of other luxuries: 'That's sheer luxury having Sky. I don't have any other luxuries in my life. I don't think that's an extravagance.' Here, Sky television, George's one luxury, was justified and given greater significance in the absence of other pleasures. Talk of a single luxury also became a defence against accusations of excessive consumption. It was common for interviewees with lower living standards to engage in such moral talk about luxury purchases, noting their relative rarity, their status as extraordinary consumption or their position as a solitary category of indulgence. As Vic (Interview 108) suggests: 'We have DVDs. That's our one extravagance, is DVDs.' Arguably, the democratisation of luxury means that even those at the lowest levels of living standards are entitled to at least one luxury, even as those with greater living standards may experience luxury across many facets of their lives.

Regardless of living standard, those who made an occasional or irregular purchase of an item they regarded as a luxury highlighted the enjoyment they drew from such purchases. Many with poor or moderate living standards mentioned the pleasure derived from the anticipation of acquiring the good or service, and the pleasure in saving or waiting for it. Opal, Vic's wife (Interview 108) talked about the anticipation of buying perfume, an act of consumption enabled by a gift from her sister:

> And there's this perfume I've had my eye on for years and I'm going to buy myself a bottle of perfume. But normally no, we just use 'run of the mill' stuff, you know ordinary soap . . . Yes I've waited for years for it so I'm going to buy it.

For those with lower living standards, the distinction between 'run of the mill' and luxury items provides an opportunity to sample luxury as part of moderate sensibilities and careful consumption. Here the exclusivity of the perfume is used to mark it out as desirable, and its exclusivity brings pleasure to the purchaser. For those of lower living standards, access to such limited items of luxury cannot be used to shore up their social status as a consumer, as Veblen might understand the purpose of luxury. Instead, consumers with lower living standards gain different rewards from purchasing small luxuries: they gain a sense of control through making a long anticipated luxury purchase. The experiences of choice and control are among the few benefits such limited items of luxury provide for those with low living standards.

Having choices was valued highly by all participants. Guiren (Interview 96, lower living standard) talked in his interview about his love for, and appreciation of, good quality books, which for him are a luxury item at a cost of over NZ$40.

> I bought it. Why? Because the shop was going bankrupt, closing down. On sale again. Five dollars, ten dollars. I quickly paid for that. I don't buy the forty-five dollar, fifty dollars. No, of course not. On sale, always. Closing down. If I want to I can go to Borders [international book store], they've got many beautiful ones but they cost fifty dollars, forty-five dollars, some eighty dollars but it's a really beautiful one, still new, but I know I can't afford so I don't think of it but wait, I always wait. In some suburb, some bookshop closing down and I go and check if they have it and then I buy it. You know, once I got it for five dollars in Warehouse [a major NZ discount outlet], a good one. Why? It had been there so long on the rack. Nobody wants it. I notice it. I spotted that one. I quickly paid the five dollars. It makes me happy. When I'm at home I look at it.

Here, by narrating a story that is recognisable as a hunting account, Guiren fashions his identity at the intersection of an appreciation of the finer things in life and living circumstances characterised by limited resources. Guiren appreciates fine books, but to achieve what he desires he must bide his time. He navigates closing down sales strategically and acts quickly when he spots valuable items overlooked by others. Guiren's pleasure in finally obtaining a desired book is bound up with his restraint and choice not to purchase from

Borders. His eventual purchase of the 'beautiful book' in a closing down sale demonstrates the virtues of his 'choice', his patience and his abilities as a knowledgeable and skilled consumer. The pleasure derived from the luxury comes as much from the astuteness required to attain it as the object's beauty itself.

However, for those who identified conventionally understood luxury goods and services as desirable, but unobtainable, the pleasure which might be derived from these was simultaneously acknowledged and dismissed. When asked what she would do with the money if she won the lottery, Lila (Interview 1) observed how pleasurable it would be to attend a ballet or concert: 'Wouldn't it be wonderful, being able to go to a ballet or concert, wouldn't that be wonderful.' In common with others on restricted incomes, Lila commented that such luxuries were unaffordable, but also in common with many other interviewees, remarked that she is coping and satisfied with what she has: 'I don't know because I've always gone scrounging, made do and, I don't think I'm too badly off.'

Guiren (Interview 96) exemplifies this moral talk, when he discusses satisfaction as the key to happiness, a happiness that means he does not think of purchasing luxury cars for instance.

> If you feel satisfied then you are happy. Satisfaction that makes you feel happy. No matter how much money you own, you possess, if you are not satisfied you won't be happy. Satisfaction, that makes you happy. Now I'm living in Auckland here, the thing that I have, I'm satisfied with the thing that I have. I feel contented. I never think of getting a [unintelligible] car, getting a BMW. So, I don't mind. Never think of that.

Guiren frames satisfaction as something available to all and unrelated to the resources that offer access to luxury goods. Similarly, Seth (Interview 70) acknowledges that while the possession of more expensive luxuries could bring pleasure, those commodities are not necessary. 'It would be nice to have a beautiful car that cost about $30,000 but that is not important to me. I am all right with a bicycle.' Seth and Guiren connect luxury with pleasure but uncouple luxury from satisfaction and personal importance, aspects of life they regard as available to all.

Having the capacity to choose was a key element of the construction of items of luxury. For those on higher incomes, power to choose was expressed differently, with interviewees reframing luxury in terms of the choice *not* to consume and viewing luxury as attainable and, perhaps therefore, unimportant.

Those at the top end of the living standards spectrum worked hard in their talk to suggest that items some might regard as luxuries were in fact necessities. For example, Peta (Interview 15) partly justifies her decision to buy an expensive car through the argument that it offers increased safety for her daughter:

> *Peta*: My car when I, oh the car I had before this one was a big, big Pajero [a Mitsubishi Sport Utility Vehicle] and that was I think something like 48,000 [dollars]. Basically I got that for my daughter to drive because she drove a lot and she tend to hit things so I thought she better come off first, not second best. And then when she went I changed it for a smaller Pajero but Piers always just buys what he wants.
> *Interviewer*: Right
> *Peta*: The money's there, why not? But not, you know I'm not really into these people who go and sort of, have you seen our latest car. It's an SJ6 with da de da, da and, you know to me a car is getting from A to B and should be trustworthy.

Peta describes her car as safe and trustworthy, rather than as a way to fashion her identity as wealthy. Peta openly disparages those who brag about their latest cars, positioning herself as sensible and practical in her purchase of a vehicle many compatriots would regard as luxurious.

While many wealthy participants noted their 'entitlement' to luxury consumption – as Peta does above by saying 'The money's there, why not?' – few participants talked about the purchase of luxury commodities purely for self-gratification, enjoyment or indulgence. Often descriptions of luxury spending were minimised by the wealthy, or mentioned apologetically as Neil (Interview 64) does, when talking about the numerous overseas trips he has had in retirement: 'I'm afraid we only travel business class these days.'

Even when extravagance was identified, the purchase and possession of luxury items tended to be framed in terms of entitlement. This moral construction of luxuries as earned or deserved was evident in participant talk, but the justification of luxury spending was expressed differently from those at the lower end of the living standards spectrum. As Helen (Interview 65) describes, entitlement for the wealthy derives from hard work and money management skills:

> *Interviewer*: So are there any things you feel you can't do because of financial restrictions?
> *Helen*: No, there haven't really, there aren't now and there really haven't been any because we earned two good salaries. We did a lot of travelling. I actually made a list the other day and we've been to

30 different countries. But, we haven't had any money gifted to us; it's just how we've used our money I suppose.

In direct contrast to Veblen's assertion that status increases as distance from the effort required to acquire wealth increases (Trigg 2001), moral justification of luxury lifestyles in today's neoliberalising societies often requires recourse to the personal effort expended to secure the resources that allow access to luxury. Following Veblen (1975 [1899]), status is maintained by the judgements others make about one's position in society, and in contemporary society these judgements are often based around perceived effort. In the social and political contexts of neoliberalism, which valorise individual success and personal responsibility for outcomes, luxury is thus moralised as a fair reward for individual success and thrift.

One consequence of viewing luxury as a just reward for individual success and thrift was a tendency among the wealthy participants to repudiate any entitlement those on lesser incomes had to items that might be considered luxuries. Catherine (Interview 23), with high living standards, began this conversation with a critique of one of her (less wealthy) friend's 'extravagant' consumption practices. Catherine links moral entitlement to economic resources. Catherine enjoys a drink of whisky daily: it is a 'little luxury' she enjoys and one to which she feels entitled as she can 'afford it'. Ironically, while whisky drinking is a luxury choice available to Catherine, she suggests that this (and smoking) should not be an option taken up by those who cannot afford it.

> *Interviewer*: So I guess again it's a choice people make?
> *Catherine*: It's a choice people make, and it's, if you want to drink whisky well then drink it if you can afford it. And if you can't well then don't do it. I mean it's not necessary for that to live.
> *Interviewer*: Sure, sure.
> *Catherine*: You know like smokers. I mean, I don't know how people can afford to smoke, apart from the health things, I mean I don't know how they can actually afford, and it's usually the people that can't afford it that are smoking themselves silly.

In this way, the pleasure of a singular luxury that those with low living standards defend as a choice which enables a sense of control and mastery is reframed by the wealthy as indicative of immorality and a lack of control.

While some of the wealthy disparaged the 'uncontrolled' and/or wasteful practices of the poor in indulging in commodities beyond their means, they were also keen to demonstrate their own restraint in purchasing and their lack of materialism. Consequently, talk about their luxury purchases was often contradictory, as Peta's interview reveals. She acknowledged that she didn't see 'life as necessarily associated to money', but realised this was because 'it's always been there'. She spoke at length of the pleasure derived from purchases she acknowledged were part of her privileged lifestyle (these included opera, concerts, exclusive restaurants, travel, and expensive jewellery and cars). Yet Peta likes to shop in charity shops: this extends the range of consumption options open to her, a fact highlighted by the existence of her husband's account at an expensive department store and her skill in obtaining 'tremendous bargains' as a knowing shopper (Gregson, Brooks and Crewe 2001).

> Yeah. And it's a rummage. It's, you know it's like yeah you get a surprise for what you can find, you know sometimes you will really get tremendous bargains. A lot of people though, like my husband who has a standing account at [expensive department store], think it's absolutely terrible, so he never comes op shopping, but yeah.

Peta uses the example of 'op shopping' here to mark herself out as different from others in her social coterie, as above and beyond the vulgarities of those who shop in expensive department stores and 'get their face done' (Interview 23). Peta's choice to refuse to buy high-end fashion clothing exclusively and to 'op shop' to the chagrin of her friends was a choice made freely in the context of her substantial economic resources: it enabled her to get pleasure from her bargains. Ironically, while spending time shopping (discerningly) for clothes in second-hand stores was a 'luxury' for her, that same consumption practice by many on lower incomes was out of necessity rather than choice (as we saw from the example of Guiren's hunt for inexpensive books). Peta differentiates and distinguishes herself from others in her group of apparently high social standing. She refuses some of the trappings popular among her social group and frames her distinction by claiming as a sign of taste an activity that is usually a signifier of economic restriction.

Material Matters in Luxury Consumption: Attributes, Places and Things

For study participants what counted as 'luxury' appeared to be influenced by the socially constructed and material dimensions of commodities and the places in which they were situated. The material properties of commodities influenced their consumption as luxury goods. Recent writing on the socio-technologies of consumption (Hand, Shove and Southerton 2007; Watson and Shove 2008) has emphasised the ways in which the material properties of things matter to how they are consumed, possessed and divested. Commodities such as expensive cars or art imply different gestures, actions and obligations for their consumers in terms of maintenance, storage and repair for example, with such demands and obligations (e.g. additional fuel consumption, suitable display space) relevant to their construction as luxuries. The material properties of places provide other imperatives for both the consumption of luxury and its narration as something justified, as Ying's purchase of increasingly large televisions demonstrates. Ying (Interview 98), on a moderate income, noted that the size of her sitting room, the increasing size of 'standard' televisions and her failing eyes meant she needed to purchase a large-screen television.

> And in the old days of course, you started off with a 24 inch T.V. then you go up to a 29 inch and now, because our lounge is quite big, we have actually got a 50 inch TV. And especially for our old eyes, we need it.

Ying's remarks point to the social construction of luxury commodities and practices in the context of particular place settings. When asked about her spending, Peta (Interview 15) confirms the importance of place in her choice to wear costume jewellery rather than her valuable 'genuine' jewellery when she goes out. She prefers to keep the authentic gems in a business vault because she believes the combination of conspicuous display and keeping her jewellery at home could prove attractive to thieves.

> *Peta*: Yeah that's interesting. Most of my jewellery is inherited from both sides of the family and it's so valuable I leave it in the vault in town in my husband's vault, or in the bank vault . . . And I wear trash I pick up from op shops. I think it's mainly cause a lot of places I work or are mixing, I mean not yes we have but a lot of places I don't like to be seen as over consumptive. I mean to me in a, living in a welfare state or socialist nation, of a nature it's conspicuous consumption is what attracts criminals no end. That's why [names suburb in Auckland] has the highest burglary rate in New Zealand. But yeah someday I'll get around to getting them out and wearing them I guess.

Peta's assessments about luxury consumption, and where and when its display is 'out of place' are not just about her fears of theft, but about the way in which her taste might be received in particular contexts. She has both taste and money, which enables her to wear 'trash' and costume jewellery if (and where) she chooses. Ironically while she attributes differences in access to commodities (and criminal desires) as symptomatic of the problems of a welfare state, in which she believes she still lives, such inequalities are more likely a product of the neoliberalising society in which she actually resides, a point which takes us to broader notions of place and context.

As noted at the outset of this chapter, the study participants were older residents of New Zealand/Aotearoa, most of whom have, over the course of their lifetimes, first been subject to a welfare state and protectionist economic policies and then, since the mid-1980s, have experienced radical neoliberalisation (Kelsey 1999). New Zealanders over the age of 65 are entitled to a universal fortnightly pension (National Superannuation) that remains as a legacy of earlier welfare state provisions, and so they are caught between a pensioner identity and one which controversially sees them as part of a 'selfish generation' which has arguably benefited disproportionately from the operation of the welfare state (Thomson 1991). Of course, many older New Zealanders have also lived through times of austerity – the Depression, the Second World War and various financial crises. Consequently while many participants acknowledge their entitlement to and the pleasure derived from luxury, they were keen to refute extravagance or wastefulness in their consumption choices. For example, Catherine's (Interview 23) frugality can be situated against locally specific generational influences which have meant she has always lived a life where many forms of consumption deemed to be 'luxury' are seen as excessive, even though she can afford to pay for them:

> *Catherine*: And food, I will buy whatever I want but at the same time I will not necessarily go and buy it at [an expensive delicatessen] when I can get the same thing at the supermarket and there's a dollar difference. Why would I go to a fancy shop? But I've never been like that.
>
> *Interviewer*: Okay, so, so you . . .
>
> *Catherine*: I'm not, I don't know what it is, we, another friend of mine she said it's our background you know. It is our background. We're hoarders of money. We, sort of for the rainy day which may never come but it's our background . . . You never spent what you didn't have and you went without until you had the money to have it and we, that was our upbringing. And also for women in New Zealand, there was no way that you could, until you were sort of like 21 or something, there was no way that you could have borrowed money or bought anything that you didn't just pay for.

Underpinned by the neoliberal ideologies of successive Labour and National governments since the mid-1980s, deregulation of New Zealand's economy has reinforced the roles and responsibilities of citizens as consumers. Deregulation has exposed firms, voluntary agencies and residents more directly than ever before to the unforgiving operation and effects of the 'market' and globalisation. Despite the continued existence of National Superannuation, the effects of the global financial crisis, the collapse of several high-profile finance companies (in which many of our participants had invested savings), and increasing media and political rhetoric about the need to save privately for one's retirement appear to have contributed to heightened financial and ontological insecurity among interviewees (Mansvelt, Breheny and Stephens 2014). Such changes potentially influence (re)constructions of what counts as luxury, including one's moral sense of entitlement to luxuries for both self and others.

> *Interviewer*: Yeah. And you're able to fill all your prescriptions?
> *Andrea*: Much as I resent the amount it costs me I'm fortunate that we did save and I resent the fact that I've lost about half of my savings through investments.
> *Interviewer*: Oh golly.
> *Andrea*: Other people took my money and spent it and then, yeah but never mind I've got enough to live.

Andrea's (Interview 86) consumption of luxuries is vastly different after the global financial crisis, now that her pension has become her main source of income rather than a supplement. Her revised luxury spending decisions now occur in quite different moral and financial contexts where she is more aware of the need to make prudent decisions to ensure she has sufficient income to last her lifetime.

Interpretations and Intersections

If, as Alain de Botton is said to have opined, 'The materialistic view of happiness of our age is starkly revealed in our understanding of the word "luxury"' (http://dailyquoted.com/quotes/46324), then an interrogation of how luxury is talked about and practised is imperative. Our analysis of interviews with older New Zealanders reveals that the ability to purchase goods and services deemed to be luxuries was a choice valued by all. Across living standards a sense of pleasure and enjoyment was derived from the purchase, use and possession of diverse commodities described as luxuries, from a \$40 book to an expensive SUV. Access to a single item they regarded as luxurious was sufficient for some with low living standards to exhibit their access to a wider world of consumption. For those people for whom expensive items and experiences were unobtainable, narrating a sense of satisfaction and contentment with small luxuries was an important part of shaping their identity as a person with access to all that really mattered in life. Expectations of appropriate and achievable luxury consumption were managed in the context of restriction, rather than being abandoned altogether. Across living standards a sense of pleasure and entitlement to luxury was expressed, though materialism, wastefulness and lack of self-control in luxury consumption were carefully avoided. In examining aspects of talk around commodity meanings, rather than focusing on more objective qualities of luxury commodities themselves, our study has revealed the role of moral ascription in the consumption of commodities, demonstrating how narratives of justification and entitlement to forms of luxury consumption provide means of shaping identities as responsible, controlled and autonomous consumers.

Bourdieu's writings on distinction, habitus and forms of capital (e.g. Bourdieu 1986) provide a way of understanding how luxury can be understood and pursued outside the realm of those with considerable wealth. At the intersection of his opposition between the 'taste of necessity' characteristic of the lower classes and 'taste of luxury' based on the freedoms available to the wealthy (Dolan 2009), those with low living standards claim the 'necessity of luxury'. However, Bourdieu's suggestion that what counts as luxury for the poor will be viewed negatively by those with more economic resources (Trigg 2001) was not generally found in this study. While the poor's moral entitlement to buy cigarettes, drink alcohol or gamble might be questioned, many of the commodities and services regarded as luxuries by those with limited resources (for example, good quality chocolates or trips to the ballet) may be taken for granted and regarded as ordinary by the very wealthy, but are not necessarily disdained. Bourdieu offers an understanding of the cultural constitution of luxury across individuals of different social classes, but like Veblen, who emphasised the conspicuous consumption of the leisure classes, his theorisation provides limited insights into how specific attributes of the material world and the material properties of things might produce valued forms of capital directed towards luxury consumption – an area worthy of further investigation.

Luxury tastes and practices vary not only across class, but also across time and in place. The luxury tastes, practices and aspirations of the older New Zealanders in this study have been framed by changing global relations and New Zealand/Aotearoa's unique political economy and cultural geography. Media, culture, commodity networks, state and economy have combined to produce both desires for, and access to, commodities. Luxury consumption practices intersect with media and cultural discourses of distinction, novelty and status, and combine with the material aspects of the things themselves to facilitate the capacity of luxuries to give pleasure in ways which are 'out of the ordinary' (e.g. to relieve, refresh, or discipline the body). While the democratisation of consumption may mean commodities deemed 'luxuries' are available to a wider range of consumers, our research has shown that leisure commodities are differently valued, pursued and understood by consumers across the living standards spectrum. Democratisation may be associated with fewer negative associations of engaging in luxury consumption, but our study of the talk and practices of a particular generational cohort of New Zealanders reveals that luxury consumption across the living standard spectrum is associated with moral prescription, particularly with regard to the entitlement of self and others to certain forms of commodity. Moreover, regardless of the ways in which luxury consumption is justified, this study of older New Zealanders across a range of living standards has revealed that the purchase of (so-called) luxuries is universally valued, providing a sense of pleasure and contributing to autonomy and well-being. Understanding the moral and social imperatives of consumption practices as they are produced in particular time and place contexts consequently provides a basis for explaining why even those with limited incomes need to be able to claim to enjoy 'life's little luxuries'.

References

Agnew, J. (1987), *Place and Politics: The Geographical Mediation of State and Society*, Winchester, MA: Allen and Unwin.

Berg, M. (2005), *Luxury and Pleasure in Eighteenth-Century Britain*, Oxford: Oxford University Press.

Berry, C. J. (1994), *The Idea of Luxury: A Conceptual and Historical Investigation*, Cambridge: Cambridge University Press.

Bourdieu, P. (1986), *Distinction: A Social Critique of the Judgement of Taste*, London: Routledge.

Cherrier, H. and Murray, J. (2002), 'Drifting away from excessive consumption: a new social movement based on identity construction', *Advances in Consumer Research*, 29 (1): 245–7.

Cresswell, T. (2009), 'Place', in R. Kitchin and N. Thrift (eds), *International Encyclopedia of Human Geography*, Oxford: Elsevier, pp. 169–77.

Cresswell, T. (2014), 'Place', in P. Cloke, P. Crang and M. Goodwin (eds), *Introducing Human Geographies*, 3rd edn, London: Hodder Arnold, pp. 249–61.

Danziger, P. N. (2011), *Putting the Luxe Back in Luxury*, Ithaca, NY: Paramount Market Publishing.

de Mooij, M. (2014), *Global Marketing and Advertising: Understanding Cultural Paradoxes*, 4th edn, Thousand Oaks: Sage.

Dolan, P. (2009), 'Figurational dynamics and parliamentary discourses of living standards in Ireland', *The British Journal of Sociology*, 60 (4): 721–39.

Faiers, J. (2014), 'Editorial introduction', *Luxury: History, Culture, Consumption*, 1 (1): 5–14.

Featherstone, M. (2014), 'Luxury, consumer culture and sumptuary dynamics', *Luxury: History, Culture, Consumption*, 1 (1): 47–70.

Flatters, P. and Willmott, M. (2009), 'Understanding the post-recession consumer', *Harvard Business Review*, 87 (7–8): 106–12.

Frank, R. H. (1999), *Luxury Fever: Weighing the Cost of Excess*, Princeton and Oxford: Princeton University Press.

Goss, J. (2005), 'Consumption', in P. Cloke, P. Crang and M. Goodwin (eds), *Introducing Human Geographies*, 2nd edn, London: Hodder Arnold, pp. 253–66.

Gregson, N., Brooks, K. and Crewe, L. (2001), 'Bjorn again? Rethinking 70s revivalism through the reappropriation of 70s clothing', *Fashion Theory*, 5 (1): 3–28.

Hand, M., Shove, E. and Southerton, D. (2007), 'Home extensions in the United Kingdom: space, time, and practice', *Environment and Planning D: Society and Space*, 25: 668–81.

Hemetsberger, A., von Wallpach, S. and Bauer, M. (2012), '"Because I'm worth it": luxury and the construction of consumers' selves', *Advances in Consumer Research*, 40: 483–9.

Husic, M. and Cicic, M. (2009), 'Luxury consumption factors', *Journal of Fashion Marketing and Management*, 13 (2): 231–45.

Kelsey, J. (1999), *Reclaiming the Future: New Zealand and the Global Economy*, Wellington: Bridget Williams Books.

Kemp, S. (1998), 'Perceiving luxury and necessity', *Journal of Economic Psychology*, 19 (5): 591–606.

Mansvelt, J., Breheny, M. and Stephens, C. (2014), 'Pursuing security: economic resources and the ontological security of older New Zealanders', *Ageing & Society*, 34 (10): 1666–87.

Ricca, M. and Robins, R. (2012), *Meta-Luxury: Brands and the Culture of Excellence*, Basingstoke and New York: Palgrave Macmillan.

Silverstein, M. J. and Fiske, N. (2003), 'Luxury for the masses', *Harvard Business Review*, 81 (4): 48–57.

Stephens, C. and Breheny, M. (2013), 'Narrative analysis in psychological research: an integrated approach to interpreting stories', *Qualitative Research in Psychology*, 10 (1): 14–27.

Thomson, D. (1991), *Selfish Generations? The Ageing of New Zealand's Welfare State*, Wellington: Bridget Williams Books, 1991.

Trentmann, F. (2006), 'The evolution of the consumer: meanings, identities, and political synapses before the age of affluence', in S. Garon and P. L. Maclachlan (eds), *The Ambivalent Consumer: Questioning Consumption in East Asia and the West*, Ithaca, NY and London: Cornell University Press, pp. 21–44.

Trigg, A. B. (2001), 'Veblen, Bourdieu, and conspicuous consumption', *Journal of Economic Issues*, 35 (1): 99–115.

Veblen, T. (1975 [1899]), *The Theory of the Leisure Class*, New York: Augustus.

Watson, M. and Shove, E. (2008), 'Product, competence, project and practice: DIY and the dynamics of craft consumption', *Journal of Consumer Culture*, 8 (1): 69–89.

Wilson, E. (2014), 'Luxury', *Luxury: History, Culture, Consumption*, 1 (1): 15–22.

Yeoman, I. (2011), 'The changing behaviours of luxury consumption', *Journal of Revenue & Pricing Management*, 10 (1): 47–50.

Chapter 6

The Object and Art of Luxury Consumption

Mike Featherstone

A central aspect of luxury is value. Luxuries proclaim value: they suggest things that can readily be valued above others. Luxuries embody the promise of special things: not merely things of quality, scarcity and wonder that are beautifully made, but also eventful and sensory fulfilling experiences. Indeed, some luxury goods are deliberately made to be noticed: to embody authority and announce their experiential dimension. It is this power of luxuries to offer more, to hold out the promise of a process of familiarisation which unfolds new aesthetic and sensory dimensions, that can evoke strong and even threatening social feelings about their exclusiveness, social cost and wastefulness. The making of luxuries can involve a seemingly excessive investment of time and money, beyond apparent social need. The distinction between everyday necessities and luxuries is generally seen as central to the understanding of luxury. The dynamic of modernity is regarded as one in which many luxuries whose consumption was formerly restricted to aristocrats, courtiers and upper-class groups, become widely available (tea, sugar, spices, silk, dyes, etc.). In pre-modern times luxury goods were generally prohibitively expensive and only available in limited quantities until European colonial expansion, the development of the slave trade and the opening up of the Americas increased both the supply and the range of substitutes. This resulted in price falls, opening up the possibility of more widespread availability and the 'democratisation of luxury'.[1] One of the dynamics of luxury, then, is to produce copies and cheaper substitutes to extend the market. But this tendency also produces the opposite move, which is at the heart of luxury, the concern to possess the original, which has unique qualities and rarity.[2]

From another perspective anything can become an indulgence, desirable or pleasing: hence anything can become a luxury. People may well have different hierarchies of goods and experiences they value at particular times of life, and hence a range of different luxuries they can enjoy or desire. These may range from the 'little luxuries', the little treats mothers provide,[3] to lottery-winner dreams of fulfilment and enjoyment replete with the finest things money can buy. The contemplation of luxuries draws on a rich discourse and imagery of comfort, sensory pleasures, elegance, style, prestige, glamour and excessive indulgence. In contemporary consumer culture there is a range of related thematics that are often associated with luxury such as beauty, romance and exotica, which can readily be found in advertising imagery. We are constantly subjected to publicity, which not only proclaims the allure of luxuries, but seeks to persuade us that we deserve them or should feel compelled to provide them for others. Luxury is a potent quality to be attributed to things and experiences, and for this reason within consumer culture the terminology, discourses and imagery of luxury are overused and can be found practically everywhere. The Internet and social media are currently adding a further dimension, by acting as a new set of resources for the presentation of information and images of sumptuous luxury goods and experiences. There is an expanding number of websites that constantly seek to outbid themselves in proclaiming superior levels of quality and distinctiveness, along with a high price tag: luxuries give way to ultra- or super-luxuries.

Most definitions of luxuries emphasise comfort, but elegance is usually mentioned and also expense. In effect the luxury object has been fashioned to provide maximum value with little concern for the amount of labour involved or the final price. This is particularly so with the type of ultra-luxuries designed for and purchased by expanding strata of wealthy people and the increasingly visible rich and super-rich. Such luxuries can be made to cater for direct sensory pleasures such as eating and drinking, but also bodily comforts as we find in tactile pleasures and proprioceptive feelings. Here we think of the touch of sumptuous fabrics, or other sensory elements such as relaxing sounds and music, careful subdued lighting and perfume to stimulate the senses, all of which help generate a certain mood and sense of care and warmth. The emphasis is on elegant and stylish craftsmanship, good design and careful construction, as in furniture, *objets d'art*, interior design and architecture. But also clothing and adornment, through the care, skill and workmanship evident in the crafting, cut and design.

In addition, along with the general tendency in consumer culture to supplement goods with experiences, and to encourage the direct purchase of experiences, can we speak of luxurious experiences? Certainly advertising copy would suggest this is the case. Again the qualities shade into each other – comfort, elegance, memorable events, adventure, excitement, exotica become the repertoire to be drawn upon in the descriptions of luxury vacations/once in a lifetime cruises/adventure holidays/destinations not to miss before you die, all inevitably proclaiming their luxurious credentials. Likewise the purchase of expensive items with expert guidance and levels of personal service that provide tutorials and back-up on how to enjoy the new car, or choose the Savile Row suit, which not only confirm the status of the products as luxuries, but confer the status of having arrived on the owner – something which can be particularly important for new rich purchasers.

Furthermore, health and body care need to be considered. Body maintenance and health check-ups have their routine and mundane aspects, but the settings, the décor and interior design of top-end private hospitals, clinics and gyms can provide very high levels of comfort, service and personal care from staff. In major global cities that are home to the rich and super-rich, the expectation is not just of high levels of technical competence and equipment, but also of comfort and service, with the price less important (the Harley Street area of London being a good example). Health and body care can also be seen as 'facilitators', necessary preconditions for enjoying the full the range of luxury lifestyles available to the wealthy. Like technological investments in transport such as private jets or luxury cars, along with advanced digital communication devices, they offer everyday savings of time for people with overflowing schedules and over-optioned lives. Communications technologies, then, can also be regarded as facilitators, to enable more efficient time economies.

A related issue is whether wealth itself can be thought of as luxurious. There are cases where people grow up in upper-class or aristocratic households and learn how to handle and take for granted many of the objects, settings and experiences normally assumed to be luxuries. In effect habitual use of some luxuries can turn them into taken for granted necessities. Yet, for the vast majority of people and the nouveau riche in particular, money itself connotes luxuriousness. Certainly, money opens the door to a life replete with possibilities: the dreams can be realised, the goods, sensations and experiences sampled. Having a lot of money makes it possible to hire professional expertise and services, which can take the risk element out of choice, and make the selection process an interesting and reassuring status-confirming experience itself. In this sense money is the prime facilitator to unlock the treasure house of luxuries.

But it has also been argued that there is a more direct process at work: people do not just want the things money can buy, they want money itself (Yuran 2014). They want the fetish-conferring and life-opening-up qualities money itself provides. In consumer culture, then, we don't just gaze longingly at the luxuries on display: the price tag also does some work. There are of course top-end shops in the wealthy areas of global cities that never have price tags for the goods on display, yet the fact that it can be readily ascertained that the goods are expensive adds a certain exclusivity, which for many people takes them into the category of 'special purchases' and gifts. In contrast, there are many instances of everyday consumption, where careful budgeting and price-sensitive purchasing are mandatory. Yet in the case of special purchases and luxuries the price may matter much less. Indeed, the knowledge that a certain item is extremely expensive itself confers status. This is something that Veblen and Marx in their different ways noted: 'things are effects of money' (Yuran 2014: 7).

While the fetishising effect of money has been the subject of a good deal of analysis (Baudrillard 1981; Dant 1996; Silva 2012; Hornborg 2014), in the way that high price can summon up desire for goods, it is also possible to see the opposite process taking place, whereby the objects desired or purchased take on a special quality, irrespective of monetary value. Walter Benjamin's depiction of the thrown-away consumer packaging and material such as train tickets, handbills, confectionery wrappers, etc., the discarded objects found in the street or junk shop, points to the potential for ordinary everyday goods to take on additional properties and retain a value (Benjamin 1999, 2010; Featherstone 2007). In such cases goods may develop a particular aura or affective charge, which becomes central to the desire for ownership, or possession. Indeed, it can be said that possession is reversed and it is their capacity to possess the owner, which is the attractor. There is a dynamic, then, which points us to consider the life history of objects and their movement in and out of luxury status and the way some can accrue value and attain the special quality of becoming powerful desired things. Some everyday objects, which were mundane and unremarked in past ages, may end up in the museum and attain high cultural value – their special quality is that they have survived and are originals from a different time. They can be treated with extreme reverence and even fetishised and provide enormous pleasure for the connoisseur or expert who has the privilege of handling them, or even just being in their presence. At the same time as museums can be part of the process of creating luxuries, drawing things to attention and making them desirable *objets d'art*, such luxury objects can also be transformed into high craft value reproductions to adorn the apartments of the wealthy. It is also, of course, possible in the life history of objects for the reverse process to take place, for objects to become seen as outmoded and for them to disappear into the storeroom, or even be discarded as rubbish (see Appadurai 1986; Brown 2004; Boscagli 2014).

What must luxuries do if they want to attain even higher value? The answer is: become art. This leads to some interesting scenarios in terms of today's luxuries, for to have the status of art conferred on luxury goods is, for many of the predominantly craft-based sectors, the highest accolade. Yet, from the art side, there has often been a feeling of superiority (and even contempt on the part of some avant-garde artists) towards the luxury sector. At the same time there has been a good deal of back-door and carefully controlled exchange mediation, given the financial power the luxury sector possesses. More recently, art museums have become increasingly commercial as opposed to educational enterprises, so such tie-ups and sponsor-ship deals can prove attractive. For the luxury houses, considerable prestige is conferred – often with the blessing of cultural establish-ments who may designate them as a boundary sub-category of art and welcome displays of 'classic' or 'avant-garde' luxury objects. To get closer to art and the art museum, one strategy is for the luxury houses to set up their own luxury brand museum, or sponsor exhibi-tions of artistic or related material which is significantly close or resonates well with the brand. In such cases, the expectation is that there will be some transference of the aura and special status of art. There is, therefore, an interesting set of dynamics involving luxury objects that will be examined in the following sections of the chapter.

The Object of Luxury

In some cases luxury objects may have such high investment value potential that the process of accruing additional value may be so compelling and attractive that the owner decides to relinquish or delay their actual consumption or use. Some luxury objects, then, such as rare crafted objects from early civilisations, or paintings or jewellery, may be deemed so valuable that they are locked away in bank vaults. Or if displayed, this is done so only when elaborate securing measures have been put in place. Their high monetary value gives them exclusivity, which means they are treated as special by retailers, customers and marketers, irrespective of their actual quali-ties. Their desirability can feed the expectation that they will provide an emotional charge and open up a range of pleasures.

Some objects such as food and drink seemingly offer immediate pleasure; they are there to be consumed. For the rich and the super-rich, the capacity to sample and explore taste is a central aspect of the consumption possibilities that wealth opens up. On one level this offers the opportunity to explore the direct taste of fine food and drink. As the worldwide market for luxury food and drink expands with more and more brands and individual producers seeking to provide specialist gourmet food and beverages to be sold in high-end shops or featured in restaurant dishes, the pressure is on to produce new levels of taste experience for the extremely wealthy. This provides the opportunity for some luxury brands to diversify and cross over into different fields to develop new markets – a move which can appear particularly attractive at a time when sales of Italian luxury goods (handbags, shoes, clothes, accessories, etc.) have stabilised, whereas Italy's premium food industry has been steadily growing and enjoys a high reputation for its artisanal and biodiversity qualities. Many of the medium-level luxury brands around the world are seeking such diversification and consolidation, as the opportunities to expand continue. Over the past twenty years the number of luxury-goods consumers worldwide has more than trebled to 330 million. The shares of luxury companies in the S&P Global Luxury Index have outperformed the S&P 500 by over 50 per cent since the 2008 financial crisis (Unger 2014).

The expansion of the luxury market and the more general 'democratisation of luxury' (Featherstone 2014; Pinkhasov and Nair 2014) not only means that luxuries are everywhere, it also creates pressures to develop even more exclusive goods, stimulating ultra-luxury brands and the bespoke luxury market.[4] The £10 million solid gold diamond-encrusted iPhone, created by British designer Stuart Hughes, is just one example of the excessive adornment of an everyday object, especially one with a limited lifespan.[5] There was an estimated total spend on luxuries of $1.8 trillion in 2012, a trend which has seen the rise of a series of luxury brand billionaires, such as Bernard Arnault of LVMH and François-Henri Pinault of the Kering Group (Bain and Company 2014). The demand for luxury consumables such as food and drink, then, can be bolstered if there is the assumption of a high level of quality crafted into them (Sennett 2008). Their value is not only enhanced by scarcity, but also by rarity. For example, an individual bottle of rare Bordeaux wine can be valued at hundreds of thousands of dollars.[6] This is even the case when an exceptionally rare bottle, such the 1787 Chateau Lafitte, has survived for over two centuries but is now clearly undrinkable, suggesting that its valuation at over $300,000 has to be understood in terms of its rarity value for a wine collector. This would also make it potentially attractive to display in a wine museum, or foyer of an exclusive wine merchant. In this case immense prestige value was added not only by the fact that it was the sole survivor from over 200 years ago and produced by a top Bordeaux premier cru label, but also by the evidence that it had been owned by Thomas Jefferson. The fact that it is undrinkable, with all resemblance to fine wine gone, is overridden by its value in the abstract table of great wines, also compounded many times by the fact that it survived intact. This adds enormously to the immense delight of the collector or connoisseur who can gaze on such an extraordinary object, or even contemplate its purchase and the fact it would take pride of place in his or her collection.[7] Again aura is at work along with distinction; but also property: the capture, ownership and possession of the item is also important.

An opposite case could be the lack of reverence shown to highly expensive items, whose consumption is direct, immediate and excessive and by no means carefully contemplated or judiciously anticipated. Rather, it is their high symbolic and financial value that makes the consumption of the finest and rarest festive food and drink important. The gesture of excessive generosity ('only the best will do'), and the wanton act of consumption, or even destruction, becomes a sign of the special nature and high value of the group of people involved. Price is decidedly no object and pales in significance against the need to demonstrate allegiance and social solidarity by acknowledging the group's luck and good fortune: effectively recognising their debt to fate by consuming particular expensive festive drinks, such as champagne, to excess. There are echoes of carnival reversals in which expensive wine flows freely, or the potlatch festivals of destructive feasting and gift and counter-gift giving here (Bataille 1988).

These examples raise a series of interesting questions about value accumulation, the nature of collecting and connoisseurship, as well as the disposability and persistence of particular objects. Luxury food and drink provide fascinating case studies as they have relatively short lifespans and are produced with high levels of expertise and crafting to provide discernible quality taste. Yet in the case of champagne, there has been the accumulation of additional symbolic value, not only in the beverage's deemed appropriateness or necessity for specific ceremonies (weddings, anniversaries, receptions, openings), but also in the case of events where the wine is deliberately poured away or destroyed in a rite to induce good fortune, as in ship launches. Another type of wasting and excess takes place at sporting events, notably Formula One Motor Racing, where there is a good deal of playful spraying around on the podium when the victors celebrate. Champagne may also appeal to the nouveau riche as a sign of wealth and luxury, that one can afford to waste it, to delight in the transgression in the deliberate wastage of a luxury, as in the case of the billionaire's super-yacht fitted out with showers that spray champagne not water (see Featherstone 2013a, 2013c).

There is a further dimension that needs to be considered before addressing the special quality of the luxury object, namely its place in the wider set of objects we handle and use in everyday life, along with their typical lifecycle: their durability, trajectory and transformations. It is possible to posit a continuum with at one extreme durable objects, which are highly crafted and sustain high value, diamonds being a good example. In the middle are everyday objects we have bought, some of which are in use, some of which hang around as stuff, things we might use but are generally deactivated; yet they still enjoy the status of things not objects (Brown 2004; Miller 2005; Boscagli 2014). Towards the other extreme are items of junk, former possessions that became stuff, then made their way into the storeroom, attic or shed. Finally, there are the thrown-away things that become seen as used-up objects and discarded as rubbish. Then, there is the afterlife of things as waste, which in some cases can have complex journeys, from the local rubbish tip to recycle plants in Africa or China where the waste is turned back into more indeterminate materials.[8] The speed with which objects pass down the line to become waste can vary a great deal, with luxury objects tending to have a slower cycle, given the fact that they are able to retain their value for longer. But our example of champagne also points to the existence of disposable luxuries.

It is the social scarcity and adjudged intrinsic qualities of the luxury object which can make it desirable. It may also gain a great deal of attractiveness by being seen as part of a set, as having a particular place in the histories and genealogies of particular types of luxury goods. For the connoisseur and collector it is this place within the symbolic hierarchies and grids of a particular classification of luxury items, often condensed into a definitive catalogue, that is important. There is the pleasure in knowing how it can be contextualised and located, its authentic pedigree. But there is also pleasure in the object itself, in its thingness, in the way it engages our senses and pulls us towards it and seemingly wants to be handled and gazed at lovingly. The capacity to handle and know the object can of course be more easily sustained in close proximity to the thing itself and indicates the importance of ownership. In his famous essay 'Unpacking My Library', Walter Benjamin (1970a: 258) suggests that for book collectors 'ownership is the most intimate relation that one can have to objects' as this relation bypasses their functional and utilitarian value. Property, the ownership of things, as in the case of objects of art and paintings by famous artists which adorn the apartments of the wealthy, creates the conditions for familiarity and the capacity to get to know objects in their fullness and potential.

In recent years, there has been a growing interest in themes such as 'the allure of things', 'the primacy of the object', the need to 'save the particular', along with the need to investigate the nature of fetishism, objectification and techno-animism. These are themes that have engaged theorists from Benjamin and Adorno onwards (see Miller 2005; Schiermer 2010; Jensen and Blok 2012; Silva 2012; Hornborg 2014; Lütticken 2014). More recently, there has also been the emergence of new materialism (Bennett 2010; Coole and Frost 2010) and object-oriented ontology (Introna 2009; Bryant 2011; Harman 2011; Bogost 2012). These concerns also resonate with the rise of interest in affect theory (Clough 2008; Blackman and Venn 2010; Featherstone 2010). There is, then, an increasing sense that we need to move beyond the human-centred frame of reference (things for us) to focus on 'thing-thing' relations, the power of things to affect each other, as well as how they entice and enchant us. This focus on 'thing-power' (Bennett 2010) builds on the previous set of formulations which emphasised 'the sex-appeal of the inorganic', the investment of libidinal energy or charge in the object (Buci-Glucksmann 1994; Benjamin 1999; Perniola 2004; Johnson 2006: 70); glamour (Gundle 2008); and aura (Hansen 2008; Benjamin 2010).

Walter Benjamin, for example, was long interested in aura, in the ways in which inanimate objects could possess a strange power and even seem to look back at us (Buck-Morss 1989; Benjamin 1999; Hansen 2008). He wanted to explore ways of saving objects from the commodification process and developed a theory of the porosity of things to show how the wasted commodity object was capable of agency and affect. For Benjamin the commodity was multifaceted and doubled as a poetic object, one that had the power to overcome the subject. As Boscagli puts it 'Instead of being seduced by the sex-appeal of the inanimate, so that he himself becomes frozen into thingness, the subject is fascinated and made alive by the wonders that the object, now re-envisioned as an object closer to the anthropological fetish or medieval relic, can perform' (2014: 50; see also Spencer 1985; Buci-Glucksmann 1994; Benjamin 1999). Benjamin emphasised the way that objects have the potential to produce happiness, and here he was influenced by Marcel Proust's discussion of how particular objects can act as signs that summon up involuntary memories that activate intense vivid experiences and moments of joy (Benjamin 1970b; Deleuze 2008; Featherstone 2013b, 2014: 60). Benjamin wanted to apply these insights to the fragments of discarded mass consumer objects abandoned in the city, or the things piled up in the second-hand shops in the arcades, things replete with potential which could be induced to open up to us and provide glimpses of happiness. While Benjamin wanted to take this in a particular direction, which we will return to shortly, it is evident that this type of auratic charge has often been associated with fine and rare objects: luxuries, objects of art and of course art itself.

The Art of Luxury

W. J. T. Mitchell (1996, 2005) asks the question 'What do pictures want?' The answer is 'they want us to love them'. Mitchell is interested in opening up a discussion about our desire for images in an effort to better understand the power images have over us: the uncanny vitality and animation often attributed to pictures. It is possible to extend the question from pictures to other art objects, and there are numerous discussions of the capacity art has to attract and hold us through its auratic and generative powers. If we ask the related question 'what do luxuries want?', the answer could be 'they want to become art'. In effect, they want to develop, or be seen to embody, the same powerful affective charge to that which is attributed to art. Then, they will express and deliver value in both the economic and cultural senses.

The promise of increasing the prestige and value of luxury goods through a closer association with art has long been seen as advantageous by the large luxury firms and conglomerates. Luxury houses in particular are attracted to the art world, with Louis Vuitton, for example, publicising its many collaborations with artists such as Takashi Murakami, Olafur Eliasson, Richard Prince, Yayoi Kusama and Daniel Buren (see Vuitton and Jacobs 2009). At the same time, the art market has become a luxury goods business, being cited in luxury indexes such as the Knight Frank Wealth Report, with greater numbers of high net worth individuals seeking to invest in artworks. Business companies in the United States, Britain, France and other places are given tax relief if they purchase works of art. The association with art confers great prestige practically throughout the luxury sector, with various institutions, such as luxury hotels, competing to hold exhibitions or become associated with art. For example, in September 2014, the Ritz-Carlton Laguna Niguel, California, presented Club Level guests with the 'once-in-a-lifetime opportunity' to see an exhibition of Pablo Picasso's works, drawn from several collections, including pieces on loan from Belgium's Galerie Moderne. Deanne French, director of public relations at the hotel, commented 'We anticipate it to be an exhibit that guests will want to experience so they will plan a visit to the resort just so they can view these famous works by one of the greatest and most influential artists of the 20th century.' The emphasis upon an exclusive experience is interesting; club class wealthy guests at the resort hotel have the privilege of seeing art in a different setting away from the crowds and noise of the masses who stream through popular metropolitan exhibitions.

There are increasing numbers of collaborations between art museums and luxury houses to set up exhibitions and longer-term art education projects. In addition to promoting exhibitions of famous artists, luxury houses also seek to create their own mythologies by highlighting the closeness of their founders or directors to art and the art world. The French fashion house Christian Dior, for example, presented a series of articles in its online magazine *DIORMAG* in 2014 which took readers through the founder's experience with art and how it influenced his fashion career. Again the experiential aspect was highlighted, with the introductory article in the series on 21 July 2014 beginning by telling consumers 'We're setting off on a voyage...' (Jones 2014). Dior regularly holds exhibitions that feature its own work and narrate its history. Some are held at its own Musée Christian Dior, as was the case with 'Dior, The Legendary Images' (May–September 2014); others move around the world, such as the Shanghai 'Miss Dior Exhibition' (June–July 2014), which attracted unprecedented numbers of visitors, or the 'Esprit Dior Exhibition' (October 2014–January 2015) in Tokyo, which explored the founder's fascination with Japanese culture and relation to famous artists of his time.

Some of the luxury house or fashion house exhibitions are staged at conventional museums, as we find with the 'Alexander McQueen: Savage Beauty' exhibition at the Victoria & Albert Museum, London, March–August 2015,[9] or the Louis Vuitton exhibition 'Voyages' at the National Museum of China in Tiananmen Square, May–August 2011. This demonstrates that there is a good deal of public interest manifest in the capacity to draw in the legions of dedicated followers who want to explore the world of haute couture and bespoke accessories, formerly restricted to the very rich. Such exhibitions bolster the image of luxury brands and involve storytelling to enhance the craftsmanship and design skills of the founders to enable people to contemplate fashion and accessories displayed as art. As Sydney Toledano, CEO of Christian Dior, remarked about the Dior exhibition in Russia in 2011, which enjoyed a record-breaking attendance: 'The 150,000 people who go to the Pushkin understand that Mr. Dior was an artist and that there is a way of contemplating the dresses with fine art' (cited in Pellegrin 2014).

This is an indication of the importance of the persona standing behind the brand and the attempts to present the founder or creative director as the key source of the brand's aura. In effect the charisma of the founder becomes central to luxury. This is the argument developed by Dion and Arnould (2011), who prefer to speak about 'charismatic experience management' based upon the persona of the leader. In addition, there is a range of related strategies which invite consumers to be involved in the processes whereby the magic is generated. These include visits to the flagship store, the brand museum, fashion shows and Internet sites, to experience and witness the creative alchemy behind the brand. All this is designed to highlight the aesthetic vision of the creator, their uniqueness and capacity to explore radical difference and experiment. Hence the dramatic styles of self-presentation and the transformative powers of successful figures such as John Galliano, Alexander McQueen, Karl Lagerfeld and Marc Jacobs. These artistic directors are seen to stand apart in their dedication, personal sacrifice and force of will. They also face regular 'tests' to demonstrate their charisma and magical touch, such as the twice-yearly fashion shows.

In their study of luxury brands, Pinkhasov and Nair (2014: 35) remark that 'Fashion is fast, seasonal and obsessed with imagery. Luxury is deep, timeless and obsessed with quality.' This assumption proves to be more complicated in the case of the luxury fashion houses, which are pulled both ways, but also attracted to go beyond luxury and into art, to seek to enhance the value of their brand by associating the name with art. This in turn will depend to some degree on the extraordinary qualities demonstrated by the flow of auratic works from the gifted charismatic creator. There is a range of dynamics at play here. Luxury and fashion houses tend to have to look a number of ways: towards endorsement by cultural establishments, to wealthy rich and super-rich clientele, but also to the mass market. Items produced for the fashion shows are orientated towards the museums, to be preserved and displayed as experimental cultural prototypes. They need endorsement by cultural gatekeepers, intellectuals, artists, critics, curators and cultural intermediaries. The rich and super-rich will purchase exclusive top-end luxuries, not always for sale in the city centre and airport shops frequented by the public. Louis Vuitton accessories can of course be purchased more cheaply on the Internet, or at outlet stores such as Bicester Village in the UK, or the range of outlet stores in Italy, the United States and other places, which enjoy considerable popularity.[10] For young women in particular, the first cheap £100 Vuitton bag purchase could indeed be an expensive luxury, an item which could carry a good deal of projected aura and represent a first step towards the intricate learning and purchasing curves that open up the new world of experience provided by the luxury brand.

Concluding Remarks

In a world that is forever producing new consumer goods driven by the dynamics of fashion and technological innovation, luxuries could be seen as a point of stability. They stand out as goods produced through fine craftsmanship and an obsession with quality; they are things that tend to retain their value. Many traditional luxury goods purchased and used by aristocrats would fit this description. The luxury brand houses want to feed off this image of tradition and quality, in which goods appear singular and bespoke, individually crafted by the human hand and not the machine. Next to the craftsman stands the artist. If it is possible for the luxury house to appropriate the aura of the artist and artistic production in the ways we have just discussed, then the prestige of their goods will necessarily rise. Yet this move can be played out in a number of ways. The luxury brand houses may elect to increase prestige and move nearer to art and endeavour to maintain their reputation for creativity, originality and exclusiveness. Or they may be drawn to the potential of the new luxury markets, which have emerged over the last twenty years or so for the new rich and middle classes. Yet catering for the democratisation of luxury by producing more affordable brands may well undermine their hard-won reputation for high craftsmanship, artistic creativity and exclusiveness. The danger is that the move towards mass luxury can devalue the brand narrative. Luxury houses and other purveyors of luxury goods such as luxury car manufacturers play out this dilemma and often engage in a dual strategy. For example, BMW, which produces a range of premium and prestige vehicles under the BMW brand, is also owner of Rolls Royce motorcars.

For those in the know – the expert, collector or connoisseur – the differences between models are apparent, given their knowledge of the 'back catalogue', the relational grid of the full range of different objects produced over time and awareness of the similarities, differences and distinctiveness of each set within a particular field. The relational grid provides the contextual knowledge, but it also points to the distinctiveness of the particular luxury item in question. This can involve appreciation of the 'thingness of things' and 'thing-power' Bennett (2010).[11] It can involve the distinctive features which engage the senses: the smell of expensive leather in the new car, the deep-throated throb of a high-powered engine, the proprioceptive push of the body back into the seat with acceleration. These are the distinctive features that advertisers endeavour to capture in advertisements, which go beyond an image or photograph and ocular-centric vision, being more multisensory and synaesthetic. They are most strongly evident in proximity to or involvement with the object. Here the object engages the body in an affective relationship. In part the affective response is shaped by the object's structure and capacities that are built, or 'crafted', into it. In part, the response is also shaped by the specifics of the encounter and how the particularities of the object reveal themselves.[12] It is this promise that, first, technical experts and craftsmen seek to design into the object; and, second, advertisers seek to accent, emphasise and promote within a broader context involving complex imagery, word and sound-play, to make the prospective object encounter 'eventful'. It is this combination that helps to develop the fascination for the object and its 'seductive' qualities. In Baudrillardian terminology, this is the excess of 'sign-value' that can become attached to objects, but tends towards overload and detachment. This process of fetishising the luxury consumer object works in much the same way for the work of art as for the luxury object such as a motorcar or handbag. But in many ways it is not the object which is being marketed by the advertisers, but a range of desired qualities or properties – comfort, beauty, prestige, freedom, romance, style, uniqueness of experience – which are more intangible marks of distinction, which can be contrasted to the common, average functional and utilitarian everyday models.

This is evident in the way some luxury motorcars embody excess – not in terms of the quality of their luxury interior passenger comfort, but in terms of the power of the engine, as is the case with top range sports cars.[13] The luxury sports car is a long way from an efficient safe utilitarian vehicle to move around urban areas. Yet as Bataille (1988) has argued, excessive expenditure can be considered in a positive light when contrasted with the production and circulation of commodities in our dominant 'restrictive economy' with its emphasis on acquisition and saving. In contrast, the 'general economy' aims not at necessity but luxury: at the expenditure and consumption of wealth.[14]

The luxury object, like art, offers the promise and the dangers of excess. It points to the strong affective forces working within social life, which at times can be destructive and even catastrophic. Governing excess and handling the tension between saving and wastefulness, between calculation and expressivity, between restricted expenditure and exuberance, between economy and luxury, is at the heart of social life. Yet there is another side of luxury to the wasting of energy involved in excessive consumption: there is also the promise of indulgence and security. It is this dimension that Peter Sloterdijk points to when he remarks:

> Luxury makes humankind possible and it is also through luxury that our world is born. Humans are, and have been since the very beginning, animals that mutually indulge and exonerate themselves by taking care of each other and by treating themselves with more security than any other living creature could ever dream of enjoying. Humankind arises through its secession with Mother Nature. We can then relate the birth of humankind with the spirit of taking-care-of. (Sloterdijk 1993: 334; cited in Elden 2011: 14)

For Sloterdijk, who wrote these remarks well in advance of his discussion of foam in Volume 3 of *Spheres* (Sloterdijk 2004), there is an onto-anthropological propensity towards luxury. This suggests the need for a theory of 'constitutive luxury' as a means of conceptualising the origin and endpoint of mankind (Sloterdijk 2004: 676). Luxury involves discharge and exoneration, but also indulgence (Elden 2011). The Western-inspired Crystal Palace, the 1851 exhibition which brought the goods and exotica of the world under one roof as 'the world interior of capital' (the title of another of Sloterdijk's books [2013]), signals the way luxury started to seize more extensive social power. These issues remain highly contemporary; they still point to the difficulty of reconciling the claims of those who live in poverty and scarcity and can only look at the consumer luxury world through the glass panes of the crystal palace, or through the ubiquitous screens of mobile media, while those inside still wander in fascination amidst the world of goods, trapped in the perpetual 24/7 mall. For both, luxury objects are important powerful motivating forces that speak to human care, indulgences and pleasures. Yet the questions of access to luxuries, the sustainability of their production, their just distribution and the possibility of a space beyond still remain compelling.

Acknowledgement

I would like to thank Couze Venn and the editors for their helpful comments on earlier versions of this chapter.

Notes

1. See the discussion in Featherstone (2013c) on how sumptuary laws gave way to fashion systems and the eventual development of consumer culture and extension of luxury (see also Clunas 1991; Burke 1993; Berg and Clifford 1999; Pomeranz 2000).
2. For an argument that sees substitutability as central to the definition of luxury, see Berry (1994: 41; also Armitage and Roberts 2014 for a critique).
3. See the description of Sunday afternoon tea Richard Hoggart (1958) provides in his portrait of life in a working-class city in the north of England.
4. The term 'ultra-luxury' has been applied to 'classic cars', which have become the top luxury-good investment over the last ten years with 'ultra-luxury brands' such as Bentley, Lamborghini, Rolls Royce, Maserati, Ferrari and Aston Martin enjoying an unprecedented sales record in 2014. It is also predicted that this segment will grow by 40 per cent in the next five years. See Cieferri 2015.
5. Inside its special shell, the phone is no different from any iPhone in terms of hardware components. The iPhone was commissioned by an unnamed Chinese businessman (*Luxo* 1 April 2013; available at www. luxuo.com/most-expensive/iphone-5-black-diamond.html, accessed 20 March 2015; see also the discussion in Armitage and Roberts 2014).
6. One of the most expensive bottles of wine on record is the 1787 Chateau Lafitte, selling for $160,000 in 1985 (equivalent to $315,000 today) to Malcolm Forbes – allegedly part of Thomas Jefferson's collection with his initials on the bottle. The 1947 Chateau Cheval Blanc sold for $304,375 by a Swiss collector at an auction at Christie's in Geneva is said to be one of the greatest Bordeaux of all time and is still drinkable and will keep for another fifty years ('12 of the world's most expensive bottles of wine', *Huffington Post*, 10 November 2011, updated 18 December 2014; available at http://www.huffington post.com/2011/11/10/most-expensive-wine_n_1084988.html, accessed 23 March 2015).
7. See the discussion of a Chinese Ming collector's feeling on handling a rare bronze in Featherstone 2014.
8. Waste has become an increasingly complex category through recent research on waste dynamics (see Cubitt 2015; Hird 2015; Reno 2015).
9. The exhibition was first staged at the New York Metropolitan Museum

     with some 661,409 people visiting over five weeks, ranking it alongside the museum's top ever exhibits: the 1963 Mona Lisa and the 1978 tour of King Tutankhamen's treasures (Byrnes 2011).

10. The cheapest Vuitton handbag from a quick Internet search was the 'authentic Louis Vuitton pochette bag' priced at £103.76 from Diannas Boutique (https://www.etsy.com/uk/listing/221789784/authentic-louis-vuitton-mm-crossbody?utm_source=google&utm_medium=cpc&utm_campaign=shopping_uk_en_gb_bags_and_purses_mid&gclid=CISWjer sz8QCFQf4wgod6FIAsg, accessed 30 March 2015). The Louis Vuitton website contains a warning about purchasing cheap Vuitton handbags online as they will be fakes and it directs people to its stores and official website.

11. Bennett notes that thing-power 'gestures towards the strange ability of ordinary, man-made items to exceed their status as objects' (2010: xvi), along with their capacity to animate and engage us.

12. It is possible to conceive this process from the perspective of object-oriented ontology and new materialism, in ways which stress the selectivity of object-object encounters and play down the psychosocial understanding of affect (see Bogost 2012; Ash 2014).

13. The Ferrari Testarossa sports car featured in the popular television series *Miami Vice* had a 5-litre 12-cylinder engine which produced 380 hp with a top speed of almost 180 mph. This type of car is driven around urban areas with 30 mph speed limits, such as the London district of Knightsbridge, where predominately Middle Eastern young men and boys from super-rich families parade their cars on a regular basis each August. Generally the cars cost hundreds of thousands of pounds, with one Dubai-registered Bugatti costing £1 million (Spillet 2014).

14. As he puts it: 'it is not necessity, but its contrary "luxury", that presents living matter and mankind with their fundamental problems' (Bataille 1988: 12).

References

Appadurai, A. (1986), 'Introduction', in A. Appadurai (ed.), *The Social Life of Things: Commodities in Cultural Perspective*, Cambridge: Cambridge University Press, pp. 3–63.

Armitage, J. and Roberts, J. (2014), 'Luxury new media: euphoria in unhappiness', *Luxury: History, Culture, Consumption*, 1 (1): 113–32.

Ash, James (2014), 'Affective transmission: encounter, force and perturbation', *Theory Culture & Society* website, 30 September 2014. Available at: http://theoryculturesociety.org/james-ash-on-affective-transmission (accessed 29 October 2015).

Bain and Company (2014), *Annual Global Luxury Study*. Available at: http://www.bain.com/publications/articles/luxury-goods-worldwide-market-study-december-2014.aspx (accessed 28 July 2015).

Bataille, G. (1988), *The Accursed Share, Volume I*, New York: Zone Books.

Baudrillard, J. (1981), *For a Critique of the Political Economy of the Sign*, St Louis: Telos Press.

Benjamin, W. (1970a), 'Unpacking my library', in *Illuminations*, ed. Hannah Arendt, London: Cape, pp. 61–9.

Benjamin, W. (1970b), 'The image of Proust', in *Illuminations*, ed. Hannah Arendt, London: Cape, pp. 197–210.

Benjamin, W. (1999), *The Arcades Project*, Cambridge, MA: Harvard University Press.

Benjamin, W. (2010), 'The work of art in the age of its technological reproducibility', *Grey Room*, 39: 11–37.

Bennett, J. (2010), *Vibrant Matter: A Political Ecology of Things*, Durham, NC: Duke University Press.

Berg, M. and Clifford, H. (eds) (1999), *Consumers and Luxury: Consumer Culture in Europe 1650–1850*, Manchester: Manchester University Press.

Berry, C. J. (1994), *The Idea of Luxury*, Cambridge: Cambridge University Press.

Blackman, L. and Venn, C. (2010), 'Introduction to affect', Special Issue on Affect, *Body & Society*, 17 (1): 1–5.

Bogost, Ian (2012), *Alien Phenomenology: Or What it is Like to be a Thing*, Minneapolis: University of Minnesota Press.

Boscagli, M. (2014), *Stuff Theory: Everyday Objects, Radical Materialism*, London: Bloomsbury.

Brown, B. (ed.) (2004), *Things*, Chicago: University of Chicago Press.

Bryant, Levi R. (2011), *The Democracy of Objects*, Ann Arbor: Open Humanities Press. Available at: http://openhumanitiespress. org/Bryant_2011_The%20Democracy%20of%20Objects.pdf (accessed 29 October 2015).

Buci-Glucksmann, C. (1994), *Baroque Reason: the Aesthetics of Modernity*, London: Sage.

Buck-Morss, S. (1989), *The Dialectic of Seeing: Walter Benjamin and the Arcades Project*, Cambridge, MA: MIT Press.

Burke, P. (1993), '*Res e verba*: conspicuous consumption in the early modern world', in J. Brewer and R. Porter (eds), *Consumption and the World of Goods*, London: Routledge, pp. 141–61.

Byrnes, Theresa (2011), 'Alexander McQueen's Savage Beauty at the Metropolitan Museum of Art', *Daily Mirror*, 22 August.

Cieferri, Luca (2015), 'Golden Age for ultra luxury brands', *Automotive News*, 1 March. Available at: http://www.autonews.com/article/20150301/RETAIL01/303029986/golden-age-for-ultraluxury-brands (accessed 23 March 2015).

Clough, P. (2008), 'The affective turn: political economy, biomedia and bodies', *Theory, Culture & Society*, 25 (1): 1–22.

Clunas, C. (1991), *Superfluous Things: Material Culture and Social Status in Early Modern China*, Oxford: Polity Press.

Coole, Diana and Samantha Frost (eds) (2010), *New Materialisms: Ontology, Agency and Politics*, Durham, NC: Duke University Press.

Cubitt, Sean (2015), 'Integral waste', *Theory, Culture & Society*, 32 (4): 133–45.

Dant, T. (1996), 'Fetishism and the social value of objects', *Sociological Review*, 44 (3): 495–506.

Deleuze, G. (2008), *Proust and Signs*, London: Continuum.

Dion, Delphine and Arnould, Eric (2011), 'Retail luxury strategy: assembling charisma through art and magic', *Journal of Retailing*, 87 (4): 502–20.

Elden, Stuart (2011), 'Worlds, engagements, temperaments', in S. Elden (ed.), *Sloterdijk Now*, New York: Wiley, pp. 1–16.

Featherstone, M. (2007), *Consumer Culture and Postmodernism*, 2nd edn, London: Sage.

Featherstone, M. (2010), 'Body, image and affect in consumer culture', *Body & Society*, 17 (1): 193–221.

Featherstone, M. (2013a), 'Super-rich lifestyles', in T. Birtchnell and J. Caletrío (eds), *Elite Mobilities*, Oxford: Routledge, pp. 99–135.

Featherstone, M. (2013b), 'Mass culture', in Masamichi Sasaki, Ekkart Zimmermann, Jack Goldstone, Stephen and A. Sanderson (eds), *Concise Encyclopedia of Comparative Sociology*, Leiden: Brill Publishers, pp. 252–61.

Featherstone, M. (2013c), 'The rich and the super-rich: mobility, consumption and luxury lifestyles', in Nita Mathur (ed.), *Consumer Culture, Modernity and Identity*, New Delhi: Sage, pp. 3–44.

Featherstone, M. (2014), 'Luxury, consumer culture and sumptuary dynamics', *Luxury: History, Culture, Consumption*, 1 (1): 47–69.

Gundle, S. (2008), *Glamour: A History*, Oxford: Oxford University Press.

Hansen, M. (2008), 'Benjamin's aura', *Critical Inquiry*, 34 (2): 336–75.

Harman, Graham (2011), *The Quadruple Object*, London: Zero Books.

Hird, Myra J. (2015), 'Waste, environmental politics and dis/engaged publics', *Theory, Culture & Society*, first published online, 29 June 2015, doi:10.1177/0263276414565717

Hoggart, R. (1958), *The Uses of Literacy*, Harmondsworth: Penguin.

Hornborg, Alf (2014), 'Technology as fetish: Marx, Latour and the cultural foundations of capitalism', *Theory, Culture & Society*, 32 (4): 119–40.

Introna, L. (2009), 'Ethics and the speaking of things', *Theory, Culture & Society*, 26 (4): 25–46.

Jensen, C. and Blok, A. (2012), 'Techno-animism in Japan: Shinto cosmograms, actor-network theory, and the enabling powers of non-human agencies', *Theory, Culture & Society*, 30 (2): 84–115.

Johnson, Barbara (2006), 'Passage work', in Beatrice Hanssen (ed.), *Walter Benjamin and the Arcades Project*, London: Bloomsbury, pp. 66–86.

Jones, Sarah (2014), 'Dior explores art heritage in summer-long content series', *Luxury Daily*, 25 July.

Lütticken, Sven (2014), 'Autonomy as aesthetic practice', Special section on Rancière', *Theory, Culture & Society*, 31 (7/8): 81–95.

Miller, Daniel (ed.) (2005), *Materiality: An Introduction*, Durham, NC: Duke University Press.

Mitchell, W. J. T. (1996), 'What do pictures *really* want?' *October*, 77: 71–82.

Mitchell, W. J. T. (2005), *What Do Pictures Want?* Chicago: University of Chicago Press.

Pellegrin, Betrand (2014), 'Selling fashion as art: how luxury brands use "heritage" marketing to convert customers', *Bertrand on Brand Blog*, 23 December. Available at: http://www.bonbrand.com/blog/selling-fashion-as-art-luxury-brands-use-heritage-marketing-to-convert-customers/#.VRG9-ULZe-I (accessed 20 March 2015).

Perniola, Mario (2004), *Sex Appeal of the Inorganic: Philosophies of Desire in the Modern World*, London: Athlone.

Pinkhasov, Misha and Nair, Rachna Joshi (2014), *Real Luxury: How Luxury Brands Can Create Value for the Long Term*, London: Palgrave Macmillan.

Pomeranz, K. (2000), *The Great Divergence: China, Europe and the Making of the Modern World Economy*, Princeton: Princeton University Press.

Reno, Joshua Ozias (2014), 'Toward a new theory of waste: from "matter out of place" to signs of Life', *Theory, Culture & Society*, 31 (6): 3–27.

Schiermer, Bjørn (2011), 'Quasi-objects, cult objects and fashion objects: two kinds of fetishism on display in modern culture', *Theory, Culture & Society*, 28 (1): 81–102.

Sennett, R. (2008), *The Craftsman*, London: Penguin.

Silva, Sonia (2012), 'Reification and fetishism: processes of transformation', *Theory, Culture & Society*, 30 (1): 79–98.

Sloterdijk, Peter (1993), *Weltfremdheit*, Frankfurt: Suhrkamp.

Sloterdijk, Peter (2004), *Sphären III: Schäume*, Frankfurt: Suhrkamp.

Sloterdijk, Peter (2013), *In the World Interior of Capital: Towards a Philosophical Theory of Globalization*, Cambridge: Polity Press.

Spencer, L. (1985), 'Allegory in the world of the commodity: the importance of Central Park', *New German Critique*, 34: 32–58.

Spillet, Richard (2014), 'Streets of Knightsbridge are jammed with Arab-owned supercars as wealthy Middle Eastern playboys flock to London for the summer', *Daily Mail*, 5 August.

Unger, Brooker (2014), 'Exclusively for everybody', *The Economist*, 13 December. Available at: http://www.economist.com/news/special-report/21635761-modern-luxury-industry-rests-paradoxbut-thriving-nonetheless-says-brooke (accessed 25 March 2015).

Vuitton, Louis and Jacobs, Mark (2009), *Art, Fashion and Architecture*, New York: Rizzoli Publications.

Yuran, Noam (2014), *What Money Wants: An Economy of Desire*, Stanford: Stanford University Press.

II Art, Design, Media

Chapter 7

Experiments in Suchness: Hiroshi Sugimoto's Silk *Shiki* for Hermès

Thomaï Serdari

Collaborations between artists and luxury firms have had a long tradition that began before the Second World War and reached a peak in the last fifteen years. This is an application of a long-lived strategy implemented by luxury names throughout the twentieth century – propelled, however, by the necessity to create original products worthy of the brand's name. Despite the general consensus that this is nothing new (Cartier would have had little to show without the work of Jeanne Toussaint or Aldo Cipullo), the market's economic pressure on contemporary luxury firms to achieve growth and higher revenues has forced the practice to acquire greater dimensions. The anonymity that characterised the artistic contributions to luxury product lines has been lifted.

Today, artists achieve high levels of recognition in society, including among the non-buying masses, which, nevertheless, aspire to participate in the art world. While art objects are still wrapped in mystery and often present intellectual challenges to those without a formal training in art history, artists enjoy new levels of fame and popularity in a world that turns artists' identity into brands. These brands are ripe for consumption even if the actual artwork is well beyond the purchasing power of the public. The masses aspire to be associated in some way with their favourite artist's brand and are willing to finance the acquisition of objects that bear the artist's signature. These objects can be anything from accessories to fashion, decorative items or electronic appliances. More often than not, they are the result of collaborations between luxury houses and contemporary artists in the form of limited editions. The proliferation of this practice, especially during the last fifteen years, raises the question of whether it has resulted in solutions that have lost their power as creative paradigms. It creates the need for a re-examination of what luxury truly is, how and why it relates to art; an assessment of the theoretical frameworks developed to evaluate the meaning, usefulness and identity of luxury; and, finally, research on artists whose work with luxury houses shifts the discussion away from commercialism and back to the nature of two important concepts that evade definition: art and luxury.

Hiroshi Sugimoto (1948–), primarily known as a photographer, is a Japanese artist of a deeply spiritual nature. His affinity for art began as a philosophical quest through the surrealist writings of modern artists and solidified based on a Duchampian approach to capturing concepts rather than representing objects (Sugimoto 2004). A philosopher, therefore, as much as photographer, painter, sculptor and architect, Sugimoto practises his art as both an intellectual and practical activity that systematises the study of time and transience.[1] His scientific observation of impermanence demands a consistency of means that itself reveals Sugimoto's attention to craftsmanship and his exhaustive understanding of materials, processes and techniques.

A trained economist, seasoned art dealer and collector with an interest in the natural sciences, Sugimoto enjoys a reputation built on his deeply conceptual aptitude for abstraction, hard work and sensorial sensitivities all expressed in finely crafted art pieces, regardless of choice of medium. The last thirty years of his life have been dedicated to an intense production schedule, one that has led to a large number of gallery and museum exhibits, often as many as four or five per year. These have been documented, critiqued and interpreted in hundreds of scholarly articles, essays and catalogue entries by renowned scholars, while Sugimoto himself has already produced twelve artist's books.

Impressive as Sugimoto's body of work is, he is not a name recognised by the masses, the uninitiated to art. His brand is very strong within the circles of the cognoscenti but practically unknown to outsiders. His brand appeals to a more sophisticated audience, and his work elicits great admiration from those who understand it. For example, he has been friendly with the Dumas family for several years, especially with the late Jean-Louis Dumas, former artistic director and chairman of the Hermès group from 1978 until 2006, who, himself, was an avid photographer. It comes as no surprise that talks about a potential collaboration between the artist and Maison Hermès started a few years ago, even if it actually materialised only after Jean-Louis's death (in 2010) with the full support of Pierre-Alexis Dumas, heir to Jean-Louis and current artistic director at Hermès.[2]

'Colours of Shadow', the third, and latest so far, artist/Maison Hermès collaboration in limited edition scarves (*carrés d'artiste*), represents a ten-year-long body of work for Sugimoto who embarked on an observational experiment with an old Polaroid camera. Informed by Newton's *Opticks* published in 1704, Sugimoto's work is the artistic manifestation of a scientific experiment that documents spans between colours, or intracolours. Concerned with the very intellectual processes that propelled Newton's methodical enquiries and Goethe's philosophical studies, Sugimoto's art consists of meticulous execution and fine craftsmanship, which, in this case, resulted in twenty different designs (chosen out of 200 photographs) of silk intracoloured scarves, each in a limited edition of seven. The 140 numbered silk scarves, printed in giant format (measuring 56 inches square) have been exhibited around the world and are available for purchase online or at the Paris flagship Hermès store (and previously made available to art collectors at the Basel Art Fair in June 2012 where the collection debuted).

The Field of Luxury Studies

When examined as part of Sugimoto's artistic and intellectual work, these scarves offer a great opportunity to illuminate aspects of luxury production that have not been examined in the literature of the field, mainly because the frameworks that have already been developed rely heavily on subjective theories that shift with time. While the goal is not to affect patterns of consumption, or to promote particular artists or luxury firms, the structure of the argument that ensues explains the power that luxury exerts over humans and why this is still relevant on both the experiential and discursive level.

Additionally, the originality of the study set forth underscores its deviation from all the previously published studies that have attempted to elucidate the concept of luxury and its impact on individual or collective behaviour, regardless of academic discipline. Before referencing the most important ones, it should be noted that in every case the discussion is primarily concerned with the relationship between consumers and luxury items, without questioning the nature of these items. It is taken for granted that objects are classified as luxury based primarily on their high price or on an outside authority's opinion that establishes them to be such.[3] In other words, scholars have not questioned the nature of the objects but only the relationship between object and consumer, and by extension society as well.

Furthermore, this approach to the study of luxury has been consistent through time and across disciplines. It closely resembles reception theory, a type of literary theory that originated in the

1960s (Jauss 1982), and which emphasises the reader's reception of a literary text or the viewer's reception of a visual work of art. Wolfgang Kemp's seminal work, 'The Methodology of the Aesthetic Reception', suggests that because the history of a field is built on information produced by subsequent generations of scholars some sort of 'creative misunderstanding' occurs both inadvertently and within 'specific historical circumstances [where] it is both deliberate and a necessary attitude' (Kemp 1998: 181). In other words, like artists who observe, absorb and utilise signs and images which they have encountered in other artists' work, so too scholars influence each other and promulgate specific ideas as givens. Kemp also makes a good point about the role of institutions that contribute to the circulation of works of art (collectors, dealers, museums) and act as authorities in establishing an 'authentic history of taste' (Kemp 1998: 182). To extrapolate from Kemp's reasoning, similarly to the history of art, in the history of luxury there is a prevalent trend that would like to be considered the authentic history of taste, and it is characterised by analysis that derives from the fields of politics, sociology and economics. Finally, Kemp notes that there is a difference between the aesthetics of reception and the psychology of reception. The former focuses on the work and its power to impact interpretation. The latter makes the spectator its focus. In luxury studies, the focus is placed on the consumer of luxury without proper regard for the luxury object other than the fact that it has been the catalyst of a discussion on consumer, and consequently, social behaviour.

These observations explain the proliferation of philosophical, sociological, anthropological, psychological, political, economic and religious approaches to understanding luxury. They do not explain, however, the lack of an art historical perspective, one that is specifically object-based and that aims at deriving conclusions about the concept of luxury through examining works that showcase characteristics associated with the definition of luxury. Therefore, this chapter is the first attempt to complete our understanding of luxury in the sense that it will articulate a discussion that revolves primarily around the object rather than the person. It focuses on the processes that made the object exist in its physical form rather than on the multiple types of private or public behaviours associated with its consumption.

Jean-Jacques Rousseau (1750), Thorstein Veblen (1899), Max Weber (1905), Pierre Bourdieu (1979), Christopher Berry (1994), Jeremy Jennings (2007), Jean-Noël Kapferer and Vincent Bastien (2009) and Pierre Berthon (2009) represent about 250 years of collective knowledge on the subject of luxury, an idea that apparently has been on our mind throughout modernity. Their works form the foundations for any new insights on luxury. These authors analyse the philosophical implications of luxury and its treatment in various historical periods, different geographic locations, a range of political regimes, a multitude of financial markets and diverse cultural landscapes. The questions upon which they have expanded are well resolved. To introduce the present enquiry is also to suggest no objection to the ideas that these authors have articulated but rather to offer a new perspective on the knowledge of luxury, one that would take the debate away from the social and the collective and would shift focus to the individual and objective experience of luxury. The goal is not to contradict but rather to complement their work. Therefore, I present this chapter as an intellectual exercise that shifts the prism away from the notion of consumption through which luxury is usually viewed in historical and contemporary debates.

The challenge becomes apparent when the reader is asked to place the emphasis on the production of luxury objects rather than their consumption. Throughout the aforementioned literature, the definition of luxury is binary and understood as something that implies excellence and excess. Excellence is easy to define, and it simply means of the highest quality. Traditionally, luxury goods are known to be of the highest quality both in terms of materials but also in terms of construction. Conversely, excess is usually understood as a negative trait of human personality triggered by greed and consumption. The common definition of excess speaks of a departure from reason, extravagance, outrageous conduct and intemperance in eating or drinking. All of these states relate to consumption. Nonetheless, there is another meaning of the term that qualifies excess as the process of exceeding something else in amount or degree, preponderance, superiority in moral weight, power, influence and importance. This definition, when seen as part of the creative production or artistic process, is the reason why it is indeed excess that propels creative thinking, craftsmanship, art and production of timeless objects with cultural significance.

A New Framework for Understanding the Meaning of Luxury

Let's think of luxury as a universal certainty that may involve any or several of our senses and that implies beauty, culture and scarcity. This means that objects or events that are beautiful (for example a sunset) are perceived as luxury when they are scarce (for example a sunset in a place where it usually rains). It also means that the event's (or object's) inherent beauty alone is not enough to impress the individual, unless the individual possesses the culture that allows one to perceive the uniqueness of the item. While scarcity is a constant through which luxury is defined, beauty and culture are also essential, yet equally elusive notions. As a consequence, luxury is a concept heavily relying on personal conditions and experiences. For example, beauty is identifiable by vision and its signals to the human brain (Starr 2013), while luxury requires engagement of the person's intellectual capacity and interpretation of various cultural cues that may include instances of humour, for example, or feelings of the sublime and so on. In other words, while luxury is mostly felt through the physical world, it is fully appreciated intellectually. If this is the case, to achieve excellence in producing a particular object is to master technical knowledge and perfect it. Perfection is finite. It is the end of a process. Therefore, it is not excellence that propels creativity. It is excess in stretching the imagination, in questioning things, in testing the limits of materials, ideas and processes. Excess is a condition that defines creative production.

In the recent documentary 'Hearts and Crafts', produced by Hermès to showcase the talent of the company's artisans across the industries within which the firm operates, a saddle maker confirms the necessity of always testing the limits of materials because in fact 'it is not the rules of mounting [horses] that have changed. It is the materials we are using today that make our work exciting.' Hella Jongerius, a renowned Dutch industrial designer who explores both industry and craft, traditional and contemporary, and who has acted as creative director for several premium brands, asserts that the only reason the profession of product designer is still relevant today (when practically all objects have already been designed and most problems have found at least one solution) is the privilege of the designer to work excessively on ideas that allow her to test the nature of materials as well as to stretch the boundaries that define human interaction with objects of daily use. One can distinguish degrees of difficulty between the excess of materials that lead the saddle maker to innovate in his studio and the work of Jongerius who pursues excess in terms of both materials and ideas (Schouwenberg 2011).

To build up the positive aspect of excess in the materialisation of new ideas and the creation of new forms to which each material can be stretched, it suffices to recall designers Marc Newson and Jony Ive who are currently the creative forces at Apple. During their interview with Charlie Rose in November 2013 on the occasion of their collaborative auction RED, which took place at Sotheby's, both designers dismissed the commonest approach to learning about things by asking who did what and when and replacing these questions with 'how did they do that?' What process is behind the creation of an object, the designers ask, especially iconic objects of great beauty and luxurious character such as the Henning Koppel pitcher created by Georg Jensen in the 1940s. Newson and Ive proclaim themselves to be 'excessively curious and inquisitive', mainly about processes, which led them, for example, to 900 prototypes of a Leica camera before approving the final model they produced for the RED auction.

These three powerful examples of excess in testing the limits of materials, ideas and processes prove that objects of timeless beauty that resonate strong emotions across cultures exist regardless of whether they are consumed or not. They also prove that what is required is not merely technical but practical knowledge, a term I am borrowing from Adamson (2013) and which involves application, observation and reflection on respective successes and failures. When excellence is the only objective of the craftsman, technical knowledge is enough. But practical knowledge is closely connected to emotional and intellectual excess that in turn reverberates through a physical creative state that could be understood and appreciated by everyone on a universal level as long as they are qualified to relate to it. But not everyone is. Like art, luxury is not democratic. It may be consumed but not fully experienced without the adequate cultural capital (Bourdieu 2010).

The more steeped in culture we are, the more we base our assessment of luxury objects on their qualitative (physical) traits. Our understanding of the culture within which an object is created enhances our ability to utilise all our senses to experience the object and to further refine our appreciation of its physicality but also its cultural meaning and intellectual rigour. This is a process that can happen regardless of whether we own the object, plan to purchase it, or simply observe it. It happens because subject and object encounter each other in time. In other words, that encounter triggers several parts of the individual's accumulated knowledge and may even provoke emotional responses which, perhaps, are in their turn analysed, and so the process continues internally to one's full satisfaction and even to one's happiness. And this is another important point about luxury: luxury satisfies the individual exactly because it offers sensorial experiences. For example, the thickness of a luxurious carpet surprises the person who walks on it, invites them to prolong the experience and offers a new definition of what satisfaction can be. Or, the lightness and precision of a luxurious writing instrument, the smoothness of the ink on the paper, delight the person who holds it. Objects with excessive physical traits that bring out unexpected and pleasing physical experiences absorb the person fully in what that experience is. They may isolate the individual from the social, and therefore from questions of equality and inequality, fairness and injustice, deprivation or gluttony, and impose an appreciation of the moment during which this physical exchange takes place. To speak of an experience that has not been commercialised, think of a sunset in which one becomes completely and utterly lost in contemplating its beauty, creating a connection that lasts for a few minutes but that in essence can be experienced as either of a very long or a very short duration. The meaning of time can be different in our experience of luxury than in that of everyday life, in the world of ordinary objects.

Ordinary objects, large numbers of them, define contemporary life. To appreciate that abundance of objects, no matter how commonplace they are, is to acknowledge that humanity has made leaps of progress in the fields of science, engineering and design. It is the constant flow of ideas from one field to the next (and in that particular order) that allows technology to progress and industry to produce so many different types of items. When humanistic thought (art) is introduced into that constant flow between the other three disciplines (science, engineering and design), the object that ensues is not just innovative but is also imbued with creativity. It often induces amazement, provokes excitement and encourages reflection. All man-made objects (ordinary or extraordinary) are the result of the constant flow of ideas between these four fields (Plate 1). In fact, the great depth in studying each one of these fields is the result of the clear demarcation of academic disciplines. University life is spent at the college of arts and science, at the college of engineering or at design school. A classification of knowledge consistent with the trends of the late nineteenth century became the norm in the organisation of our institutions, both cultural and of learning (Adamson 2013). The museum, for example, is a type of institution that clearly reflects the rise of the natural sciences in the nineteenth century along with the split that occurred between visual and decorative arts (Belozerskaya 2005), or, as most scholars of the twentieth century would put it, between fine arts and minor arts.

While the nineteenth and twentieth centuries witnessed tremendous progress in each of the academic disciplines, the end of the twentieth century, and our time in the twenty-first, is characterised by a shift between the previously insulated four fields (art, science, engineering and design), a flow of ideas that happens at a greater pace, a fluidity of thought that borrows methodologies from more than one discipline, and a production of objects or systems that are truly interdisciplinary and could not exist without that blending of frameworks and processes from distinct fields. The Internet is a text-book example of how the four fields coalesce. An idea that started as a philosophical quest (philosophy is part of the arts), found its anchors in science (mathematics and physics), was built into a system through engineering and was made usable thanks to designers that conceived of the user interface and the machine through which to access it. There is a myriad of similar examples among the ordinary objects that abound in our world.

In that sense, the previous representation of the four fields of Plate 1 can be better expressed with a new figure (Plate 2). Here it becomes clear that these four fields are not insulated, which implies that knowledge gained in one of the four can easily be applied in the other three. While it is reasonable to imagine that the flow of ideas happens in a clockwise movement at the outer rings of each circle, the circles intersect. These areas (regions shaped like asymmetric lenses) are characterised by higher activity in exchange of ideas, quicker application of ideas and a multitude of technological innovations. For example, the question of gravity had been of a philosophical nature since antiquity and until Sir Isaac Newton, mathematician and physicist of the late sixteenth and early seventeenth centuries, applied his scientific knowledge in solving it. Consequently, know-ing how to calculate the centre of gravity of any object became fundamental in engineering new systems, which were then applied in various industries, from agriculture to aeronautics. Applied physics led Nicolas-Joseph Cugnot, a French military engineer, to 'build a steam-powered tricycle for hauling artillery'.[4] Today, innovations in the automobile industry happen where the two circles of engineering and design intersect.

Luxury objects that maintain their aesthetic value through time are produced where all four circles intersect and, specifically, where all asymmetrical lenses intersect. In other words, true luxury objects are those that result from processes that are based on art, science, engineering and design. Watches are a very good example of that reasoning. The scientific understanding of how to measure time led to the engineering of the movements of watch components. Movements can be very sophisticated in their design and extremely complex. Their complexity stems from the watchmaker's excessive seeking for new ways to push the limits of the materials used, of the processes through which they are transformed and of the ideas expressed in the timepiece's precise manufacturing.[5] Overcoming material limitations and inventing new movements that work harmoniously together to create very pleasing visual and tactile effects and an accurate mechanical body can be likened to poetry or art. Considering that all artists aim for works that remain eternal, it comes as no surprise that a luxury watchmaker would choose materials of the highest quality (and rarity), all of which contribute to making the watch a perfect example of a true luxury object produced where the four fields coalesce.

True luxury stems from that four-sided, well-defined area where all four fields intersect. As a result, unique processes of production (engineering and design) are a luxury producer's catalyst of innovation and represent a luxury firm's competitive advantage. They are customarily proprietary and continuous, and as such become the true cornerstone of a firm's heritage. To contribute to a firm's resilience, these processes need to evolve with time. A firm's legacy in innovating within its respective field and market is its heritage – a word most often misused by companies, the popular press, and the public and diminished to a one-sided view of its meaning, that of history. To prove that heritage means more than a 'long history' and directly references the evolution of proprietary production processes, one may recall Wedgwood, the legendary English company that produces earthenware. While the brand's founder, Josiah Wedgwood, was innovative in his studio processes, a tastemaker with his designs and a brilliant marketer – as all businesses ought to be – the brand failed to remain contemporary after Josiah's death. Wedgwood, the brand, deprived of Josiah's excessive intellectual curiosity and subject to several new owners, failed to evolve either in terms of processes or in terms of designs. This meant that it failed to remain contemporary. Wedgwood today is a nostalgic reminder of what the original brand once was, and borderline kitsch. Heritage alone is not the marker of luxury (Koehn 1997).

Ironically, Wedgwood's nemesis, French porcelain maker Sèvres, in business in the town of Sèvres since 1756, preserves its heritage by regular infusions from contemporary artists who test the material, along with their ideas and production processes, and allow the brand to resonate with the public's quest for 'newness', 'mystery' and 'wonder'. In other words, the Sèvres brand's business model is based on the amalgamation of science, engineering, design and art. Sèvres has produced excellent and contemporary products from 1756 to the present day. No wonder then that a Sèvres object, a porcelain skull with long chains of rosy-coloured eyeballs that spill over and around it, found its way into the exhibition space of the Museum of Art and Design in New York City. In our age of hyper-commercialism, haunted by visions of a post-apocalyptic world as described by fashion designer Alexander McQueen and artists Damien Hirst and William Delvoye, perturbed by problems of ecological disasters, persistent wars and the reality of certain death, the Sèvres skull remains as luxurious in nature as it is deep in meaning and contemporary. Sèvres was founded to reinforce exports of French luxury goods in the eighteenth century and remains at the forefront of luxury production today. Based on their business model and creative explorations, they should be among the top luxury brands tomorrow and in another 200 years (Pinot de Villechenon 1997).

By then, and while our bodies may have been replaced or supplemented by high-tech parts, our physical experience of luxury will be totally different. Knowing that true luxury producers operate within that area where art feeds science, which propels engineering and drives design, it comes as no surprise to realise that they are already experimenting with technology, which is an important means of production and complements – rather than contradicts, as some superficial press reports claim – handicraft (Adamson 2013). As a case in point, consider another luxury object shown in 2013 at the 'Out of Hand: Materializing the Post Digital' exhibition at the Museum of Art and Design in New York: a three-dimensional printed necklace designed by Marc Newson and produced by French High Jewellery house Boucheron.[6] The piece, a physical representation of the Julia mathematical formula in three-dimensional printed platinum, studded with over 2,000 sapphires and diamonds, is the perfect manifestation of excess in all three areas we explored earlier (materials, ideas and processes) and an experiment in far-reaching design that takes into account science, engineering and design. In that sense, it respects cultural heritage but also allows the perception of luxury to evolve as our own living conditions change.

Hiroshi Sugimoto's Experiments in Art, Science, Engineering and Design

Sugimoto was raised with Christian principles in Japan and discovered the teachings of Zen Buddhism in Los Angeles in the 1970s. While this may be confusing for the rest of us, it actually imbued Sugimoto's thinking with the certainty that knowledge imparted to us through teachings is not always credible (Sugimoto 2004: 25). The only certainty he fathomed, the unity of time, he pursued through two major experiments. Photographs of cases displaying prehistoric narrative scenes at the American Museum of Natural History were crafted in such fine detail that Sugimoto's camera managed to erase the lines between past, present and future. With these photographs, Sugimoto transports the viewer to each one of the scenes captured, blurring not only the borders between fake and real but also the certainty of time's linear progression.

This concept achieved its aesthetic zenith with two other projects in which Sugimoto tested the exposure of time. In 1976, he began photographing the interiors of movie theatres by keeping the shutter open throughout the entire movie. His images showed white, empty spaces. The irony is that the emptiness of the white is filled with hours of 'real time' and hours of 'fictional time' on the screen. The white is a capsule of boundaries that have collapsed but also a gateway to the continuity of time. Similarly, Sugimoto's 'Seascapes' began with photographs of the Caribbean in 1980. In this series he captured the certainty of time's cyclicality through equally long exposures that are marked on the photographic paper as a single horizon, a true (or is it?) division between sea and sky, between types of matter in the process of becoming one another (Brougher and Müller-Tamm 2010: 21).

Most people, including photographers, look at the world around them and retain its physical expression: persons, man-made cities and nature. Sugimoto is not interested in what resides on the surface. He wants to make the viewer aware of what lies within and beyond the surface. He uses his camera to discover and uncover the inner workings of the universe. He works with light but his subject is time. A 'theoretician and cultural anthropologist in three fields of scientific inquiry' (Sugimoto 2004: 23), the photographer works in mathematics, geometry and mechanics to illuminate the sublime forces that rule the universe. In his body of work entitled 'Conceptual Forms' (Sugimoto 2004), he captures a series of stereometric models made of plaster, produced about 150 years ago, as a tool of instruction in institutes of mathematics and the natural sciences. 'Mathematical Forms: Surfaces' and 'Mathematical Forms: Curves' are essentially irrefutable documents demonstrating that what we have traditionally known as philosophy turns into science.

Photography itself happens through a mechanical apparatus that uses chemistry to capture instances of time. The process implies the use of science, engineering (in the camera itself) and design (in the way the photographer stages his views). In Sugimoto's case, it also incorporates philosophical enquiries of a humanistic nature that aim at articulating the aesthetics of knowledge in familiar shapes and forms. 'Lightning Fields' is an investigation in the physics and chemistry of the invisible: electric power. A spark, or beam of light, captured on a photosensitive plate pays tribute to the history of photography (recalling the earliest experiments of the eighteenth and nineteenth centuries) but also to the trajectory of contemporary art (referencing Walter de Maria's land art project with a similar title). With the use of a generator, Sugimoto produced electrical flashes that appear out of the dark and quickly fade. The photosensitive plate captures every single moment in the life of the beam and renders them in amorphous shoots that contrast against the dark background but remain out of focus since no one single moment is more important than another. Once again, the cyclicality of time leads Sugimoto's experiments. The optical devices he uses allow him to interpret philosophy through the visualisation of abstract concepts and to make art out of things with no artistic intentions.

Drawing on his expertise as a collector of meteorites and fossils[7] (both of which interest him because they capture matter at particular points in time and deliver it unchanged in space and time), Sugimoto likens photography to a 'fossilization of time' (Sugimoto 2014: 17). References to time and matter reveal that Sugimoto's art is based on science, technology, design and religion in similitude to the art of the Renaissance, when 'artists were stirred by a profound religious faith while also engaging in serious scholarship' (Sugimoto 2014: 47). To work along these lines suggests a desire to understand the world as a unity, in the past, present and future.[8] It also suggests intellectual and artistic activity in that small but well-defined area at the centre of the Euler diagram in Plate 2. His life resembling a cabinet of curiosities for the incurable collector en route to discovering the secrets of the universe, Sugimoto is a polymath whose art helps us learn about our future by looking at our distant past. The age of darkness remains a constant compass for Sugimoto, who, fascinated, asserts: 'before the human mind started to apprehend matter through the laws of physics the world was filled by a sacred mystery. If we think about it, the great myths of humankind are all wonderful poems, really a form of art' (Sugimoto 2014: 47). When it comes to light, the inner beauty of its structure and the beauty it outlines in the world around us, Sugimoto takes its study all the way to Newton's physics rather than limit his knowledge to the pioneers of nineteenth-century photography, such as Talbot and Daguerre.[9] In doing so, he also absorbs contemporary criticism of Newtonian experiments, including Johann Wolfgang von Goethe's lyrical interpretation of the universe, in which he vehemently argued for a sensorial experience of natural phenomena – even if these were not yet quantifiable, measurable and, therefore, applicable at the time.

The inexplicable turns into the magical. And magic turns into worship. This applies both to awe-inspiring natural phenomena and to man-made beautiful and opulent objects, classified as luxury. When discussing luxury and beauty, Goethe would have wanted to account for their impact on the human psyche.[10] He was not mistaken but did not have all the facts either. Gabrielle Starr's work is directly applicable here especially since she addressed questions about the relation of emotions to aesthetic experience and how such experience differentiates individuals. Conducting laboratory work in neuroscience, Starr exposed the brain's default mode network during a process of emotional movement that involved images of beauty and related to the individual's aesthetic experience (Starr 2013). To extrapolate, the individual can experience luxury internally without the prerequisite of collective imperatives or expected social behaviours.[11]

Sugimoto's work, an intellectual and practical activity that encompasses the study of the universe, its structure and behaviour, through observation and experiment, captures the universally poetic and condenses it in verses of opulent beauty. What he sees, and invites us to see, is not the finite but the transient. Excess is his driver (and not excellence) because excess implies change in matter, methods and concepts. It implies 'becoming', rather than 'being', several instances of suchness through time.

The suchness of colour (*shiki* in Japanese) in the atmosphere is the focus of his project for Hermès, for which Sugimoto contributed twenty photographs of the empty winter sky of Tokyo at dawn (from a large number of Polaroids that he painstakingly produced every single day over a long period of time). By capturing the ether's immateriality at the break of dawn, Sugimoto systematised the exploration of the multitude of colours that had not been classified among the seven defined by natural science. His Polaroids gave shape to the immateriality of the spans between colours, or intracolours, as he called them. They also revealed to him that prolonged staring at a single colour results in the perception of the exact opposite one, which means that human experience of the world is highly dependent on the individual and the human body's physical response to natural phenomena through our senses. In other words, the aesthetic experience stems from a physical one (an idea that has now been proven by Starr's work). It is the rigour of the aesthetic experience that the artist manipulates to rouse intellectual responses and thus enjoyment in the work.

The work itself, an edition of seven scarves for each Polaroid, numbered by hand from one to seven, made of 100 per cent silk twill plume with a hand-rolled hem, are what Hermès calls 'giant scarves', measuring 56 × 56 inches (140 × 140 cm) each. They are sold in a cylindrical case (as a painterly canvas often is and very different from Hermès's regular production of scarves, which are folded square and placed in the company's signature orange boxes).[12] They come with a certificate of authenticity and a book that documents the entire project, the complete set of Polaroids (Hermès 2012: 43).[13]

Scarf 075 (Plate 3, Polaroid 075) evidences the difficulty of the concept's execution on silk. Hermès is known for its excellence in silkscreen printing, a technique that uses a mesh screen to support an ink-blocking stencil in order to create the desired image when colour is poured over the mesh (and the fabric). The firm's long tradition of working with silk in its Lyon[14] factory has been showcased in Coleno (2010), in the documentary 'Hearts and Crafts' (2012), and during an itinerant show that took place in 2013 in various cities in the United States where the company exhibited the equipment (of each 'métier' or craft) along with the skilled artisans who work at the various production facilities. Silkscreen printing of the elaborate designs produced by Hermès for the 'carrés' is a complex process that involves several employees at each stage (a single scarf may require as many as 190 screens for the separation of colour hues). Scarf 075 seems to capture thousands of intracolours. How does silkscreen printing work for so many colours with no definition of contour?

It does not. This is precisely where the value of this collaboration lies. With Victor Borges at the helm of the Lyon silk facility, and after several discussions with the artist,[15] it was decided to experiment with inkjet printing. Let's think of the Euler diagram of Plate 2: an artistic concept that draws heavily on the history of science and manifests itself through the application of natural laws through engineered optical devices is designed to attain material form as scarves. This is already at the centre of intersecting circles. Additionally, a new type of machine needs to be invented (an inkjet printer of appropriate size and with the technical capacity to ensure accuracy in the transferring of the Polaroid image onto silk).[16] When the machine was perfected to the specifications, the process had to be tested multiple times to ensure precision in variation of tone, colour and hue (Plate 4, Polaroid 005). From inception to production, the project took a little over two years. It enabled the artist to find another channel for the dissemination of his ideas. It empowered the company to prepare for technological changes, to question established processes of production and to innovate in anticipation of the unknown future. It confirmed that heritage in the context of luxury does not mean stagnation but rather continuity in experimentation, endurance in a changing world, and stability even at the centre of a constant flow of ideas (referring to the Euler diagram again and the changes that occur in the sciences and technology because of progress). The type of experimentation this collaboration propelled cannot be measured in financial terms. To experiment for two years on a new inkjet printing machine and to invent a method that preserves the accuracy of colour and hue is an immensely costly operation. Yet, at €7,000, the scarves are fairly priced considering their conceptual value, and far from recouping the company's capital investment in producing them. This collaboration concerns the preservation of French heritage, the company's alignment with vigorous intellectual figures of the contemporary art world,[17] and long-term strategic thinking in business. It has nothing in common with the multitude of collaborations flooding the market every so often where the initials of a famous artist, or a minor intervention on an existing product, pose as art and are appropriated by 'luxury' brands that are entirely preoccupied with short-term growth and revenues.

Conclusions

> A quality of beauty is that it gives deep satisfaction to the mind
> without arousing lust for possession. (Umberto Eco)

The reality of our branded lifestyles coupled with the intensification of stardom in the art world has created a new opportunity for luxury firms. They are now in a position to capitalise on their ability to produce artist's limited editions that respond to people's hunger for brand consumption. Whether a brand is product-driven or celebrity-driven matters very little when businesses are motivated exclusively by short-term gains.

While these attitudes raise fascinating questions that relate to the consumption of brands and specifically luxury brands, the present chapter has differentiated itself from the ongoing discussion on luxury consumption and shifted the conversation to questions of luxury production. In doing so, it also articulated a new framework through which luxury can be studied. This new method of study is object-based, drawing heavily on art historical methods of research and analysis. It also incorporates philosophical debates and recent findings in how neuroscience can aid our understanding and appreciation of art. A focus on Hiroshi Sugimoto's highly conceptual work for the luxury house Hermès allows the reader to test the framework and to ascertain its validity and merit in the existing literature on luxury.

The economists' interpretation of luxury products as strictly

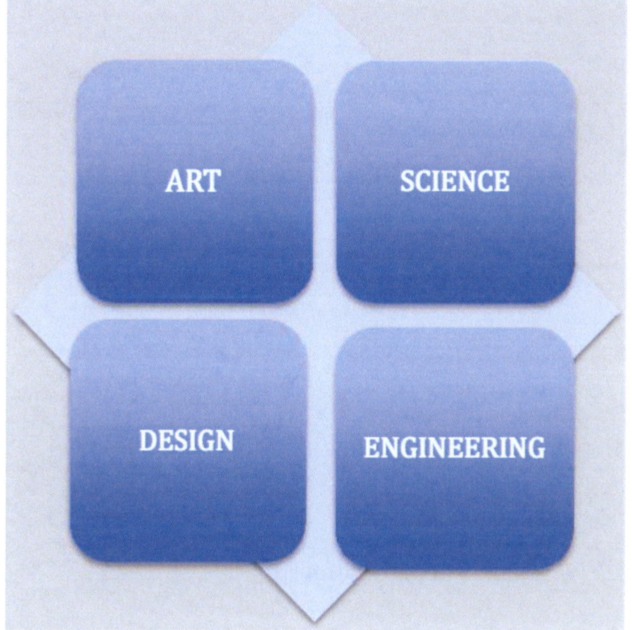

Plate 1 The four distinct fields through which knowledge evolves. (Thomaï Serdari, 2015)

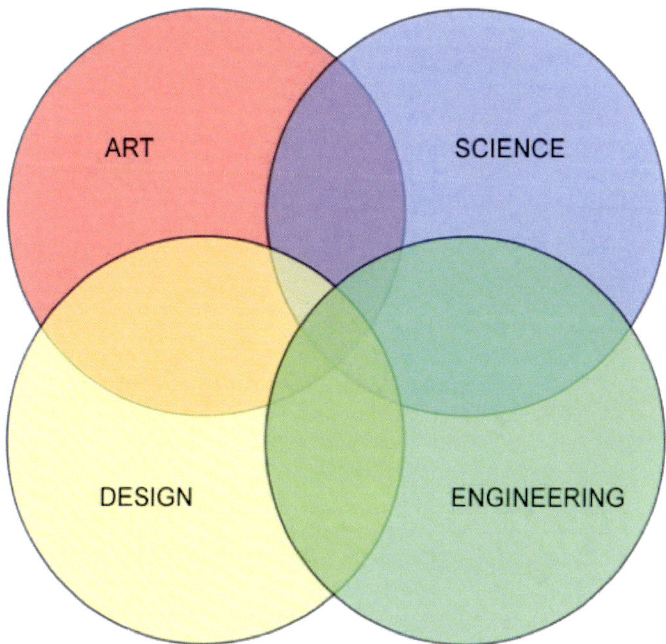

Plate 2 The four fields of knowledge in a Euler diagram configuration that explains the evolution of knowledge for the design and production of material objects. (Thomaï Serdari, 2015)

Plate 3 Hiroshi Sugimoto, Polarized Colours 075, 2010. Polaroid (7.7×7.9 cm). © Hiroshi Sugimoto, courtesy Pace Gallery.

Plate 4 Hiroshi Sugimoto, Polarized Colours 005, 2010. Polaroid (7.7×7.9 cm). © Hiroshi Sugimoto, courtesy Pace Gallery.

unnecessary expenditures that are used as a means to generate economic profit for the elite and its advancement in political power is limited. The identification of luxury with either history or preciousness or even scarcity alone is also limited and certainly superficial. Perhaps a better way to comprehend the power of luxury over our individual sensory system is to accept that luxury delights us, both physically and intellectually, because it allows us to absorb, occasionally observe and perhaps reflect on the outcomes of excessive creative presence. Businesses that design systems to support that type of creative output are not mere custodians of cultural heritage. They are mainly, and foremost, contributors to human progress. They employ innovation as a means to economic prosperity and long-term social engagement through scalable distribution.

Hiroshi Sugimoto's work Hermès represents the coalescing of art, science, technology and design. Where these four fields meet, Sugimoto's work is the expression of the universal certainty that involves any or several of our senses and that implies beauty, culture and scarcity. As such, it qualifies as luxury. Additionally, and based on recent neuroscientific experiments, it elicits direct neurological responses of pleasure and brain activity in the individual. Therefore, true luxury (at the heart of the Euler diagram proposed in this chapter) can be defined before it enters the social, political and economic debates that explain how it is used, consumed or communicated in the service of power or other motives an individual might have in society. An object-based study of luxury explains the encounter between the object and the individual as well as the individual's neurological and emotional responses to it. What happens later, when the social self takes over, is the subject of a different discussion.

Notes

1. Interview with Hiroshi Sugimoto at his New York City studio on 15 May 2014.
2. Interview with Sugimoto, 15 May 2014.
3. Kapferer recognises six authorities on luxury: the public (democratic approach); the aristocracy (elitist approach); the producer of luxury; the experts on luxury; the empirical approach (of observation); the authoritative approach of a committee (such as the Comité Colbert, for example, which has been defining luxury since 1954) (Kapferer 2009).
4. Ask History: Who built the first automobile? Available at: http://www.history.com/news/ask-history/who-built-the-first-automobile (accessed 12 December 2014).

5. Watchmaking is an art that closely relates to Belozerskaya's discussion of the importance of the alchemist as the person in charge of scientific knowledge, engineering methods, design techniques and artistic inclinations.

6. Marc Newson, *Doudou Necklace*, 2009 (sapphires, diamonds, white gold) made by Boucheron. The design is drawn from a mathematical function, the Julia set, named for the French mathematician Gaston Julie (1893–1978). This set belongs to a category known as fractals, which display complex, repeating patterns. The stones, comprising over 2,000 sapphires and diamonds, were carefully selected to capture the subtle gradations of colour found in Julie set fractals.

7. Sugimoto refers to fossils as 'pre-photography time-recording devices' (Sugimoto 2014: 17).

8. Interview with Sugimoto, 15 May 2014.

9. *H3 Hiroshi Sugimoto: The project*. Available at: http://editeur-en. hermes.com/editions/h3-hiroshi-sugimoto/couleurs-de-l-ombre-2.html (accessed 14 December 2014).

10. 'Colours', Goethe argued, 'appeal directly to our senses; red and blue have effects upon the human psyche that will not submit to mechanistic quantification'. *H3 Hiroshi Sugimoto: The project* (http://editeur-en. hermes.com/editions/h3-hiroshi-sugimoto/couleurs-de-l-ombre-2.html; accessed 14 December 2014).

11. Collective imperatives and social behaviours are different facets of luxury, well covered in the literature of the field as explained in the review section of this paper.

12. The collection has travelled to and been exhibited in museums and galleries around the world.

13. By 'complete' I am referring to the Polaroids Sugimoto decided to assign to the collaborative project with Hermès. The artist owns countless more but did not include them all in his selection for the collaboration.

14. Lyon has been the centre of silk production in France since the early sixteenth century when the city became the capital of the European silk trade and boosted French exports of luxury goods to reduce France's trade deficit.

15. Interview with Sugimoto, 15 May 2014.

16. Interview with Sugimoto, 15 May 2014.

17. The first edition by Hermès Editeur was based on work of Josef Albers who died in 1976 and whose creations can be produced through the traditional silkscreen printing process. So do the scarves in the second edition comprising works by French contemporary artist Daniel Buren, whose images are representational. The breakthrough in the series comes with the work of Hiroshi Sugimoto, who truly challenged the established production processes.

References

Adamson, Glenn (2013), *The Invention of Craft*, London: Bloomsbury Press.

Belozerskaya, Marina (2005), *Luxury Arts of the Renaissance*, Los Angeles: The J. Paul Getty Museum.

Berry, Christopher J. (1994), *The Idea of Luxury: A Conceptual and Historical Investigation*, Cambridge: Cambridge University Press.

Berthon, Pierre, Pitt, Leyland, Parent, Michael and Berthon, Jean-Paul (2009), 'Aesthetics and ephemerality: observing and preserving the luxury brand', *California Management Review*, 52 (1): 45–66.

Bourdieu, Pierre (2010 [1979]), *Distinction: A Social Critique of the Judgement of Taste*, London: Routledge.

Brougher, Kerry and Müller-Tamm, Pia (2010), *Hiroshi Sugimoto*, Ostfildern: Hantje Cantz.

Coleno, Nadine (2010), *The Hermès Scarf: History and Mystique*, New York: Thames and Hudson.

Hermès (2012), *Annual Report: Overview of the Group Review of Operations*, Paris: Hermès.

Jauss, Hans Robert (1982), *Aesthetic Experience and Literary Hermeneutics*, Minneapolis: University of Minnesota Press.

Jennings, Jeremy (2007), 'The debate about luxury in eighteenth and nineteenth century French political thought', *Journal of the History of Ideas*, 68 (1): 79–105.

Kapferer, J. N. and Bastien, V. (2009), *The Luxury Strategy: Break the Rules of Marketing to Build Luxury Brands*, London: Kogan Press.

Kemp, Wolfgang (1998), 'The work of art and its beholder: the methodology of the aesthetic reception', in Mark A. Cheetham (ed.), *The Subjects of Art History: Historical Objects in Contemporary Perspectives*, Cambridge: Cambridge University Press, pp. 180–96.

Koehn, Nancy F. (1997), 'Josiah Wedgwood and the first industrial revolution', in Thomas K. McGraw (ed.), *Creating Modern Capitalism*, Cambridge, MA and London: Harvard University Press.

Pinot de Villechenon, Marie Noëlle (1997), *Sèvres: Porcelain from the Sèvres Museum, 1740 to the Present Day*, London: Lund Humphries.

Rousseau, Jean-Jacques (1750), *Discours sur les sciences et les arts*, Geneva: Barillot & fils.

Schouwenberg, Louise (2011), *Hella Jongerius*, London; New York: Phaidon.

Starr, Gabrielle G. (2013), *Feeling Beauty: The Neuroscience of Aesthetic Experience*, Cambridge, MA: MIT Press.

Sugimoto, Hiroshi (2004), *Conceptual Forms*, Paris: Fondation Cartier pour l'art contemporain.

Sugimoto, Hiroshi (2014), *Cahiers d'Art*, 38th Year, No. 1, Paris: Éditions Cahiers d'Art.

Veblen, Thorstein (1899), *The Theory of the Leisure Class: An Economic Study of Institutions*, New York: Macmillan Company.
Weber, Max (1958 [1905]), *The Protestant Ethic and the Spirit of Capitalism*, New York: Scribner.

Websites

Charlie Rose Interviewing Marc Newson and Jony Ive (air date 11 November 2013): http://charlierose.com/watch/60303885.
Hella Jongerius (2013), 'Why Create Another Piece of Furniture': https://www.youtube.com/watch?v=qROeUj_3AEE.
Hermès Editeur Online Gallery-H3 Hiroshi Sugimoto: http://editeur-en.hermes.com/editions/h3-hiroshi-sugimoto.html.
Hermès International (2012), Hearts and Crafts: http://www.lesmainsd-hermes.com/en.

Chapter 8

Libeskind in Las Vegas: Reflections on Architecture as a Luxury Commodity

Adam Sharr

Around the time that the Guggenheim Museum in Bilbao opened in 1997 – a memorably sinuous building designed by the office of architect Frank Gehry – journalists coined the term 'starchitect'. It is now used to refer to the famous architects of 'signature' buildings, to Gehry and also Zaha Hadid, Jean Nouvel, Norman Foster, Renzo Piano and Rem Koolhaas. It is not new to promote the idea of the genius architect. Historians have, for centuries, likened architects to solitary artists despite the teams of people who are inevitably involved in designing and making buildings. What is new, however, is that big-name architects are no longer just designers of spaces and traders in cultural capital but also part of a group of global luxury brands whose aura can be attributed, at least in part, to the mutual interdependence and reinforcement of those brands (Klein 1999; Klingmann 2010). Prada have hired Herzog and DeMeuron and Rem Koolhaas's OMA to design stores for them, for example, to mutual commercial benefit.

The soubriquet 'starchitect' is, arguably, most often applied to Daniel Libeskind. Formerly seen as an intellectual, as a 'paper architect' who did not build, he shot to fame with the completion of the Jewish Museum in Berlin which opened in 2001. Its jagged forms and choreographed experiences derived from powerful ideas about commemoration, where absences evoke presences and presences evoke absences. Dramatic millennium projects around the world fostered the idea that 'iconic' buildings could be catalysts for urban regeneration, helping Libeskind's studio, and his personal imprimatur as designer, to become a global brand. Libeskind is now most famous for museums, including Imperial War Museum North in Salford, UK (2002) and dramatic alterations to the Military History Museum in Dresden, Germany (2011). The studio has also produced various commercial projects including apartments in Singapore (2011) and Westside Shopping and Leisure Centre in Bern, Switzerland (2008).

This chapter is about another Libeskind project: another shopping mall, opened in Las Vegas in 2009, deploying what have become the architect's trademark crystalline shapes. Named 'Crystals at CityCenter', the mall's branding derives its name and its luxury credentials from Libeskind's signature contribution.

What follows will examine Crystals at CityCenter as an example of the millennial phenomenon of the starchitect-designed iconic luxury building. It will explore the origins of Libeskind's architectural brand forms in the architecture of trauma in Berlin and, by contrast, the re-use of those forms in service of high-end retail on the Las Vegas Strip. Thanks to Robert Venturi, Denise Scott-Brown and Steven Izenour's 1972 book *Learning from Las Vegas* – a herald of postmodernism which studied the so-called ordinary buildings of the Strip according to semiotics – that city's architecture has become understood in terms of signs and symbols. I will argue, following this characterisation of the architecture of Las Vegas in the 1970s – and the construction of super sized theme hotels there in the 1990s and 2000s which turned buildings into super signs – that Crystals at CityCenter is also an example of architecture as sign. This time it is a sign of architecture referring only to itself, of architecture imagined as a luxury commodity.

Libeskind in Berlin

To appreciate how Libeskind's architecture operates in Las Vegas, it is important to begin by recounting the roots of that studio's trademark buildings, with a brief but necessarily detailed account of the Jewish Museum in Berlin (Figure 8.1) – an exceptional project which has secured a place in the single-volume histories of architecture. This is required, first, to establish the credentials of brand Libeskind and, second, because I will discuss later tropes that recur in the Las Vegas project which first appeared at this extraordinary site of architectural invention.

Since the fall of the Iron Curtain in 1989, Berlin has, arguably, become the capital of contemporary memorial architecture. Acts of public atonement for the Nazi past now figure prominently in the cityscape. These range in scale from the field of mute blocks comprising the Memorial to the Murdered Jews of Europe, designed by Peter Eisenman and Richard Serra, to individual brass cobbles, *Stolpersteine*, that quietly mark the buildings from which people were deported to their deaths in concentration camps. Arguably the most striking of Berlin's contemporary memorials is the Jewish

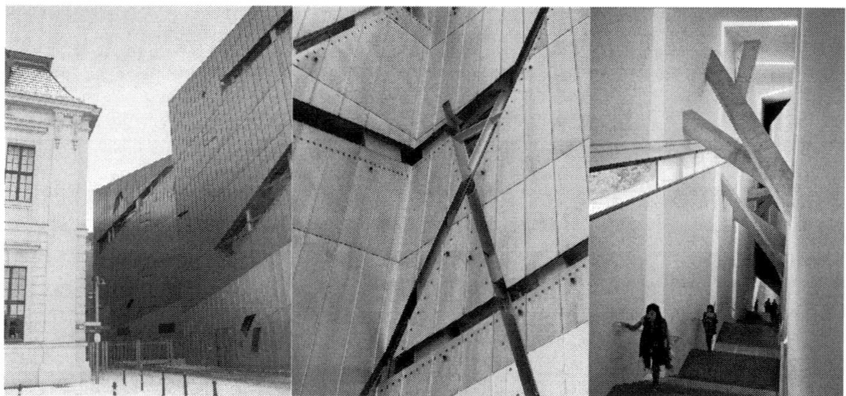

Figure 8.1 The Jewish Museum in Berlin designed by Studio Libeskind: its junction with the adjoining neo-classical museum (left); the façade showing windows which appear slashed through the zinc cladding and the bullet-hole cladding drainage detail (centre); and the 'Axis of Continuity' with structure crashing through the stairwell. Images from Wikimedia Commons: © Jorge Royan (http://www.royan.com.ar) (left); dalbera from Paris, France (http://creativecommons.org/licenses/by/2.0) (centre); Schlaier (public domain) (right).

Museum, in the district of Kreuzberg, which commemorates not just the persecution and murder of six million European Jews in the city where the Nazis planned many of their atrocities, but also celebrates Jewish life and culture before and after the Holocaust. Studio Libeskind won the project in an architectural competition in 1989. Opened some twelve years later, the building's construction and the fit-out of its exhibitions did not always proceed smoothly. But, if visitors are in a receptive frame of mind, the resulting building provides one of the most intense experiences that architecture can offer.

The Jewish Museum's jagged floor plan is hard to appreciate from the street except as a series of strange shapes. Its coordinates instead make sense from above, as a zig-zag reputedly derived from a series of lines plotted on a map connecting the addresses of deported Jews (Libeskind 1990). The sharp-edged volumes that result, leaning backwards and forwards from the vertical plane, are clad with reflective zinc sheets with carefully articulated seams. These seams are fixed diagonally, animating the façades with an effect that is at once static and restless. Seemingly slashed through them are a series of slit windows, recalling gun emplacements, whose organisation follows another order, an 'irrational and invisible matrix' once more deriving, reputedly, from addresses in the city (Libeskind 1990). The zinc sheets are also punctured by lines of holes, like bullet holes, which, practically, serve to drain condensation out of the cladding's construction.

After the building's dramatic first impression, the visitor may search in vain for an entrance. As if to emphasise that the trauma which the building commemorates can't be easily accessed or commodified, the neighbouring neoclassical museum building serves as an entrance. The interiors of the Jewish Museum are reached only through a connecting tunnel. Passing through that tunnel, the visitor is presented with a choice of three routes. Each of these echo what Libeskind called 'three realities in the history of German Jews' (Libeskind 1990). The first and longest route, named the 'Axis of Continuity', opens to a stair leading up to the exhibition levels – through which structural beams crash diagonally – that ultimately terminates at a blank wall, paradoxically representing the continuity of Berlin's history. The second, called the 'Axis of Emigration', is a corridor whose walls and floor are disconcertingly slanted, leading, through a heavy door, to the destabilising 'Garden of Exile' where daylight penetrates a series of forty-nine concrete columns built, unsettlingly, at 12° to the vertical. The third route, the 'Axis of the Holocaust' is a dead end, its glass cases filled with artefacts from the personal lives of murdered Jews, terminating at the chilling Holocaust Tower whose clanging door reverberates behind you when it closes. The Jewish Museum is also punctuated by five bare concrete voids, vertical atria which can be seen from the gallery levels. With one exception, these voids are empty, representing 'that which can never be exhibited when it comes to Jewish Berlin history: Humanity reduced to ashes' (Libeskind 2000: 14). This account highlights that the architecture is intended to unsettle expectations, to trade in metaphor and meaning, where metaphor is constituted not just in applied ornament but in the organisation of the plan and the surfaces of the building.[2]

The Jewish Museum's power follows from Libeskind's fastidious pursuit of that commemorative programme on that site in relation to the map of that city. The urban form of Berlin and its history were interpreted to produce an architecture that remains both particular and remarkable. Nevertheless, Libeskind's subsequent projects, including Crystals at CityCenter, quote – sometimes heavily – from this project. Maybe this is to accept Theodor Adorno's claim that 'to write poetry after Auschwitz is barbaric' (Adorno 1967: 19), that the Holocaust marked the end of the Enlightenment project of beauty and that all art forms, architecture included, must be remade anew: that all architecture cannot now be anything other than architecture-after-the-Holocaust? Or maybe the Jewish Museum is more simply understood as the progenitor of brand Libeskind, as the source of a series of signature architectural forms that have subsequently been redeployed in service of different clients, programmes and contexts, not least for 'high-end' shopping in Las Vegas?

Signs and Symbols in Las Vegas

If Berlin is the global capital of contemporary memorials, then Las Vegas can be imagined as the global capital of excess; the city where Guy Debord's 'society of the spectacle' is made architectural (Debord 1970). Its reputation for indulgence does not stem solely from the Strip's recent mega hotels – each one a town in its own right, the size of several city blocks, packed with slot machines, gaming tables and restaurants serving all-you-can-eat buffets twenty-four hours per day. It also comes from the environmental and logistical challenges of maintaining a city of this scale in the heat of the Nevada desert, from the huge area of air-conditioned and artificially lit spaces, and the air traffic that now supplies over half of Las Vegas's visitors, to the number of fountains, garden sprinklers and showers running constantly in one of the most water-deprived locations on the planet.

Las Vegas was founded in 1905 as a railway town. Its growth accelerated in the 1930s, made possible by the damming of the Colorado River to provide water and cheap hydro-electricity, and further accelerated by the state of Nevada's legalisation of gambling at a time when neighbouring California clamped down on betting. Martino Sterli reflects on the city's growth in the immediate post-war era to become 'an entertainment centre of world renown' (Sterli 2013: 79). 'Two factors', he suggests,

> were central in this unparalleled development. On one hand, from a sociocultural perspective, Las Vegas represents a carnivalesque antithesis to the Puritanism of American society. In contrast to the Catholic carnival tradition, with its temporary, circumscribed breaching of the rigid social order, here the Dionysian inverse and its taboo desires were territorially domesticated for American society. On the other hand, Las Vegas provided an outlet for postwar capitalism, where a middle class that had come into money could satisfy its desires for diversion. . . (Sterli 2013: 17)

The Las Vegas Strip's takeover by the entertainment industry continued in the 1940s with many of its new buildings – designed to be seen from the highway and accessed by car – owing more to the ambitious architectural modernism of Los Angeles than the informal architectures of the Nevada desert. The neon signs of the hotels – attached to façades, integrated with the buildings or freestanding on the roadside – increasingly jostled for motorists' attention. The night-time image of the city progressively outshone its daytime one. The 1950s brought nuclear testing to the nearby Nevada Proving Grounds, curiously serving to heighten Las Vegas's glamour, and the 'Rat Pack' of Frank Sinatra and his compatriots, consolidating the city's reputation as 'a place of fast (and fleeting) good fortune and love affairs' (Sterli 2013: 83). This was a new luxury for the increasingly wealthy middle classes; the decadence, danger and excess represented by the singer and his compatriots offered up for more widespread consumption.

In architectural terms, by the mid-1960s, 'the Strip had attained its "classic" form', notes Sterli. It 'presented itself as a sequence of starkly differentiated building complexes lined-up along the road like a string of pearls . . . Every hotel-casino looked out over a vast parking lot to the highway [and between them were] smaller motels, gas stations, car rental businesses, wedding chapels and souvenir shops' (Sterli 2013: 84). It was this 'classic' roadside Strip – the epitome of 'car oriented, de-centralised urban sprawl', of hotels separated from the road by vast parking lots, of access by car rather than foot, of a certain kind of American post-war urbanism – to which architects Denise Scott Brown and Robert Venturi, together with their teaching assistant Steven Izenour, brought a group of Yale students in autumn 1968.

The outcome of their studies, edited and published as the book *Learning from Las Vegas* (Figure 8.2), challenged architectural orthodoxies, simultaneously prompting admiration and provoking contempt. First published by MIT Press in 1972 and reissued in more portable form in 1977, the book has since become so famous that further books, including another one from MIT Press, have been written about it (Rattenbury and Hardingham 2007; Vinegar 2008; Vinegar and Golec 2008; Sterli 2013). *Learning from Las Vegas* was published at a time when it seemed that architects were only interested in imagining cities following the historic European model of dense, walkable streets and squares; when traditional conventions for drawing cities using figure-ground and Nolli plans[3] held sway; when modernist architectural conventions of 'form follows function' – of construction imagined as 'honest' to the construction materials used and the functions of the spaces – seemed unassailable; when famous architects and architectural academics tended to dismiss anything distant from the high culture of the field. In this context, the idea of

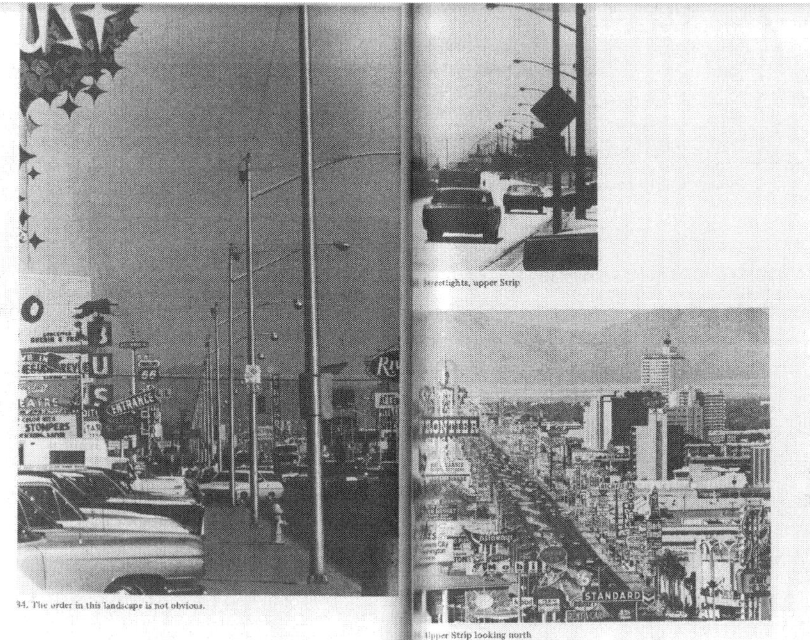

Figure 8.2 Spread from Robert Venturi, Denise Scott Brown and
Steven Izenour, *Learning from Las Vegas* (1977 edition) showing 'classic'
Las Vegas strip and sprawl. (MIT Press)

studying the 'ordinary' architecture and urban form of Las Vegas, let
alone learning lessons from it, would have seemed risible to many
scholars and practitioners.

Kester Rattenbury recounts the arguments of *Learning from
Las Vegas* following the tripartite structure of the book. 'The graphic
techniques used in the first section', titled 'A Significance of A+P
Parking Lots, or Learning from Las Vegas', she argues:

> identified many types of architectural behaviour: signs, heraldry,
> decorations, Ducks [buildings in the shapes of signs, like a hot dog
> stand in the shape of a hot dog, or a building in the shape of a
> duck], Decorated Sheds [cheap buildings with decorated, signify-
> ing façades effectively pasted onto the front] and so on. These are
> then discussed, in a far more familiar essay-type form (the content
> remains unusual) of text and illustration, in the second section 'Ugly
> and Ordinary Architecture, Or the Decorated Shed'. This second
> section develops the arguments for the recognition of the forms and
> innovations of Las Vegas as part of the *same* tradition of signs,
> heraldry, Ducks, Decorated Sheds, discoverable in the great cities
> of the past. It argues, inter alia, the sense and superiority of Ducks

over Decorated Sheds, in an age in which decoration was culturally outlawed. Modernism, in claiming to eschew ornament, had actually managed to turn would-be functionalism into a *style*, and was now designing machine-aesthetic Ducks. (Rattenbury and Hardingham 2007: 15)

Learning from Las Vegas thus argued – at a time when the norm was stripped modernist architecture whose forms were supposedly generated from function, when architectural decoration was seen as redundant – that the signifying function of architecture had been mistakenly discounted. It claimed a continuing importance for thinking of buildings as signs, suggesting that roadside signs themselves 'were the equivalent of the signs in the Byzantine and Counter Reformation churches' (Koolhaas and Obrist 2001: 615). The third section of the book, 'Essays in the Ugly and Ordinary: Some Decorated Sheds', presented design projects pursuing the idea of ordinary architecture. Rattenbury describes this section as offering:

> many more provocative and contemporary ideas . . . even though the projects are now 30 years old and few of them were built. [For example] The Crosstown Community Project, a study of supporting real, existing ordinariness ('we trust you not to try to neaten up South Street at the expense of its inhabitants', their clients told them) is a study . . . of renewed relevance in an expansionist Western world of unchecked gentrification. (Rattenbury and Hardingham 2007: 15)

The iconoclastic effects of the book's calmly presented studies of the Strip seem, in retrospect, to have been 'a bracing shower of common sense' (Rattenbury and Hardingham 2007: 16). Resonating with a contemporary concern with semiotics in other academic fields, the authors sought to renew the legitimacy of signification in architecture at a time when the discussion of aesthetics had come to seem suspiciously bourgeois, when the most appropriate discourse was that of function. *Learning from Las Vegas* opened up again the study of how buildings and their details connote visually their function, their cultural register, their entrances and their hierarchies of space. The neon signs of Las Vegas, and the city's Ducks and Decorated Sheds, showed how cheap, ordinary, ugly architecture (as the authors proudly described it) communicated. And the authors sought to give its significations the same authority as those of Ancient Rome or eighteenth-century Bath or Edinburgh. Even in 1968, thanks to Las Vegas's repeated and prominent depiction in film and its associations with stars of stage and screen, the city may have represented an exceptional instance of ordinary roadside architecture. But, where architectural signs and symbols were concerned, it was celebrated as the exception that proved the rule.

Super Hotels and Super Signs

The pace of change in Las Vegas since Venturi, Scott Brown and Izenour[4] drove out of town with their students has been no less extraordinary than that before their visit. By nearly every measure – visitor numbers, total number of hotel rooms, population, revenue, retail sales, gaming revenue, employment – the city has grown hugely. Land speculation and hospitality have also become increasingly important to the city's economy: 'In 2004 land transactions reached $30million per acre and hotel, food and beverage sales overtook gambling as the primary revenue stream at major casinos' (Smith and Tilden 2013). The city's urban form and architecture have also changed hugely. Big entertainment corporations such as MGM and Bally's have fuelled vast construction projects, and their mergers, sales and acquisitions of resort hotels have driven development. The architectural typology of parking lot and casino-hotel has been superseded by spectacular hotel super blocks imagined as entertainment experiences, many of them built right on the Strip, over the top of the original parking lots. As land values have risen, Strip and sprawl have been densified until the city's plan has begun to acquire the density of those older, more conventional cities with which Las Vegas was once contrasted. As Rem Koolhaas has put it, 'the city-as-mirage described in *Learning from Las Vegas* has, through sheer mass, become a real city' (Koolhaas and Obrist 2001: 595). And, just as Las Vegas's buildings have inflated to vast dimensions, so too has their iconography.

Writing in 1996, Venturi and Scott Brown characterised these changes in an essay titled 'Las Vegas After its Classic Age':[5]

> The Las Vegas Strip has officially been renamed Las Vegas Boulevard. This signifies its urbanisation . . . A proliferation of streets parallel and perpendicular to the Strip has produced superblocks, whose density derives from the building of larger and ever larger hotels and the replacement of parking lots with parking structures. The Strip is no longer a linear element in a desert, it is a boulevard in an urban setting; sprawl has become edge city. Traffic jams and busy pedestrian sidewalks attest to this evolution. Up front, sidewalks have been landscaped and parking lots have become front yards, their asphalt surfaces converted to Romantic gardens planned to draw pedestrians

> from the Boulevard to the hotel porte-cochère. (Venturi and Scott
> Brown 1998: 126)

In the 1990s, a series of themed super hotels were built, opening directly off Las Vegas's newly pedestrian-friendly Boulevard (Figure 8.3). The skyline of the hotel New York-New York (finished in 1997) collages together reproductions of the Empire State Building, the Chrysler Building, the former World Trade Center and others. The façade of The Venetian (1999) incorporates replica elements from the Palazzo Ducale, Piazza San Marco, St Mark's Campanile and the Rialto Bridge. Outside, gondolas are piloted along a strip of canal. Paris (1999) addresses the Boulevard with versions of Le Theatre des Arts, the Arc de Triomphe and even Montgolfier's balloon. A half-size Eiffel Tower, its feet puncturing Paris's hotel lobby, looms over the Strip, scaled down in size from the original to avoid disrupting air traffic at nearby McCarran Airport. At Paris, slot machines and gaming tables line the artificially lit interiors. Meanwhile, walls painted with generic *belle époque* architectural façades, and ceilings painted with cloudy skies, attempt to evoke Parisian streets and squares (Figure 8.4). The seedy edgy glamour of 'classic' Sin City Vegas – connoted by the tuxedos, drinking, sex and mobster violence associated with the Rat Pack – was supplanted by the international package tour, by the marketing of themed hotel entertainment experiences in the terms of mass produced exclusivity. These are luxury hotels designed for families and marketed as alternatives to trips to Florida, Disneyland or Dubai. Pools and children's entertainers supplement casinos and nightclubs. The interior design of these super hotels is contrived according to commercial logic, carefully planned to maximise catering and gambling income, intended to keep visitors inside and keep them spending. The exterior logic, meanwhile, is that of the visual spectacle.

'Las Vegas has become scenographic like Disneyland', Venturi and Scott Brown remarked in a 2001 interview (Koolhaas and Obrist 2001: 617). It has gone from 'signography to scenography'. While Las Vegas's 'classic' neon signs have been gradually removed during the densification of the Strip, the new super hotels have become super signs. Connoting New York, Venice and Paris, these hotels-as-signs have co-opted the popular reputation of world cities into the branding and marketing of luxury leisure experiences. Skylines are abstracted as outlines, scaled and remapped as signifiers of cities, with replica detail then applied. Thus, city block size hotels are dressed as signs of cities, making a tongue-in-cheek claim to the supposed glamour of their referents. Scaled, shifted and reassembled

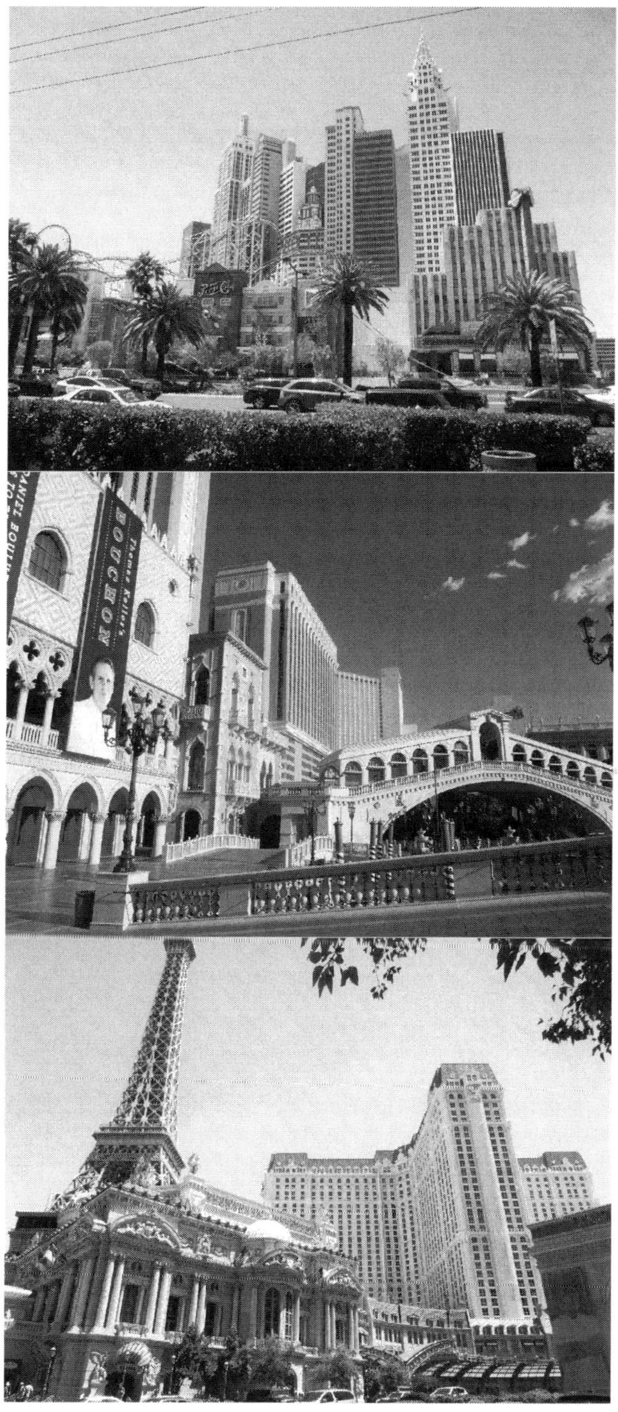

Figure 8.3 Las Vegas super hotels built in the 1990s: New York-New York (top); The Venetian (centre); and Paris (below). (Adam Sharr)

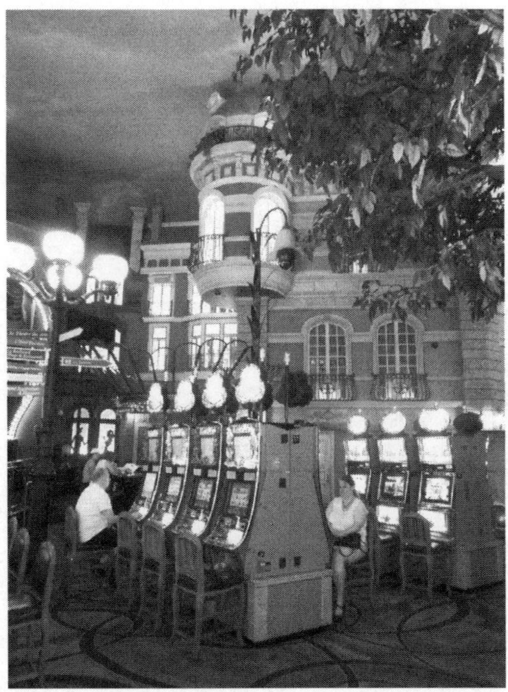

Figure 8.4 The interior of Paris, Las Vegas, showing reproduction *belle époque* façades and painted cloudy skies above rows of slot machines. (Adam Sharr)

as collages, they are not merely simulacra. The Las Vegas Strip has accepted Venturi, Scott Brown and Izenour's urban analysis in terms of signs, inflating and mutating it, resetting it in the pedestrian density of a more traditional cityscape whose claim to academic authority those authors sought to reject (Vinegar and Golec 2008). New York-New York, The Venetian and Paris perhaps represent the city of Las Vegas taking the arguments of *Learning from Las Vegas* away from Yale academics and making them its own. It can be argued that, whether or not Venturi, Scott Brown and Izenour would like it, the super hotels demonstrate back to them the fullest extent of their own thinking.

In Las Vegas's breakneck urban development, however, the era of the city-branded super hotel as super sign has itself passed. More recent developments on the Boulevard – most importantly CityCenter – seem to pursue different, more complex, significations – although, as I will now argue, they have more in common with each other than it might first appear.

Crystals at CityCenter

The foregoing discussions have highlighted how the Las Vegas Strip and its buildings remain exceptional, no matter that they were once claimed as a definitive example of ordinary American architecture. Architecture made there cannot fail to carry particular cultural baggage, loaded by *Learning from Las Vegas*. That book and its subsequent mythology now mean that the architecture of the Strip must always be the architecture of the sign. The question for new projects in that place – like Crystals at CityCenter – is about what, precisely, their architecture signifies.

Opened in December 2009 – with an 'invite-only event co-hosted by photographer Sebastian Copeland in partnership with *Vanity Fair* magazine, and attended by actors Orlando Bloom and Rosario Dawson' (Smith and Tilden 2013: 187) – the CityCenter development comprises a casino, three hotels, a shopping mall and residential towers. At the time, it was the largest privately funded construction project ever built, not just in Las Vegas but in US history.[6] For its developers, MGM MIRAGE, it represented a novel approach to the casino-hotel, imagined not as a super hotel but as a luxury resort. Commercially and architecturally, it did not take its cues from existing developments in Las Vegas but instead made a 'radical proposal: look to the east coast' (Smith and Tilden 2013: 187). Developer James Murren reflected:

> We could have designed a new themed hotel or expanded [the existing hotel] Bellagio south or developed a stand-alone contemporary hotel-casino. It would have been interesting but predictable and at the end of the day it would have just cannibalized our existing properties. CityCenter is none of that. It appeals to people who already come here, but it also will attract people who heretofore had no interest in Las Vegas, who are worldly, who travel to great cities, recognise superior architecture and design, seek out art galleries, museums and public spaces that have significance. (Smith and Tilden 2013: 39)

Just as Las Vegas's super hotels of the 1990s rejected the 'classic' form of strip and sprawl in favour of a new idea of luxury as family entertainment, so CityCenter rejected the business model and the design of those super hotels to promote a new idea of 'high-end' luxury, appealing to people imagined to have more cultural capital. European and American cities were invoked not in terms of skyline super signs but instead as sources for 'authentic' urban experiences. The development was conceived as a 'city within a city', an evocation of traditional urban architecture and urban space in the context of an increasingly densified, pedestrian-friendly Las Vegas Boulevard. The architect of CityCenter's masterplan was Ehrenkrantz, Eckstut & Kuhn (EEK). In their book celebrating the development's construction, William R. Smith and Scott J. Tilden wrote that:

> EEK's departure point was New York City's SoHo district, an area favoured by the affluent, discerning consumers CityCenter would cater to. The district's mix of mid-rise buildings, retail outlets, residences, services and public spaces was a model of successful mixed-use development . . . a vibrant downtown. It was SoHo's energy and density rather than its architectural style that inspired EEK's . . . form of urbanism on the Strip . . . 'At that moment, I think we and the client team realized that this was no longer a casino project in the traditional sense', said Peter Cavaluzzi, principal at EEK, 'But it could have the potential to become an authentic urban place. And so that was really the launchpad for the whole project. Everything began to flow from that perspective.' (Smith and Tilden 2013: 47)

To emphasise the idea of making an 'authentic' city in Las Vegas, to acquire the cultural capital that the developers saw as essential to their marketing and business plans, global architects, landscape architects and interior designers were appointed. Studio Libeskind, author of the Crystals shopping mall, may have been the only signed-and-sealed 'starchitect' on the list but others included the assured names of Kohn Pederson Fox (for the Mandarin Oriental hotel), Pelli Clarke Pelli (for the Aria Resort and Casino) and James Corner Field Operations (for aspects of the landscape design).

Libeskind in Las Vegas

Crystals at CityCenter glistens in the desert sun, its trademark jagged forms leaning towards the Strip (Figure 8.5). Despite the project's claims to high culture, its description in Smith and Tilden's book *Creating CityCenter: World Class Architecture and the New Las Vegas* begins in quantitative commercial terms:

> Crystals retail and entertainment district is located right on Las Vegas Boulevard and provides direct pedestrian access from the Strip. The 3-story, 500,000-sq.-ft. building houses 55 of the world's top luxury retailers under its multifaceted, skylit roof, from Tiffany & Co. and Bulgari to Harry Winston and Roberto Cavali, and protects shoppers from the sun with a glittering metal- and crystalline-clad façade. (Smith and Tilden 2013: 126)

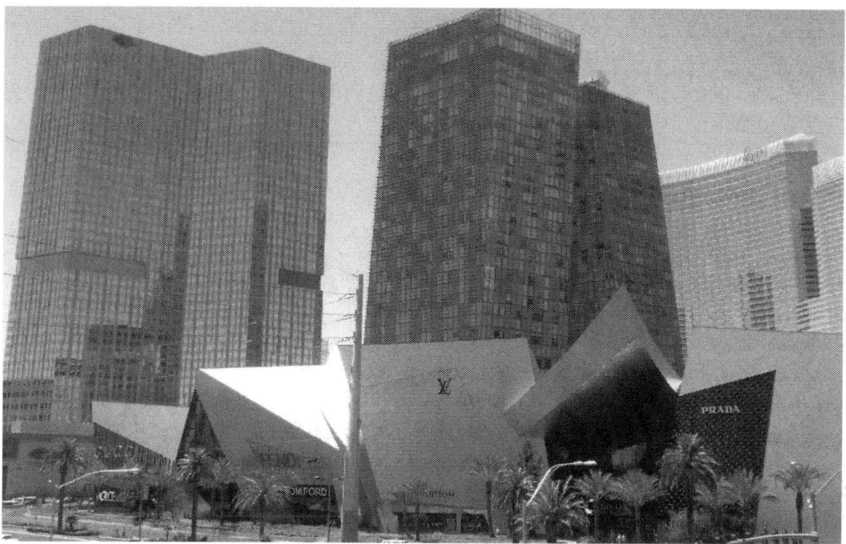

Figure 8.5 Crystals at CityCenter, designed by Studio Libeskind, seen from Las Vegas Boulevard, accessorised with the logos of designer brands. (Adam Sharr)

The authors reflect that 'World class design required facilities of equal calibre', noting that, '[c]oncurrent with the search for project designers, executives from MGM MIRAGE's retail division set out to fill CityCenter's 500,000-sq.-ft. Crystals with the finest luxury brands in the world' (Smith and Tilden 2013: 49). In the developer's value set, Studio Libeskind is equated directly with Tiffany and Bulgari as one among a series of luxury brands which could be harnessed to drive 'high-end' value. The architect's signature was intended to secure credibility for the development among both its prospective retail tenants and its imagined 'superior', 'worldly' visitors.

The architecture of Crystals makes its claims to such credibility by quoting directly from Studio Libeskind's earlier work, specifically from where the brand originated: Berlin's Jewish Museum. Seen from the street, the jagged shapes of Crystals are finished in a similar diagonal reflective cladding. However, that cladding is accessorised here with the lettering of large logos – such as YSL, Louis Vuitton, Fendi, Gucci and Dolce & Gabbana – which can be seen in the tradition of Las Vegas's signage as a distinctive heraldry, signifying the corporate packaging of luxury goods and associating a particular idea of leisure with consumption, specifically with the consumption of products that demonstrate the purchaser's wealth to others (Berry

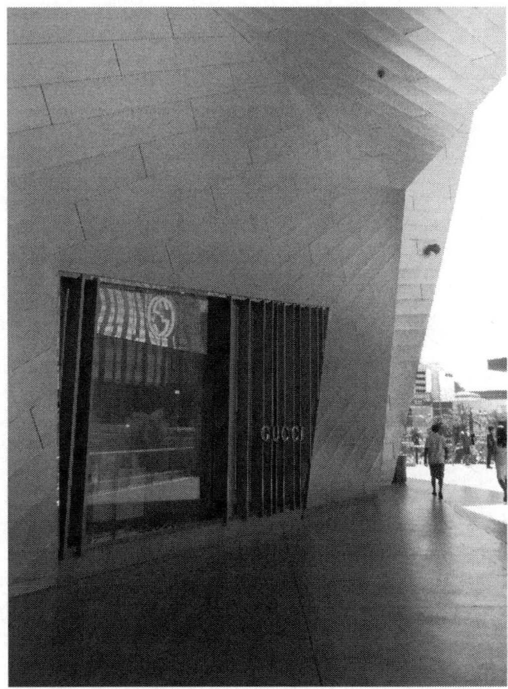

Figure 8.6 The entrance to Crystals showing diagonal cladding, plus a Gucci branded window display and banks of CCTV cameras. (Adam Sharr)

1994). The building's shapes are signifiers themselves, immediately recognisable as 'a Libeskind', as another designer product from a global brand.

The building's entrances are made apparent by the articulation of its jagged forms (Figure 8.6). The air-conditioned mall interiors are spacious, lined with expensive materials, and are, once again, dominated by the logos of retail tenants (Figure 8.7). Unusually for Las Vegas, the spaces are naturally lit and top-lit. Roof lights appear as gashes in the ceiling, echoing similar gashes across the façades of the Jewish Museum (Figure 8.8). Structure crashes diagonally through these roof lights, just like it does on the staircase of the 'Axis of Continuity'. Slots for lighting and air-conditioning extracts are also articulated as gashes in the ceiling, quoting from their Berlin referent. Interior walls are patterned with diagonal lines in the drywall (plasterboard, in British English) that ornament the interior walls, tracing out Libeskind's trademark geometries as a surface pattern. Air-conditioning inlets are formed across some of these walls in lines of circular nozzles, recalling the bullet-hole drainage device

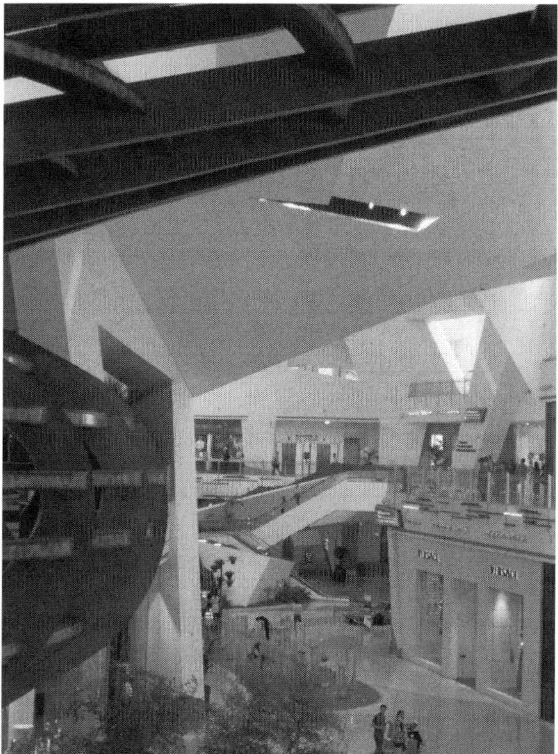

Figure 8.7 The interior of Crystals at CityCenter showing luxury retail units. (Adam Sharr)

in the cladding of the Jewish Museum (Figure 8.9). These architectural motifs – which were loaded with commemorative meaning in Berlin – seem more ambiguous in Las Vegas, where they stand as self-quotation on the part of Studio Libeskind, as repeated tropes of architectural form.

Libeskind's buildings, like those of other 'starchitects', have the aura of artworks. They are purchased by their developers not just as functional buildings but as talismans of cultural capital, as illustrated by the ideas of MGM MIRAGE's developer James Murren quoted above. They portray a sense of worldliness and sophistication, seemingly elevating the status of the people who procure and use them. This aura is frequently extended by the published ruminations of the 'starchitects' themselves, where they account for their buildings in relation to the values of high culture. Crystals at CityCenter is no different, and Daniel Libeskind's discussions of the mall have made claims to the past and the present:

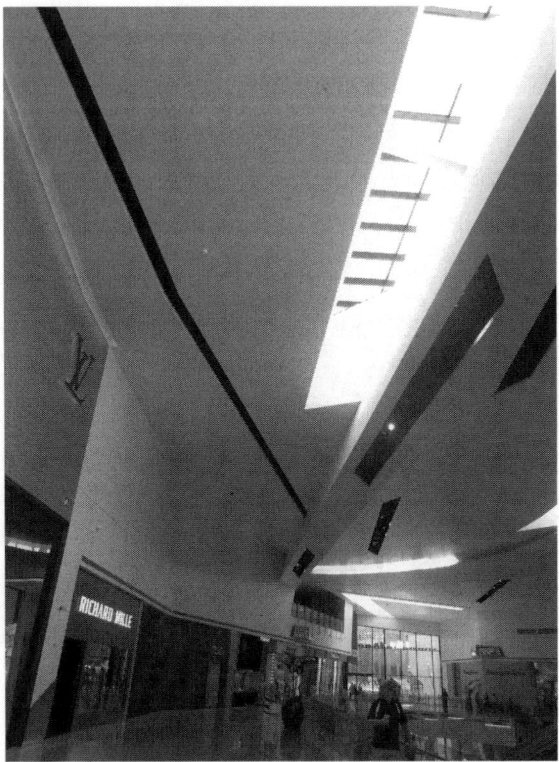

Figure 8.8 The interior of Crystals showing zones for artificial lighting and air-conditioning effectively slashed through the ceiling and roof lights with structure crashing through them – architectural quotations from the Jewish Museum. (Adam Sharr)

> 'It's not just an inert steel and glass work', he [Libeskind] says. 'To me, a good building or a city development is more like a book. It has to tell you something – a story. It tells you something about the past, something memorable. It tells you something about the future, something you didn't know, and opens a whole new world to the visitor. And that's when the building really begins.' (Smith and Tilden 2013: 126)

The architect likens the building to literature. He also links it to its Berlin referent by evoking memory and thus the project of commemoration that informed the design of the Jewish Museum. But, unlike in Berlin, it seems that the past he evokes here is not particular, merely a sense of there being something that has gone before. Broad ideas of past and future are deployed as claims to cultural authority. But what seems to matter more in Studio Libeskind's Las Vegas project is

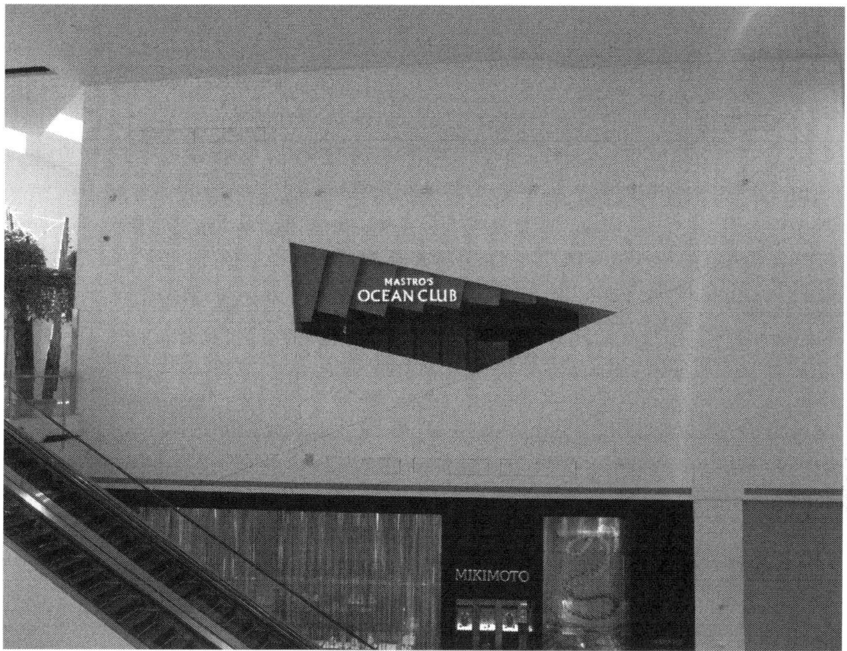

Figure 8.9 The interior of Crystals showing a line of circular air-conditioning inlets and diagonal patterns scribed into the drywall. (Adam Sharr)

the idea of an iconic building in the city, of the unfolding of a sense of architectural drama, of 'wow':

> 'The "wow" is not just picture postcard; it is the continual experience that you have when you are conversing with family and friends, just walking, and just enjoying yourself,' says Libeskind. 'And what we are creating is something really exciting – large-scale urban space, spiralling space, that creates a landscape within which you find the fantastic flagship stores, the fountains and all the amenities, but also something that takes you on an urban voyage. And you really discover the complexity of the city, and the fun and pleasures that a city experience really gives you.' (Smith and Tilden 2013: 133–4)

The Jewish Museum in Berlin sought to avoid the commodification of commemoration, its architectural sequences and the layout of its axes denying the idea of a straightforward entrance, of a linear teleology of spaces, rendering the museum's stories more ambiguous and less easy to consume. The project made a reputation for Libeskind as a critical architect, as one who was, unlike the mainstream practices of the time, able to articulate in architecture a set of values that were clearly distinct from a simple commercial response to a functional brief. The programme for Crystals at CityCenter is different, and Libeskind is, in this context, not unhappy with equating shopping at 'fantastic flagship stores' with happiness and the celebration of consumption as leisure. The complexity of the city seems to be evoked, here, more as a long history of pleasurable retail experience than as an important site of civic engagement. Predominant in Libeskind's account, however, is the mythology of originality in artistic production. A genius myth is centred on the architectural author here. Such mythologies seem to have become necessary in contemporary claims for cultural capital, and they underpin the linked phenomena of the 'starchitect' and the iconic signature building:

> perhaps the most sustainable feature of Crystals is its originality. 'To sustain novelty, you have to build a space that is really unprecedented', says Libeskind, 'a space that is not just like the Galeria [Vittorio Emmanuele] in Milan or elsewhere but a space that doesn't have a front, back or roof. Everything has been designed in this building as a gigantic sculpture and as a gigantic work of art from every angle. It changes not just with every minute but with every heartbeat. It is imbued with a spiritual quality which is endless, that is never going to be exhausted.' (Smith and Tilden 2013: 136–7)

While Crystals at CityCenter has its formal origins in the inventions of the Jewish Museum, and while it claims its authority as an artwork through its associations with that building and its details, Libeskind's account here illustrates how the two buildings diverge. In Berlin, the trademark shapes of brand Libeskind were a novel consequence of the commemorative agenda and the symbolic language of that highly loaded project. In Las Vegas, however, novelty – as expressed through the reiteration of those trademark shapes – seems to have become an end in itself. Novelty is equated with spirituality. And novelty permits claims to be made for the building as an artwork and for its distinction as a 'high-end' product.

The marketable commodity of cultural capital is thus claimed for Crystals through the tropes of history, urbanity, spatial drama and artistic originality. The Las Vegas context, I argued above, colours how architecture operates there. If architecture in Las Vegas cannot avoid being interpreted in terms of signification, then what does Crystals at CityCenter signify? The project has been imagined as a rejection of previous Las Vegas architectures, of super hotels as super signs, which themselves could be understood as a rejection of the 'ugly ordinary' of strip and sprawl. CityCenter has been portrayed as

a reclamation of 'authentic' urban form in response to the densification of the city grid of Las Vegas and also the symbolic appropriation
of cities at The Venetian, Paris and New York-New York. The building signifies an idea of the 'authentic' traditional city, imagined here
not just in terms of liveable streets and squares but in terms of those
streets and squares as a marketable commodity, as a signifier of the
idea of a civic past; an idea that can be sold to high-end consumers
as luxury. Likewise, Crystals at CityCenter seeks to claim the idea of
architecture as art, as a pursuit whose details and nuances exist for
the appreciation of connoisseurs. Primarily, then, the building is a
sign of high architecture commissioned in service of itself, signifying
the very idea of architecture. It connotes the idea of architecture
as a signifier for high culture, becoming a device for marketing to
'high-end' consumers. This enables the building to claim the status of
artwork, in order to help market products as designer goods, selling
the buying of luxury goods as leisure.

Architecture as a Luxury Commodity

As another iteration in Las Vegas's architecture of signification,
Crystals at CityCenter demonstrates that luxury is, by definition,
always a shifting commodity. The mall's claims to luxury, like
those of the generation of super hotels before it, rely on it being
distinguished as different from what went before. Christopher Berry
reflects that:

> Implicit . . . is the transient nature of luxury goods. A luxury is not
> something static, it is dynamic; it is subject to development as desires,
> and necessary attendant beliefs, are met and then fuelled with further
> qualitative modifications or refinements. (Berry 1994: 18)

To assert itself as luxurious, Crystals had to be seen as different from
Paris, The Venetian or New York-New York, which themselves had
to be seen as different from the architecture of the 'classic' Strip.
This relates to three aspects of 'the phenomenon of non-functional
demand', which Berry summarises on the basis of H. Leibenstein's
work from the 1950s: 'the "Bandwagon effect" where demand
increases due to the fact that others are consuming the product as,
for example, in the case of what is fashionable; the "Snob effect"
where demand decreases due to the fact that others are consuming a particular product, and the "Veblen effect" where demand
increases when the price is higher rather than lower' (Berry 1994:

27; Leibenstein 1950). To remain luxurious, the idea of luxury has to keep changing. Something must seem expensive, it must appear (in the imagination if not in fact) to be available only to a few, and its exclusiveness must shift and mutate as it becomes available to larger groups. This is reflected in the developer's and architect's discourses about Crystals at CityCenter, in their carefully chosen vocabulary which sought to reject ideas about predictable and formulaic design to promote exclusiveness and expensiveness.

Primarily, the discourses around Crystals at CityCenter worked to claim cultural authority for a novel architecture so that it could be sold as a luxury commodity. They illustrate the contemporary purchase of the idea of the 'starchitect' and the perceived value of 'iconic' buildings. Annette Condello, in *The Architecture of Luxury*, links this to the associated notion of the architect as a designer brand, whether in relation to the output of their studio or to the myth of genius promulgated around the signature architectural author:

> 'Luxury' is generally defined as 'a state of great comfort or elegance, especially when involving great food, dress, furniture or appliances of any kind' and 'sumptuous and exquisite food and surroundings'. At the outset [in Ancient Greece], luxury was not confined to behaviour, cuisine, objects or surroundings. It was also expressed architecturally . . . Generally speaking, at various times in the past both small and large constructions that exceeded necessity have been thought of as luxurious . . . The key changes to the term 'luxury' in modern times have been its relation to *deluxe* consumption goods, marking the buildings as brands, and as benefits for most people to enjoy, especially the middle class. (Condello 2014: 3–4)

What distinguishes the buildings of contemporary 'starchitects' from the architecture of other less famous designers, and those of multiple and more ambiguous authors, is the added cultural capital that stems from the creative reputation signified by their brand, which somehow exceeds regular building. Buildings by 'starchitects', like Crystals at CityCenter, are frequently imagined as somehow 'architecture plus something'. It is by virtue of this extra, this excess, that they conform to Christopher Berry's account of luxury goods:

> A luxury good is an indulgence . . . In abstract terms, the assumption in contemporary commercial usage is that a luxury good is a widely desired (because not yet generally attained) good that is believed to be 'pleasing', and the general desirability of which is explained by it being a specific refinement, or qualitative aspect, of some universal generic need. (Berry 1994: 40–1)

This 'something' added by the buildings of 'starchitects' is found in a particular conjunction of novelty and refinement. To succeed as luxury, that conjunction must be achieved in a way which is unpredictably predictable – it must be edgy enough to be different but also sufficiently close to mainstream taste that it can be seen as a novel refinement of existing values, forms and conventions, rather than a wholesale rejection of them. The sociologist Pierre Bourdieu, in his critique of the codes of art, has argued that this process relies on subtlety of judgement, and that there is frequently little difference between the supposedly most informed and least informed taste:

> knowledge . . . becomes increasingly specific as we go towards the more educated beholders, so that the most adequate perception differs only from the least adequate in so far as the specificity, richness and subtlety of the categories employed are concerned. (Bourdieu 1984: 231)

Bourdieu's work highlights that, in the work of 'starchitects', cultural capital emerges from increasingly subtle judgements, from a novelty predicated on being sufficiently new for the connoisseurs and sufficiently conventional for popular taste. Whereas the Jewish Museum, at the time of its construction, was perhaps too different, too loaded, for its architectural motifs to be acceptable to a commercial developer, their ongoing repetition as a set of forms has achieved a balance of novelty and familiarity where, in the context of a shopping mall, they can be safely claimed in service of the project of luxury.

The commercial function of 'starchitects' and their architecture yielding 'high-end' value – is thrown into sharp relief here. As is the potential damage they can cause to regular architects and architecture. 'Starchitects' and their 'icons' achieve disproportionate media coverage in comparison to their tiny part in the spectrum of architectural production, to the point where many people think of architecture as only being about spectacular buildings of this sort. Good ordinary buildings – let alone the 'ugly' ordinary buildings celebrated by *Learning from Las Vegas* – are in danger of vanishing behind these fantastic fabulations in the public imagination. Around 80 per cent of buildings in the UK are constructed without the services of an architect – a figure not dissimilar to that of many Western countries – and research has suggested that the idea of hiring an architect wouldn't occur to many householders (Samuel 2012). For them, architects have become perceived as a luxury, imagined as an expensive indulgence when it comes to household extensions or ordinary houses. Through their association with other luxury brands, 'starchitects' seem to be pushing everyday architects out of mainstream public consciousness. 'Starchitects' have promoted architecture as a luxury commodity among developers, the wealthy and the consumers of Sunday newspaper culture columns. But it could be argued that the more that famous architects like Daniel Libeskind promote themselves as luxury brands, the more their forms and their soaring rhetoric seem detached from everyday building, the less likely it is that the profession of architecture itself will survive. If architects become seen as a luxury rather than a necessity, they will become only a niche, boutique extension of the construction industry. Crystals at CityCenter shows that the architecture of 'starchitects' has come to signify the idea of architecture signifying only itself, architecture as a commodity where 'starchitects' are hired to reproduce replicable, marketable shapes for their international sign value. This is, however, an idea of architecture that few architects who are concerned with everyday design would want to subscribe to.

Notes

1. The term cultural capital was popularised by the sociologist Pierre Bourdieu to describe the connoisseur's knowledge of art, literature and other cultural forms, whose subtleties those connoisseurs deploy competitively to exert power, operating in a similar way to the deployment of financial capital to exert power (Bourdieu 1983, 1986).
2. The building can be seen in the lineage of the contemporary counter-monument: a monument which conspicuously rejects the traditions of the pompous memorials of the past, like equestrian statues, in favour of more complex forms and ideas, often dealing in presences which stand for absences and absences which stand for presences (Young 1992, 1994).
3. In 1748 Giambattista Nolli engraved his famous *Pianta Grande di Roma*, a plan of Rome which is now usually known by his surname. Most significantly, Nolli added to his map the interior plans of public buildings such as churches and colonnades as though they were open space. What his drawing does is to show the civic space of the ancient city making little distinction between what is outside or inside, private or open to all. The map is frequently used to illustrate an idea of urban public realm that became popular in Western Europe in the later nineteenth and twentieth centuries.
4. I reproduce here the sequence of author names as listed on the book's cover. Denise Scott Brown has written an important feminist essay about

how her name is often omitted in connection with their work, and always listed second, in favour of Robert Venturi's (Scott Brown 1989).
5. Venturi and Scott Brown summarised the argument of this essay in a subsequent interview: 'In "Las Vegas after Its Classic Age" we describe the following evolutions: from strip to boulevard, urban sprawl to urban density, parking lot to landscaped front yard, asphalt plain to Romantic garden, decorated shed to duck, electric to electronic, neon to pixel, electrographic to scenographic, iconography to scenography, Vaughan Cannon [hero of neon signage design] to Walt Disney, pop culture to gentrification, pop taste to good taste, perception as driver to perception as walker, strip to mall, mall to edge city, vulgar to *dramatique*. To simplify, the main thing is that it went from the archetype of the strip and sprawl to the scenography of Disneyland' (Koolhaas and Obrist 2001: 617).
6. 'The company used $3.2 billion of its $7 billion unsecured credit agreement with the Bank of America for the deal, leaving $3.8 billion up front, which would be offset by annual revenues of $2 billion and a projected $2.5 billion in sales at CityCenter's residential complex' (Smith and Tilden 2013: 41).

References

Adorno, Theodor (1967), 'Cultural criticism and society', in *Prisms*, trans. Samuel and Shierry Weber Nicholsen, Cambridge, MA: MIT Press, pp. 17–34.

Berry, Christopher J. (1994), *The Idea of Luxury: A Conceptual and Historical Investigation*, Cambridge: Cambridge University Press.

Bourdieu, Pierre (1983), *Distinction: A Social Critique of the Judgement of Taste*, trans. Richard Nice, Cambridge, MA: Harvard University Press.

Bourdieu, Pierre (1984), 'Outline of a sociological theory of art perception', in *The Field of Cultural Production: Essays on Art and Literature*, New York: Columbia University Press, pp. 215–37.

Bourdieu, Pierre (1986), *The Rules of Art: Genesis and Structure of the Literary Field*, trans. Susan Emanuel, Redwood City, CA: Stanford University Press.

Condello, Annette (2014), *The Architecture of Luxury*, Aldershot: Ashgate.

Debord, Guy (1970), *Society of the Spectacle*, trans. Fredy Perlman and Jon Supak, Detroit: Black & Red.

Klein, Naomi (1999), *No Logo*, London: Picador.

Klingmann, Anna (2010), *Brandscapes: Architecture in the Experience Economy*, Cambridge, MA: MIT Press.

Koolhaas, Rem and Obrist, Hans Ulrich (2001), 'Relearning from Las Vegas: an interview with Denise Scott Brown and Robert Venturi', in Rem Koolhaas and Chuihua Judy Chung (eds), *The Harvard Design School Guide to Shopping*, Cologne: Taschen, pp. 595–603.

Leibenstein, H. (1950), 'Bandwagon, snob, and Veblen effects in the theory of consumers' demand', *Quarterly Journal of Economics*, 64 (2): 183–207.

Libeskind, Daniel (1990), 'Between the lines: extension to the Berlin Museum, with the Jewish Museum', *Assemblage*, 12 (August): 18–57.

Libeskind, Daniel (2000), *Daniel Libeskind: Jewish Museum*, Berlin: Verlag der Kunst.

Rattenbury, Kester and Hardingham, Samantha (eds) (2007), *Supercrit 2: Robert Venturi and Denise Scott Brown, Learning from Las Vegas*, London: Routledge, 2007.

Samuel, Flora (2012), 'Extension stories', in Adam Sharr (ed.), *Reading Architecture and Culture: Researching Buildings, Spaces and Documents*, London: Routledge, pp. 96–105.

Scott Brown, Denise (1989), 'Room at the top? Sexism and the star system in architecture', in Ellen Perry Berkeley and Matilda McQuaid (eds), *Architecture: A Place for Women*, Washington, DC: Smithsonian Institution Press, pp. 237–48.

Smith, William R. and Tilden, Scott J. (2013), *Creating CityCenter: World Class Architecture and the New Las Vegas*, New York: W. W. Norton.

Sterli, Martino (2013), *Las Vegas in the Rearview Mirror: The City in Theory, Photography and Film*, Los Angeles: Getty Publications.

Venturi, Robert and Scott Brown, Denise (1998), 'Las Vegas after its classic age', reprinted in Robert Venturi, *Iconography and Electronics – Upon a Generic Architecture: A View from the Drafting Room*, Cambridge, MA: MIT Press, pp. 123–36.

Venturi, Robert, Scott Brown, Denise and Izenour, Stephen (1972), *Learning from Las Vegas*, Cambridge, MA: MIT Press (revised edn, 1977).

Vinegar, Aron (2008), *I am Not a Monument*, Cambridge, MA: MIT Press.

Vinegar, Aron and Golec, Michael J. (2008), *Relearning from Las Vegas*, Minneapolis: University of Minnesota Press.

Young, James E. (1992), 'The counter-monument: memory against itself in Germany today', *Critical Inquiry*, 18 (2): 267–96.

Young, James E. (1994), *The Texture of Memory: Holocaust Memorials and Meaning*, New Haven, CT: Yale University Press.

Chapter 9

Sartorial Connoisseurship, the T-shirt and the Interrogation of Luxury

Jonathan Faiers

> At first glance, everything looked the same. It wasn't. Something
> evil had taken possession of the town.[1]

Luxury is parasitic. In its action it is carcinogenic, colonising the host's body, replicating its vital organs, making itself indispensable, often undetectable, debilitating and frequently terminal. From handbags to hotels, excursions to enemas, luxury's contemporary colonisation is irresistible, infecting the very discourse we use, as terms such as luxury for all, luxury for less, stealth luxury, affordable luxury and even luxury lite pass unchallenged and are employed to camouflage luxury's essentially socially dichotomous function within a deceptive membrane of inevitability.[2]

This text will explore the invasive action of contemporary luxury production and consumption, and in order to understand its selective and often initially unrecognisable progress, fashion will provide a suitable 'host' with which to more closely observe its characteristic stages. The basic plain white T-shirt, ubiquitous, instantly familiar and apparently simple, has provided a fertile vestimentary culture in which luxury's recent diversification and adaptation can be detected. A garment as democratic, modest and undistinguished would seem at first glance an unlikely target for luxury's conquest, and yet it is precisely because of its humble and unpretentious origins that luxury finds in it its ideal sartorial colony. But before considering luxury's insidious permeation of the plain white cotton T-shirt and why this subtle – to many, invisible – appropriation of an everyday item encapsulates its contemporary expansion, it is necessary to con-textualise this within an understanding of the more easily assailable processes of refinement, embellishment and substitution.

Early in Christopher Berry's seminal text *The Idea of Luxury* he addresses luxury goods as typically understood as often having undergone a process of refinement and ornamentation. This is not to say that they lose their original function, indeed preserving their basic utility is essential to their status as luxury goods, but the apparent superfluity of added qualities such as lustre, softness or transparency, to choose typical qualities attached to luxury textiles for example, is an essential part of their recognition as luxury goods. As Berry suggests, 'The refinements that characterise luxuries are the qualitative or adjectival aspects of goods' (1994: 11). This application of the veneer of luxury, a seductive surface, has, of course, been fundamental to the manufacture of luxury goods from the earliest times, and the crafts essential to the production of these significantly luxurious surfaces is as important to today's luxury producers as it was in ancient times. If the discernment of luxury is understood pathogenically, then these qualities assume the role of symptoms, external manifestations of the contagion of luxury.

Excrescences of gold and precious stones, febrile sheens and degenerating translucency have regularly exercised literary imaginations, oscillating between moral condemnation and fascinated desire. This construction of infectious luxury was perhaps most exquisitely imagined in the symbolist reveries of late nineteenth-century Europe, where figures such as the Duc des Esseintes in Joris-Karl Huysmans' masterpiece *À Rebours* combine the liqueur-induced memory of bloody dental extraction with the realisation that his experiment to offset the tones of his oriental carpet by having his pet tortoise studded with jewels has only succeeded in bringing about the creature's demise, who expires from an invasion of luxury: 'Accustomed no doubt to a sedentary life, a modest existence spent in the shelter of its humble carapace, it had not been able to bear the dazzling luxury imposed upon it, the glittering cape in which it had been clad' (Huysmans 2003: 49). Des Esseintes' unfortunate tortoise provides a refined prototype for death by luxury, and supplanting reptile for human we arrive at one of twentieth-century popular culture's most memorable images, that of the gilded Jill Masterson, the Bond girl featured in *Goldfinger* who dies from 'skin suffocation' (a condition fabricated by Ian Fleming) after being painted entirely in gold.

If Huysmans' and Fleming's fervid visions underscore luxury's potential harm, it is of a distinctly conspicuous form, an expression of moral decay rendered corporeally visible, conspicuous contagion perhaps, to paraphrase Thorsten Veblen's celebrated term 'conspicuous consumption'. Published a mere fifteen years after des Esseintes' experiments into the limits of esoteric luxury, Veblen's *Theory of the Leisure Class* is today regularly invoked to rationalise the global cathexis centred on contemporary luxury production and consumption (Veblen 1899). However, his diagnosis of the disease of luxury understandably assumes a distinctly nineteenth-century degenerescent form, where finery as the sign of economic excess and its attendant moral decline is akin to the lesions and chancres symptomatic of that supreme nineteenth- and early twentieth-century moral indicator: syphilis.

Although the conspicuously luxurious symptoms of Veblen's leisure class can still furnish us with a rationale with which to analyse the endemic spread of global luxury and even the phenomenon of 'masstige', botanical manifestations of the infestation of luxury, which are typified by a more sustained and gradually detrimental symbiotic relationship, offer a more accurate metaphor for the current commodified union between luxury and the commonplace.[3] Mistletoe, the best-known parasitic plant, adds to the bark of its host a luxurious embellishment, the vibrant green leaves and pearl-like berries (incidentally a favourite motif of *fin de siècle* jewellers) a dazzling tumour, which by the aid of a specialised organ – the haustorium – connects the parasite to the conductive system of its host. With this organ it extracts water and nutrients, killing the portion of the branch to which it is attached, additionally stunting the growth and in some cases killing the tree it is feeding on. This complex botanical relationship replicates not only the consumer's slow economic debilitation once infected by luxury, but also the process of luxury brand extension where established brands (in this case the host) support a more showy and therefore commercially popular 'line' (the mistletoe), in a risky enterprise which puts the original authenticity and exclusivity of the host brand in jeopardy. In short, while mistletoe is visually appealing, its berries are poisonous, unlike the fruit of the tree from which it has sprung.

The consideration of luxury so far has used analogies of infection reliant on easily recognisable indicators where the carapaces of traditional luxury such as gilding, bejewelling and similar embellishments have been likened to the physically deteriorating effects of illness. But a parallel and ultimately more devastating expression of luxury's potential for colonisation is its insatiable desire to locate new territories, invading and assimilating, rendering those same territories transmogrified. This is often achieved most effectively by strategies based on mimesis and the introduction of imperceptible yet devastating variation, on mutation and sabotage, an extension of the recently coined 'stealth luxury' beyond its current usage to identify the reduction in logo-laden luxury accessories or the realisation by retailers that just occasionally wealthy people might purposely 'dress down' when going shopping.

In 2013 Kanye West, the American rapper, songwriter, producer and latterly fashion designer, generated a considerable amount of celebrity fashion press column inches when he unveiled the latest of his forays into design: a plain white T-shirt with a price tag of 120 US dollars. No doubt the sartorial indignation was engineered in part at least by West's publicity machine, but it was none the less surprising given that in that same year it was possible to purchase plain white T-shirts from Maison Martin Margiela for $215, a slightly longer version from Rick Owens for $255, and topping the list in 2013 a Dior Homme plain white cotton T-shirt with subtly rounded 'shirt tail' effect hem for $480. In 2014 Selfridges of London online offered Rick Owens' oversized (i.e. large) plain white T-shirt for £350 (equivalent to $547 at the time of writing), informing potential purchasers: 'Oversized, unconventional pieces have become a Rick Owens signature and this cotton-jersey t-shirt is a core look from the designer. Cut with a crew neck and short sleeves, the elongated silhouette supplies the designer's Italian-made, offbeat style.'[4] Leaving aside variations such as long sleeves, the addition of a patch pocket or the use of formerly utilitarian fabrics such as 'Aertex', all of which elevate the retail price dramatically, it was also possible to purchase plain white T-shirts from Alexandre Plokhov for £281.59, from Valentino 'featuring short sleeves' for £240, and the competitively priced Margiela basic T for £199.45 from the online retailing site Farfetch.[5] All of these T-shirts are completely plain, made from white cotton, have no visible logo or printing and are short sleeved with a conventional crew neck.

Berry again suggests that the status of certain luxury products and services is by no means fixed: 'Implicit here is the transient status of luxury goods. A luxury is not something static, it is dynamic; it is subject to development as the desires, and necessarily attendant beliefs, are met and then fuelled with further qualitative modifications or refinements' (1994: 18). Therefore an item may often commence its 'life' as a luxury – rare, exclusive, and innovative – and then as the demand for it grows and it becomes commonplace it can, in certain instances, shift from being a luxury to a necessity. Berry uses the example of sanitation, citing the water closet as a former luxury that is now 'a legally enforceable requirement' (1994: 18). This process appears to be operating in reverse in the case of the plain white 'luxury' T-shirt. What was once a utilitarian, basic item of clothing that served specific sanitary, economic and thermal functions has, in the examples given above, been completely transformed into a prohibitively expensive and, it could be argued, functionless garment, despite the often employed qualification of those same items as 'basic'.[6]

Look, you fools, you're in danger! Can't you see? They're after you! They're after all of us! Our wives, our children, everyone! They're here, already! You're next![7]

Constructed from knitted cotton jersey the T-shirt as we recognise it today takes its name after its shape; a 'T' formed by the body and sleeves. Although impossible to ascertain when the first T-shirt was made, or indeed worn, key moments have shaped its development. Its earliest incarnation was as a form of abbreviated underwear, the result of detaching the top half of the popular mid nineteenth-century one-piece suit of men's underwear, the union suit as it was known in the United States, or 'long johns', while the similar garment developed in England was more commonly known as combinations. By cutting the top half of these garments in two to form a separate (at this stage long-sleeved and buttoned) top and bottoms, it was possible for men working in hot environments to go bare-chested without the hazardous impracticality of having the top half of the suit hanging loose around the waist and hips. This somewhat ad hoc prototype of today's T-shirt underwent a number of modifications including shortening the sleeves, but as with many contemporary items of clothing, it was the standardisation of the garment for military wear that ensured the T-shirt's longevity. Issued at the end of the nineteenth century to troops to wear under their uniform to protect the jacket from sweat and other staining and to provide a layer of protection between body and outerwear, it became customary for troops to remove their jackets during work parties or when stationed in warmer climates, thus protecting the jacket from soiling and simultaneously 'normalising' what had originally been underwear as outerwear. The obvious practicality of this simple garment, its comfort, ease of laundering and all round convenience meant that it was swiftly adopted as the twentieth century progressed by working men in the United States and, somewhat later, in Europe.

The T-shirt retained its distinctly proletarian origins throughout the first half of the twentieth century, but by the 1950s and with an added impetus coming from popular culture, the T-shirt as a vestimentary sign of the 'working man' underwent a subtle but vital shift, and it embarked on its next journey as the sign of the 'physical' man. As worn by Marlon Brando in the 1951 film version of *A Streetcar Named Desire* (Figure 9.1), and then in *The Wild One*, the simple white T-shirt developed a new sexualised and oppositional appeal that resulted in rocketing sales of the garment both in the United States and elsewhere.[8] Already re-constructed as a garment loaded with socio-political meaning, when it was then subsequently

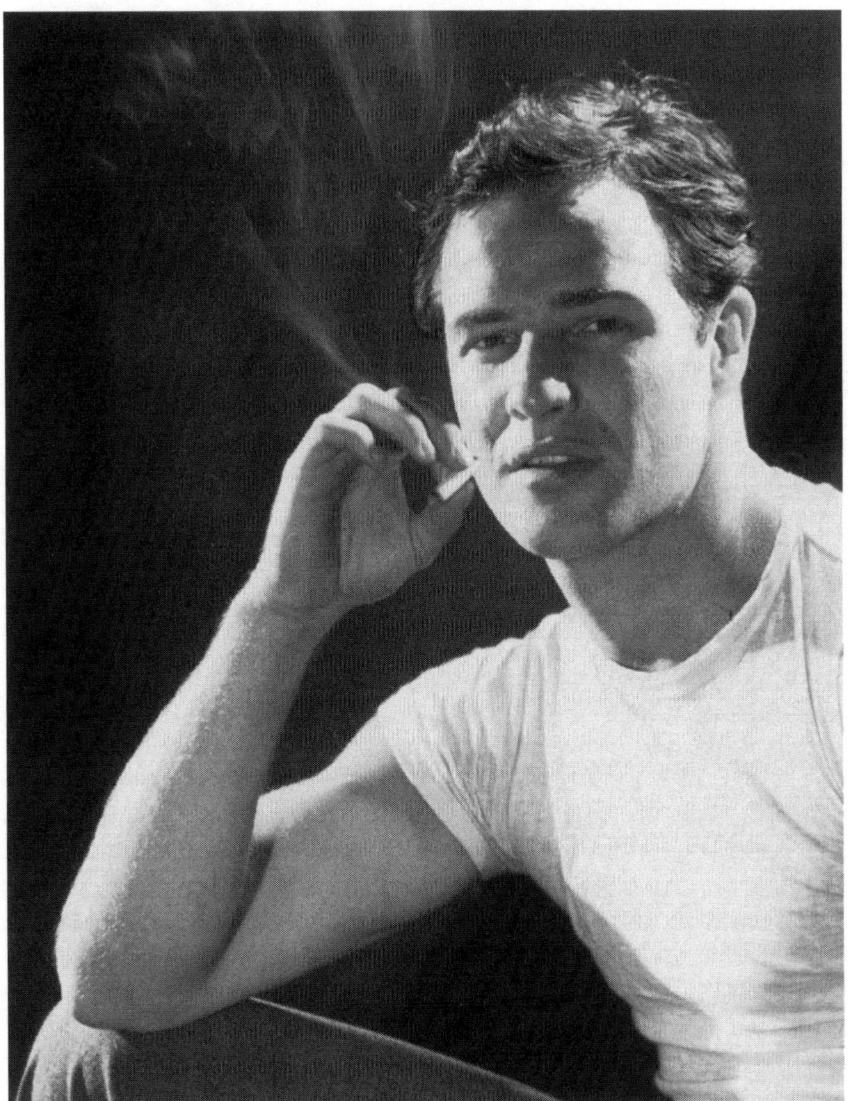

Figure 9.1 Marlon Brando, *A Streetcar Named Desire*, 1954. (Courtesy Snap/Rex)

worn by James Dean as the sartorial livery of misunderstood and rebellious youth in *Rebel Without a Cause* (Figure 9.2), the T-shirt was now able to signify rebellion, non-conformity and classlessness, and its centrality to twentieth and twenty-first century dressing was secured.[9]

So far in the history of the plain white T-shirt, this newly significant garment remained resistant to the contagion of luxury, its

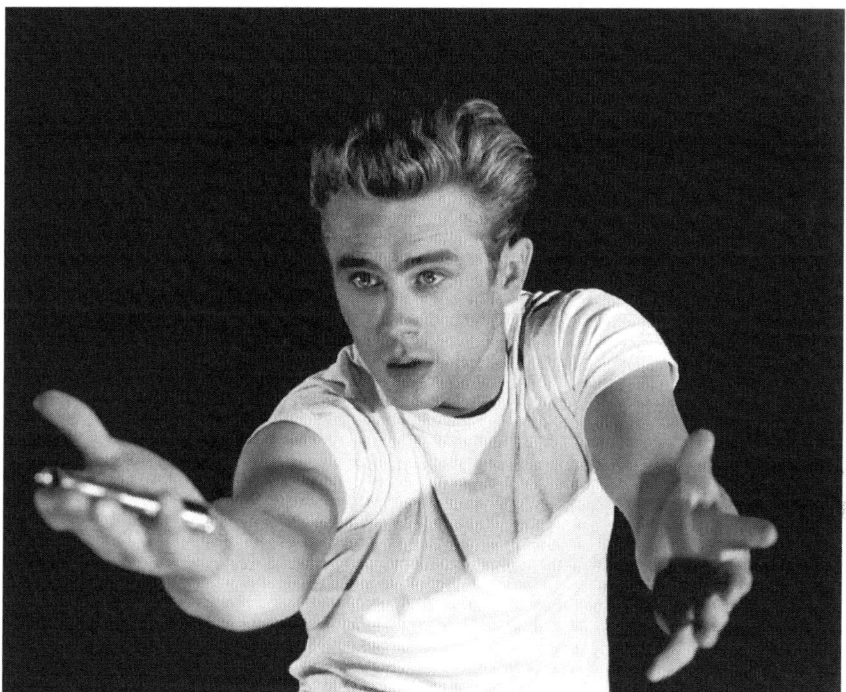

Figure 9.2 James Dean, *Rebel Without a Cause*, 1955. (Courtesy Everett Collection/Rex)

proletarian plain white cotton an unsuitable medium in which to cultivate the tumours of excess. This situation was about to change, however, due to the combination of technical advances in printing technology and the rise of global fashion branding. During the 1960s the development of screen-printing techniques, especially the rotary multicolour garment screen-printing technology specifically aimed at producing images on textiles, found its most suitable surfaces on the plain white cotton T-shirts that had by this time become ubiquitous. T-shirts became blank canvases for a bewildering variety of politically motivated, countercultural messages, alongside becoming the most profitable and effective means of advertising everything from rock concerts to restaurants. A detailed study of the early warning signs of commercial infection in the form of logo-laden T-shirts is beyond the scope of this text, which is concerned solely with the 'blank' or 'anonymous' T-shirt, but it is important to acknowledge as this technological embellishment of the plain T became the catalyst for subsequent fashion-branded shirts that provided the all-important breach in the white T-shirt's defences against the infection of luxury.

The colonisation and debilitation of the original T-shirt's

democratic message, and the replication and commandeering of its early printed anti-capitalist messages by the spread of luxury fashion logo-printed T-shirts signifying unwarranted pricing structures, exclusivity and elevated socio-economic status, can be understood as the early stages of malignant progression. The luxury logos covering every available surface of the host's body, including endlessly proliferating masses of luxury branded T-shirts, has made luxury the target of those who see this subjugation to the brand as toxic to our own sense of self. We become consumed by the all-embracing identity of the global super brand, Vuittonised, Guccied and Hermèstasised, a condition where 'the product is promoted as a "sign of me" – a signal to others of our status, aspiration or personal values' (Pavitt 2000: 44). The broken promises that accompany the display of these signs is easily targeted, giving rise more recently to a form of T-shirt détournement, the most popular examples being the 'Homiés' variant of Hermès, and the 'Célfie'/Céline shirts.[10] But as the advocates of détournement, the members of the Situationist International, themselves expressed, its very parodic methods enshrine a fundamental ineffectuality: 'The parodic-serious expresses the contradictions of an era in which we find ourselves confronted with both the urgent necessity and the near impossibility of bringing together and carrying out a totally innovative collective action' (Knabb 1981: 56). A prophecy that the T-shirt examples mentioned above exemplify, simultaneously critiquing the original luxury brands, promoting those same brands and making them known to wider audiences while the satirical shirts themselves become collector's items providing new possibilities for socio-cultural belonging or exclusion, dependent on 'getting the joke'. Luxury it seems is immune to such attacks and no amount of Homiés and Célfie variants provides effectual immunisation against luxury contamination.

> Your new bodies are growing in there. They're taking you over cell for cell, atom for atom. There is no pain. Suddenly, while you're asleep, they'll absorb your minds, your memories and you're reborn into an untroubled world.[11]

If high-end designer T-shirts bearing brand logos, embroidered, printed or otherwise can be understood as the visible signs of an infection of luxury, where the eruption of the logo on the surface of the wearer's body is akin to the physical manifestations of disease, such as discoloration, bruising, lesions and epidermal melanomas, the plain white luxury T-shirt offers an even more convincing carcinogenic analogy. As is well known, cancers are notoriously difficult to identify and diagnose, certainly in their early stages. Dubbed the 'great imitator', cancers have the ability to pass undetected, or to mimic the symptoms of other diseases. Often there are no apparent visible physical signs of their growth, and yet unobserved they are busy stimulating abnormal cell growth, 'switching off' the body's safeguarding inhibitors and invading the body's healthy tissue. Imitating, and to the untrained eye, indivisible from, its utilitarian and affordable 'host', the luxury white T-shirt wearer moves among us. Apparently the same, but subtly different, these 'imitators' conform externally to those who wear their T-shirts innocuously and consider their comfort, cost, cleanliness and practicality and little else. These sartorial aliens are a different strain, however, and evoke the figure of the replicant central to many of the most celebrated works of science fiction, from Stanislav Lem's indestructible Rheya in *Solaris*, the pods that gestate into perfect replicas of the inhabitants of *Invasion of the Body Snatchers* (Figure 9.3), John Wyndham's *Midwich Cuckoos* and of course Philip K. Dick's haunted replicants in *Do Androids Dream of Electric Sheep?*, famously translated into film as *Blade Runner*.[12] More than mere robots or artificial life forms these replicants are as real as you and I, are apparently flesh and blood, but somehow lack the full range of human emotional responses. Often needing an

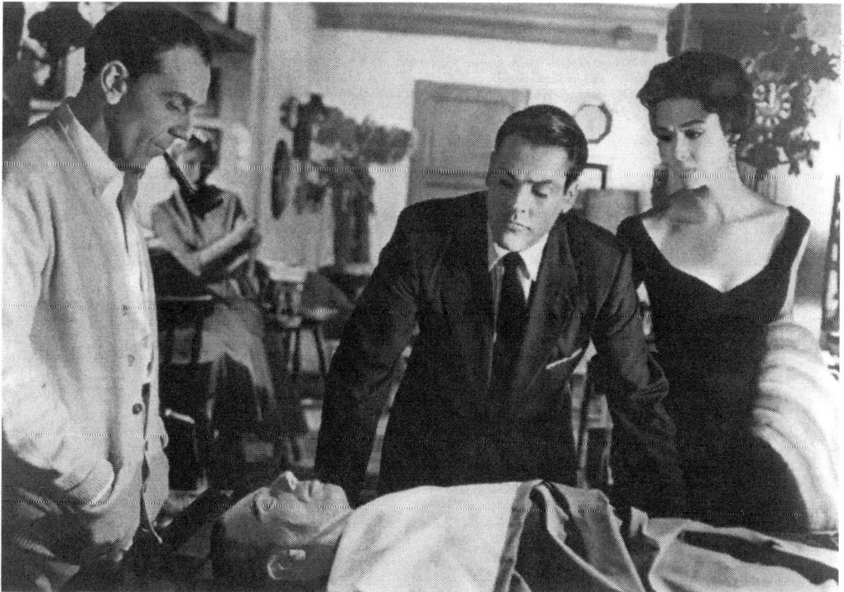

Figure 9.3 Dr Bennell examines Jack Belicec's developing replica. Still from *Invasion of the Body Snatchers*, 1956. (Courtesy Moviestore Collection/Rex)

original host to colonise and derive nutrients from, they eventually eradicate all traces of the original colony and like cancers mimic with deadly consequences their human archetypes. So it is with the luxury non-branded T-shirt, which has been spawned from the very same white cotton fibres as its egalitarian host, but replaces them with threads woven from luxury. Through the offering up of large sums of money, focused sartorial connoisseurship and brand worship, these threads go through a process of vestimentary transubstantiation, where an ordinary white T-shirt becomes a luxury T-shirt.

Huysmans' historical connoisseur, the Duc des Esseintes, provides us with another useful demonstration of what might be understood as the logical extension of stealth luxury, in the celebrated description of his plans to redecorate his apartments. Becoming bored with costly and luxurious furnishings, the sourcing and arrangement of which occupy a considerable amount of his time, des Esseintes decides to approach the problem in an entirely new, and for him, amusing manner. He elects to use the most costly and rare materials in order to create the illusion of poverty; asceticism constructed from extravagance, but which crucially for him, and for our consideration of today's luxury T-shirt, is indiscernible from the genuine, modest and affordable objects on which his luxurious subterfuge is based.

> After turning the question over in his mind, he eventually came to the conclusion that what he should try to do was this: to employ cheerful means to attain a drab end, or rather, to impress on the room as a whole, treated in this way, a certain elegance and distinction, while yet preserving its essential ugliness. He decided, in fact, to reverse the optical illusion of the stage, where cheap finery plays the part of rich and costly fabrics; to achieve precisely the opposite effect, by using magnificent materials to give the impression of old rags. (Huysmans 2003: 62)

While des Esseintes' decorative deceptions furnish us with an instructive literary referent, reflecting the fundamental dishonesty that is inherent to designer T-shirts posing as 'normal', basic garments, there are of course crucial differences. While des Esseintes utilises costly silks to imitate yellowing plaster, for example, the white shirts under discussion do not pretend to be anything other than made from simple white cotton, possibly of a finer grade, probably stitched more precisely, but intrinsically the same as their lower price 'poor relations'. The subterfuge is of a different order, less tangible and perhaps more immoral. Two and three hundred pound T-shirts that are identical to those costing a few pounds infect those who purchase and wear them with an ersatz egalitarianism, suggesting classlessness, but inwardly reinforcing economic and sartorially cultivated distinctions. These luxury T-shirts masquerading as 'casual' or 'throwaway' are of course anything but, and reflect the advanced stages of luxury infection their wearers have reached. Gone are the previous external signs of contamination, the luxury logo, the fine fabrics and distinctive styling, and in their place luxury metastasises internally, hollowing out the victim's body and principles, cloaking its deadly progress within an apparently frugal and democratic carapace. As Bourdieu suggested of culture in general, and here we might include the impossibly refined level of sartorial connoisseurship reached by the devotee of the luxury white T-shirt, 'The denial of lower, coarse, vulgar, venal, servile – in a word, natural – enjoyment, which constitutes the sacred sphere of culture, implies an affirmation of the superiority of those who can be satisfied with the sublimated, refined, disinterested, gratuitous, distinguished pleasures forever closed to the profane' (Bourdieu 1986: xxx).

Of course on one level plain white luxury T-shirts are an obvious 'brand extension', as although costly, they provide an entry level to a brand for consumers who would otherwise find its more substantial items prohibitively expensive, and they function in a manner similar to luxury perfume, or sunglasses or scarves. What sets the white T-shirt apart from the luxury accessory, however, is that these other lower priced luxury items typically provide ample opportunity for the display of logos and other distinguishing marks. Even 'luxury' perfume, typically now the first products encountered on entering the contemporary department store, and with the free availability of testers making it possible for even the layperson to cultivate a relatively subtle 'nose', means that identifying an expensive perfume from other lower priced fragrances can now be undertaken with apparent ease. The 'no logo' white T, however, requires a sartorial connoisseurship and level of expertise of a completely different order, only to be found in the historical figure of the dandy, among whose illustrious company Huysmans' des Esseintes can be included, and who is the counterpart of those cinematic and literary heroes who can spot the replicants' fatal flaws and in turn might just be able to save the world from luxury domination. The plain T-shirt's terrifying blankness makes it virtually impossible for the average mortal to distinguish between a £2.14 Fruit of the Loom white T and Margiela's basic T for £199.45, and this, it could be argued, is precisely the intention of the 'true' luxury item.[13] Real luxury should remain unrecognisable by the masses, signalling its status only to a very select group who can identify and appreciate the wearer's sartorial connoisseurship, leaving the logo-laden 'masstige' accessories to loudly declare their increasingly tenuous position as luxury for an ever-growing number of contemporary consumers.

Having invoked the figure of the dandy, it will be necessary to consider exactly whether this much-abused historical character could come to our sartorial rescue and provide an understanding and guide to the appreciation of the contemporary luxury T-shirt. Charles Baudelaire provides perhaps the most succinct formulation of the dandy, and certainly one that presents a striking proximity to today's white cotton aficionados when he writes:

> Dandyism does not even consist, as many thoughtless people seem to believe, in an immoderate taste for the toilet and material elegance. For the perfect dandy these things are no more than symbols of his aristocratic superiority of mind. Furthermore to his eyes, which are in love with *distinction* above all things, the perfection of his toilet will consist in absolute simplicity, which is the best way, in fact, of achieving the desired quality. (Baudelaire 1995: 27)

'Absolute simplicity' is certainly what is projected by Margiela's, Owens's and Valentino's T-shirts, but Baudelaire's crucial 'distinction' as a quality is perhaps more problematic. Is this distinction as difference, as merit or as worth? If difference is meant then, ostensibly, these garments do not fulfil this function, being in many cases indistinguishable from their less exclusive counterparts. Worth again seems an unsatisfactory term when considering these garments, since it is obviously too subjective, and if we understand it economically the pragmatist would certainly argue that the one yard or so of plain cotton jersey required to make a plain T-shirt is not worth £100 or more. So, perhaps an understanding of distinction as merit is most useful, with its implications of quality, excellence and importance, all epithets exhaustively employed as part of the discourse of contemporary luxury consumerism.

The recognition and understanding of the small distinguishing detail underpins a popular understanding of connoisseurship, whether that be literary, artistic, epicurean or, essentially, sartorial. Baudelaire's dandy considering a white T-shirt today would be able to recognise with ease the difference between a pure cotton and cotton polyester mix for example, the quality and tension of the sewing thread, whether the seams have been reinforced, the width of neckband and hems and so on as crucial indicators of the shirt's 'distinction'. But Baudelaire also suggests a more metaphysical, perhaps even supernatural dimension of discernment to the dandy. A sensibility so refined, attuned and innate that it expresses itself not merely in the clothes he chooses to wear but in the manner in which he inhabits them, a 'oneness' with his wardrobe, and where he is seen wearing it: 'Nothing is missed, his lightness of step, his social aplomb, the simplicity in his air of authority, his way of wearing a coat or riding a horse, his bodily attitudes which are always relaxed but betray an inner energy', a relationship with clothing that today is best, but inadequately, translated as 'personal style' (Baudelaire 1995: 29).

Philippe Perrot in his *Fashioning the Bourgeoisie* suggests that

> Clothing, like language, always happens somewhere in geographical space. In its form, color, material, construction, and function – and because of the behaviour it implies – clothing displays obvious signs, attenuated markings or residual traces of struggles, cross-cultural contacts, borrowings, exchanges between economic regions or cultural areas as well as among groups within a single society. (Perrot 1994: 7)

It is this instinctual understanding of the import of clothing and its ability to be read, deciphered and translated like a text that is fundamental to the dandy as a sartorial connoisseur. He shares this same combination of scrupulously researched vestimentary knowledge and instinctual knowing with that other great nineteenth-century figure: the detective. Conan Doyle's Sherlock Holmes, for example, places an encyclopaedic knowledge of nineteenth-century clothing production and retailing at the heart of many decisions he makes about accepting a case when first interviewing potential clients, but even more important perhaps is his intrinsic understanding of how clothing is worn, and shaped by the wearer, as clues to a person's habits and behaviour betrayed by the series of tell-tale signs left on the clothing and which underpin his celebrated 'forensic' method of detection. Numerous examples of Holmes's otherworldly, even dandaical affiliation to clothing can be found, but the following example from *The Adventure of the Blue Carbuncle* (1892) distils Holmes' dazzling technique. In the tale, Holmes constructs a man's character and habits solely from reading the vestimentary clues left behind on his hat. He proposes that the owner of the hat is highly intellectual (its size suggesting a large head, therefore a large brain), has had his hair recently cut at a barber's and uses pomade (scissor-cut ends of hair stuck together and caught in the hat's lining), has fallen on hard times recently (it is a good quality but old-fashioned style of hat), is unloved by his wife (it has not been recently brushed), rarely goes out of the house (the dust caught in the hat band is of a domestic fluffy variety rather than grittier street dirt) and probably does not have a gas supply in his house (candlewax stains suggest the use of candles for illumination rather than gas jets) (Conan Doyle 2005).[14] This bravura display of sartorial connoisseurship is of the same order as that of Baudelaire's dandy and the progenitors he pays homage to: Sheridan, Brummell and Byron.

Knowing just how revealing clothing can be, the true dandy of course will go to extreme lengths to confuse the untrained eye of the novice, laying false clues or dressing (apparently) so unremarkably as to escape consideration or notice at all. In his introduction to the third edition of Baudelaire's collection of poems *Les Fleurs du Mal*, the poet Théophile Gautier suggested, possibly apocryphally, that Baudelaire's consciousness of what Elizabeth Wilson has termed the 'unspeakably meaningful' quality of clothing meant that in order to avoid appearing vulgar Baudelaire would sandpaper the nap of his new suit so as to dull its shiny newness to make it appear more 'lived in', as contemporary sartorial discourse might express it (Baudelaire 1868; Wilson 2009: 3). This reduction of newness, the moderation of the pristine, is the process that des Esseintes took to its limits in order to construct his humble 'monk's cell' of a bedroom, where 'the ceiling was similarly covered with white Holland, which had the appearance of plaster without its bright shiny look; as for the cold tiles of the floor, he managed to hit them off quite well, thanks to a carpet patterned in red squares, with the wood dyed white in places where sandals and boots could be supposed to have left their mark' (Huysmans 2003: 62). This willingness to purposely 'dress down' can also be understood as the motivation inspiring today's luxury white T-shirt wearers, a desire to appear ordinary, a man of the people who cares little about his clothing and only for practicality, whereas in fact he, and only a very select band of observers, know the real truth, that his 'humble' white T-shirt is in fact an extraordinary garment, its blandness and unremarkable appearance achieved at great cost.

Roland Barthes' extension of Baudelaire's formulation of dandyism acknowledges it as a twofold process, not just an 'ethos' but a 'technique', the detail again understood as paramount, suggesting that the dandy sometimes

> relies on wealth to distance himself from the poor, other times he wants his clothes to look worn out to distance himself from the rich – this is precisely the job of the 'detail' which is to allow the dandy to escape the masses and never to be engulfed by them; his singularity is absolute in essence, but limited in substance, as he must never fall into eccentricities, for that is an eminently copyable form. (Barthes 2006: 67)

The eccentricity that Barthes notes is also an essential component of the development of the contemporary white luxury T-shirts under discussion. With the working-class, practical white T-shirt newly augmented as the garb of the rebellious outsider, thanks in no small part to its manifestation in mid twentieth-century popular cinema, fashion, as always, did not take long to appropriate its proletarian, or 'street', cachet. T-shirts started to appear on runways as an 'ironic twist' to more formal items of dress, a way of 'dressing down' a tailored suit or overcoat. Yves Saint Laurent's celebrated female version of a man's tuxedo evening suit, or 'le smoking' as it was dubbed, although originally teamed with shirt and tie, or worn with nothing underneath to emphasise the inherent gender play that made Saint Laurent's suit such a lasting success, was in reality worn (whether a Saint Laurent or one of the many other versions of the masculine suit for women produced by designers throughout the 1970s and '80s) by women more often with a plain white T-shirt, a less obvious and clichéd version of a shirt and tie, and less confrontational than going naked underneath.[15] The plain white T-shirt, often in costly fabrics such as silk or the finest of wools, started to make its appearance from the 1970s as a staple item, along with a good tailored trouser suit, in the wardrobes of professional women worldwide. A few years later it would find its way back onto the male body worn under the newer unstructured suits pioneered by designers such as Giorgio Armani, where a fitted, tailored shirt and tie would have looked out of place. This was then given an immediate popularity boost, as had happened when Brando and Dean wore their T-shirts as a sign of rebellion, when Crockett and Tubbs – the characters played by Don Johnson and Philip Michael Thomas, respectively, in the phenomenally successful TV series *Miami Vice* – championed the wearing of T-shirts under pastel coloured suits whose casual lightweight cut was influenced by designers such as Versace, Hugo Boss and of course Giorgio Armani (Figure 9.4).[16] The two stars' regular appearances in unstructured, pale coloured suits with the sleeves rolled up, T-shirts and loafers worn without socks (as Barthes reminds us the detail is paramount) became one of the most defining menswear looks of the 1980s, making the plain T-shirt acceptable as the vestimentary partner to the new relaxed tailoring originating from Italy and which found an appreciative audience, especially in America.

If the white T-shirt as the sign of a new informal attitude to men's dressing provided new possibilities to dress down, and indeed an antidote to the formality of suit wearing, it also suggested a certain level of social, economic and sartorial autonomy. The studied informality

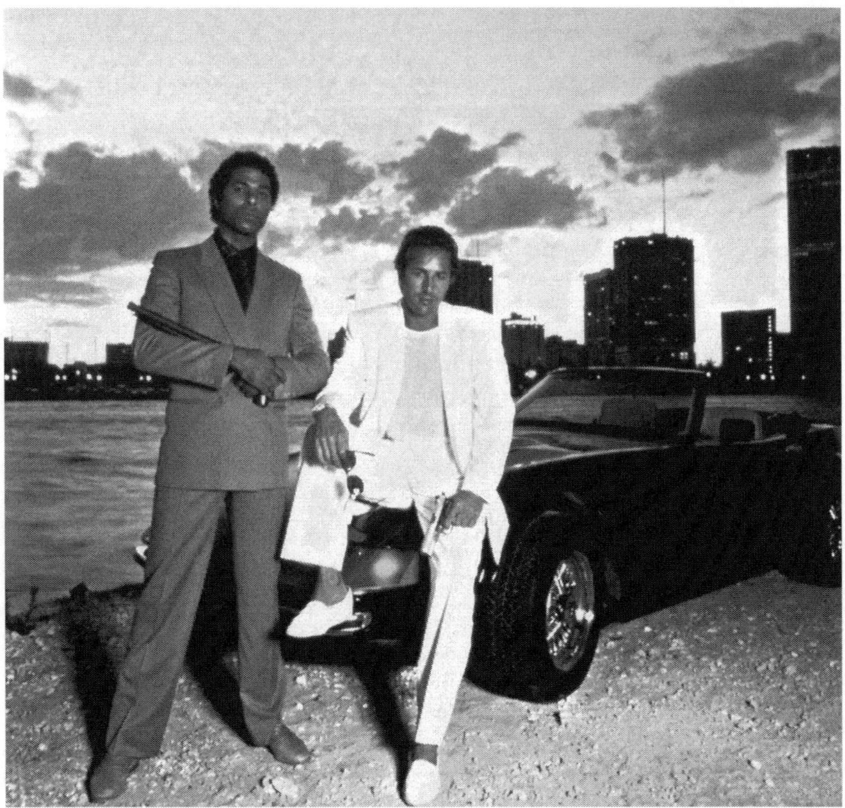

Figure 9.4 Don Johnson and Philip Michael Thomas, *Miami Vice*, 1984–99. (Courtesy Everett Collection/Rex)

proclaimed its wearers as wealthy enough to afford Italian tailoring yet also unconstrained by the more formal dress codes indicated by the conventional suit and tie; Crockett and Tubbs' maverick and hedonistic lifestyles thus find their perfect expression in their wardrobes. While the white designer T-shirt worn under a pastel suit became a metaphor for a lifestyle typified by luxury and excess, elsewhere the white T-shirt provided the ground for a much more cerebral and often more ascetic deconstruction of the parameters of the suit and of men's tailoring in general, and was championed by a new elite professional class. The so-called Japanese revolution that took Paris by storm in the late 1970s and on into the 1980s, occurred when conceptual designers such as Kenzo Takada, Issey Miyake, Yohji Yamamoto and Rei Kawakubo presented clothes on the Paris runways that directly challenged Western conventions of sexuality, tailoring and finish.[17] The plain white T-shirt provided a fundamental 'base layer' for these designers, especially in their designs for menswear, using it to contrast with the experimental interrogations of the man's formal suit and jacket they were undertaking at this time. The plain white T-shirt became the uniform for a host of new professionals in the fields of media, advertising, design (especially architecture and product design), fine art and 'thinking' rock stars, who understood the structural and conceptual testing grounds that their Japanese designer suits represented and which needed the foil of an unremarkable and ubiquitous plain white T. Asymmetric lapels, uneven hem lines, contrasting fabrics used on the same garment and unfinished or 'deconstructed' seams and hems needed the contrast of basic white cotton to offset what Barthes' would no doubt have termed their 'eccentricities', the T-shirts acting as 'straight men' to their sartorial 'funny partners'.

While both aesthetically and visually T-shirts provided a plain cotton contrast to these vestimentary pyrotechnics, they also retained an economic function by juxtaposing the obvious expense of these designer suits with the minimalism of plain cotton (although of course a plain white Commes des Garçons T-shirt from this period, as today, was not exactly a bargain).[18] They also signalled, to the uninitiated at least, that this was not a suit to be taken seriously in the accepted sense but ironically, subversively, or for those who were seduced by conceptual fashion's manifestos, as a sign of revolution. The egalitarian traces and 'residual markings' noted by Perrot, donated by the presence of a white T-shirt to these extremely costly items worn as the uniform of the new design-conscious elite that emerged in the 1980s, were essential to offset, obscure and shore up these same garments' philosophical shallowness, and the suggestion that such suits with their instantly dated detailing could ever provide a real antidote to the Western fashion system (Perrot 1994: 7). The recognition of these white T-shirts as luxury items is made manifest by the fact that they are teamed with the conspicuousness of Japanese sartorial aesthetic detailing, whose very expense is signalled by its conceptual difficulty, an expense that by extension must also spread to the T-shirts chosen to be worn with them as foils.

Returning to today's anonymous luxury white T-shirts, a consideration of which began this text, no such easy contrast is available – the lack of 'eccentric' detailing and the fact that more often than not these Ts are worn on their own, not as a context for more expensive items of clothing, makes them even harder to recognise and distinguish from their more humble and modestly priced counterparts. They require even greater powers of observation than our sartorially savvy dandy, and so it is necessary to return once more to another classic literary figure, who like Holmes possessed extraordinary powers of observation. In Edgar Allan Poe's celebrated tale 'The Purloined Letter', August Dupin, his prototype detective, deploys his powers of 'ratiocination', as Poe termed it – a combination of deductive reasoning and empathy, which allowed him to 'think' like the criminals he studied. In the tale he discusses the efficacy of hiding objects in plain sight and how the best way of concealing something is not to hide it at all, but to do the reverse and present it so obviously that it escapes attention by those expecting and looking for more obscure hiding places and clues. Here he discusses this principle by referring to a guessing game based on identifying place names on a map: 'These, like the over-largely lettered signs and placards of the street, escape observation by dint of being excessively obvious; and here the physical oversight is precisely analogous with the moral inapprehension by which the intellect suffers to pass unnoticed these considerations which are too obtrusively and too palpably self-evident' (Poe 1974: 345).

Similarly, today's luxury-loving costly white T-shirt wearers hide their sartorial expenditure in plain sight, deriving pleasure from the fact that only themselves and a very select body of observers and T-shirt aficionados will recognise their expenditure for what it is, while the rest of an unassuming populace will register their T-shirts as indistinguishable from any other. This is the embodiment of stealth luxury, undetectable; the privileged knowledge of their cost, provenance and perhaps the touch of these luxury T's is their greatest asset, where all other vestimentary clues as to their superiority and rarity have been excised – no excessive detailing, no elaborate top-stitching, no apparent 'styling'. These T-shirts operate like dysfunctional, costly linings, linings worn on the outside whose richness and opulence are known only to the wearer, but in this case the opulence is absent and yet still provides an internalised contact with luxury, understated and undetectable. As *British Vogue* noted of certain London couturiers' work in September of 1960: 'Luxury is not the kind of thing that flaunts itself . . . a costume's lining may be one of its chief attractions.'[19] This is a luxury which turns inwards, away from excessive and conspicuous displays of wealth, slowly taking over the body of its wearer with the proliferating tumours of superiority. Not for these wearers the vulgar displays of wealth, no need for the reflected glory they might accrue from the envious glances of passers-by, instead a complacency and self-righteousness born from the knowledge that the expenditure involved in these garments is only measured metaphysically and privately, self-gratifying and self-satisfying, in short, the epitome of luxury. Barthes' dandy revelled in this self-absorption:

> Furthermore, he takes distinction that bit further: its essence is no longer social for him, but metaphysical; the dandy stands in opposition not at all to the upper class and lower class, but only in absolute terms to the individual and the banal; so the individual is not a generalized idea for him; it is him alone, purified of all recourse to comparison, to the extent even that, like Narcissus, it is to himself and him alone that he offers a reading of his clothing. (Barthes 2006: 67)

Now riddled with this most insidious and internalised of luxury's endlessly replicating carcinogens, the white T-shirt wearer is inexorably emptied of all rational judgement and assumes Baudelaire's 'haughty exclusiveness, provocative in its very coldness' (Baudelaire 1995: 28). Baudelaire also suggests, most pertinently for this current volume, that dandyism is at its most widespread in periods of transition, for him expressed by the moments between the decline of aristocracy and the establishment of true democracy. Given that the figure of the dandy, or perhaps we might dub him the sartorial connoisseur, is a key figure when undertaking any serious study of luxury, can we then also understand him as central to the emerging field of critical luxury studies, which acknowledges both the historical formations of luxury (Baudelaire's sandpapered suit) as well as its constantly diversifying contemporary manifestations (Rick Owens's £350 white T-shirt)? Perhaps the greatest accomplishment of today's transitional dandy is his ultimate reproducibility, and the contagion of luxury is now so endemic that all we need do to aspire to the dizzy heights of sartorial connoisseurship is don a plain white T-shirt, imagine it to be the product of Margiela, Owens or Dior, and follow the advice given by Dr Miles Bennell, the hero of *Invasion of the Body Snatchers*:

> Keep your eyes a little wide and blank. Show no interest or excitement.[20]

Notes

1. Voiceover from *Invasion of the Body Snatchers*, 1956, dir. Don Siegel.
2. It is possible to purchase a 'luxury enema bidet seat' featuring variable spray direction, deodoriser, adjustable seat and water temperature and drying actions from sites such as www.bidetpro.com.

3. 'Masstige' is a portmanteau term consisting of mass and prestige to denote affordable or mass-market luxury.
4. From http://www.selfridges.com/en/rick-owens-oversized-cotton-jersey-t-shirt_348–3001846-RU15S4262BA11/?previewAttribute=White (accessed 9 November 2014).
5. http://www.farfetch.com (accessed 9 November 2014).
6. Many of these 'luxury' designer T-shirts are described as 'basic', a linguistic deceit that bestows on them a practical and essential quality, implying that these exceptionally uneconomical garments are somehow a necessary item in one's wardrobe.
7. Dialogue from *Invasion of the Body Snatchers*.
8. *A Streetcar Named Desire*, 1951, dir. Elia Kazan. *The Wild One*, 1953, dir. Laslo Benedek.
9. *Rebel Without a Cause*, 1955, dir. Nicholas Ray.
10. I refer here to the highly successful range of T-shirts produced by Reason, a New York based sports and casual wear manufacturer established in 2004 who 'struck gold' when they produced the first of their 'détourned' Homiés T-shirts, satirising the established French luxury brand Hermès by subverting the company's name and substituting its famous carriage logo with an American taxi cab explaining on their website: 'The French have no idea how to pronounce our American slang in just the same way we cant pronounce the names of their high-end brands. Here, we are homies, there we are Homiés' (http://reasonclothing.com/products/homies-tee-white-black; accessed 9 December 2014) The Homiés line has since been followed by Prada (Primadonna), Givenchy (Givencheap) and Céline (Céline Dion and Cénile parents) editions, all of which incorporate the distinctive typography and logos of the original brands. Numerous versions of the Céline/Célfie T-shirt are available following the singer Rihanna's much publicised and discussed selfies while wearing an original Céline T-shirt. The linguistic pun proving an obvious commercial success and also referencing the term's recent use to describe the situation where on being incarcerated the detainee produces an iPhone selfie from the prison cell, hence 'celfie'.
11. Dialogue from *Invasion of the Body Snatchers*.
12. The screenplay for the film *Invasion of the Body Snatchers* was based on the novel *The Body Snatchers* by Jack Finney (originally serialised in *Colliers Magazine* in 1954).
13. Men's white heavy cotton T-shirt available from Amazon, http://www.amazon.co.uk/Fruit-Loom-Heavy-Cotton-T-Shirt/dp/B004FKFDOE (accessed 11 December 2014).
14. For more on the forensic method and clothing and its formulation within popular culture, see Faiers (2013).
15. 'Le Smoking' was originally created by Yves Saint Laurent in 1966. It garnered immediate attention from the fashion press and swiftly secured its place within popular fashion culture. It can be considered

as paving the way for what, in the 1980s, would come to be known as 'power dressing', a move towards professional women dressing more androgynously, and, therefore, powerfully, in suits to combat the institutionalised sexism women were increasingly confronting in the workplace from the 1970s onwards.

16. *Miami Vice* was created by Anthony Yerkovich and produced by Michael Mann for NBC. The series starred Don Johnson as James 'Sonny' Crockett and Philip Michael Thomas as Ricardo 'Rico' Tubbs, two police detectives working undercover in Miami. The series ran for five seasons on NBC from 1984 to 1989.

17. The so-called Japanese revolution refers to the first (from the late 1970s to the early 1980s) Paris collections of Japanese designers Kenzo Takada, Issey Miyake, Yohji Yamamoto, Rei Kawakubo and Hanae Mori. For a detailed examination of this subject, see Kawamura (2004).

18. Commes des Garçons is the highly successful brand created and overseen by Rei Kawakubo, arguably the most influential of all of the 'conceptual' Japanese designers.

19. From the article 'Couture Clothes: Are They Worth the Money?' *British Vogue*, September 1960.

20. Dialogue from *Invasion of the Body Snatchers*.

References

Barthes, R. (2006), *The Language of Fashion*, ed. A. Stafford and M. Carter, Oxford: Berg.

Baudelaire, C. (1868), *Les Fleurs du Mal*, Paris: Michel Lévy Frères.

Baudelaire, C. (1995), *The Painter of Modern Life and Other Essays*, ed. J. Mayne, London: Phaidon.

Berry, C. (1994), *The Idea of Luxury: A Conceptual and Historical Investigation*, Cambridge: Cambridge University Press.

Bourdieu, P. (1986), *Distinction: A Social Critique of the Judgement of Taste*, London: Routledge.

Conan Doyle, Arthur (2005), *The New Annotated Sherlock Holmes*, ed. L. S. Klinger, New York: W. W. Norton.

Faiers, J. (2013), *Dressing Dangerously: Dysfunctional Fashion in Film*, New Haven, CT and London: Yale University Press.

Huysmans, J.-K. (2003), *Against Nature (À Rebours)*, London: Penguin Books.

Kawamura, Y. (2004), *The Japanese Revolution in Paris Fashion*, London, Bloomsbury.

Knabb, K. (ed.) (1981), *Situationist International Anthology*, Berkeley: Bureau of Public Secrets.

Pavitt, J. (ed.) (2000), *Brand.new*, London: V&A Publications.

Perrot, P. (1994), *Fashioning the Bourgeoisie: A History of Clothing in the Nineteenth Century*, Princeton: Princeton University Press.

Poe, Edgar Allan (1974), *Selected Writings of Edgar Allan Poe*, ed. D. Galloway, London: Penguin.
Veblen, T. (1899), *The Theory of the Leisure Class: An Economic Study of Institutions*, New York: Macmillan.
Wilson, E. (2009), *Adorned in Dreams: Fashion and Modernity*, London: I. B. Tauris.

Chapter 10

Online Luxury: Geographies of Production and Consumption and the Louis Vuitton Website

Agnès Rocamora

In their study of online action, Steven Schneider and Kirsten Foot develop the notion of a 'web sphere', that is, 'a set of dynamically defined digital resources spanning multiple web sites deemed relevant or related to a central event, concept or theme, and often connected by hyperlinks' (2005: 158). The web now abounds with sites devoted to luxury fashion, forming what can be called, drawing on Schneider and Foot, the luxury web sphere. The present chapter is devoted to one of its iterations, the Louis Vuitton website, and interrogates the ways a luxury brand produces, and reproduces, online the logics of distinction and social differentiation that underpin luxury (Bourdieu 1984; Lipovetsky 2003; Michaud 2013). It looks at how exclusivity is built into a site, and, in the process, identifies the actors who are included in, as well as those excluded from, luxury as defined by Louis Vuitton.

In the first section, I situate the brand in the context of the luxury fashion industry. I then discuss the notion of websites as hypertexts to engage with the issue of the problems that might arise from researching such texts, and to briefly reflect on my approach to the Vuitton website. In the second section, I focus on the idea of production, and in the third on consumption, for both discourses on production and consumption inform much of the website; the former by way of the various stories and histories of the making of Louis Vuitton goods that are narrated there, the latter by virtue of the site being largely devoted to the promoting and selling of goods. A commercial website is a 'space of consumption' (Currah 2003: 5). Interrogating such a space, I look at its social make-up to ask: who are its imagined consumers? Which also means: who are its absent 'others'?

The Vuitton website, however, is also a space of production, both in the sense that it devotes many words and images to the topic of the production of Louis Vuitton goods, but also in the sense that this putting into discourse is itself an act of production, a 'symbolic production' (Bourdieu 1993a). As Pierre Bourdieu reminds us, a whole system of words and images is interposed between producers and consumers of fashion. This system acts as a screen which participates in an act of 'collective belief' and 'collective misrecognition' without which fashion cannot thrive (Bourdieu 1993b: 138). Similarly Roland Barthes writes that 'In order to blunt the buyers' calculating consciousness, a veil must be drawn around the object – a veil of images, or reasons, of meanings' (1990: xi). Thus when Zygmunt Bauman notes that 'The culture of consumer society is mostly about forgetting, not learning' (1998: loc. 1285), one could add that it is also about concealing. In this chapter I show how Vuitton use the website to hide certain dimensions of the production of goods – automatisation, outsourcing and marketing – the better to construct themselves as a luxury brand. As Currah also observes, a web store is 'a culturally encoded aesthetic trap: a virtual landscape of consumption that has been constructed and displayed according to the philosophies of executive corporate actors which intend to attract, retain and transact with those surfers who are most likely to become long-term "exchange- partners"' (2003: 9).

If the section on production is about concealing, that on consumption could be said to be about forgetting; forgetting that the world is differentiated along the lines of class, gender and race, and that luxury goods, which are 'distinguished and distinctive, selected and selective' (Bourdieu 1984: 278), are central to this process of differentiation. In that section I comment on the website's implied consumers, looking at the ways distinctions of class, gender and race are articulated to support the construction of Louis Vuitton as a brand reserved for a privileged social group.

Digital Luxury

Christopher J. Berry (1994) identifies clothing as one of the categories of luxury, alongside sustenance, shelter and leisure. High fashion goods in particular, and the related category of accessories, are indeed a very visible part of what is often referred to as the luxury industry. For luxury is an industry, one which shares with capitalism a common history, commercial profit and the good of the nation having, since the nineteenth century, been invoked as a way of 'de-moralising' luxury and justifying its production and consumption (Sombart 1967; Berry 1994). Today luxury is a thriving economic sector, and luxury groups have embraced elaborate strategies of marketing (Michaud 2013: 63). Thus, €217 billion was spent on luxury in 2013 and 'More than 10m new customers are entering the market each year' (*Economist* 2014). Educational programmes have been developed – such as, in America, NYU's MBA Luxury Marketing Specialization – that train students in the business of luxury; luxury consultancy firms abound; online and offline media titles devote regular columns to the topic (e.g. the *Financial Times*' 'Luxury 360'; *Women's Wear Daily*'s 'Designer/Luxury'), when they are not themselves entirely devoted to it (e.g. *Forbes Life*; *Luxure*; *Luxuriousmagazine.com*; *Uptown*); and vast numbers of business books discuss luxury. For while luxury has received much attention from the fields of marketing and management studies, apart from a few exceptions (see, for instance, Berry 1994; Sekora 1977; Lipovetsky 2003), it has largely been ignored by social sciences and humanities scholars.

Within the luxury industry, one name stands out: Louis Vuitton Moët Hennessy (LVMH), the leading luxury group. In 2013 it generated a record sales figure of 29.15 billion euros, and a profit of 3.4 billion euros (*Challenges* 2014). The group comprises a range of divisions and related brands – 'Wines and spirits'; 'Perfumes and Cosmetics'; 'Watches and Jewelry'; 'Fashion and leather goods', the latter being the most profitable division and 'Louis Vuitton' one of its 'star brands' (Cavender and Kincade 2014; LVMH 2014).

Specialising in trunks, the Louis Vuitton company was created in 1854, after the name of its French founder. Success grew quickly correlatively to the 'transport revolution' that was taking place at the time, the company finding its customers in the high society of the Second Empire (Pasols 2005: 56). In 1997 the first Louis Vuitton website was launched, signalling the brand's entry into the web sphere. It now comes in different languages, the content being largely the same across all editions.

The luxury web sphere consists in sites that generally fall into three categories: social media; e-commerce; e-magazines. The first category includes platforms such as Facebook, blogs, vlogs, Tumblrs, Instagram, YouTube and Pinterest, where accounts are owned by brands or private individuals. The second category includes both luxury brands' e-commerce sites and multi-brand e-tailers such as Net-a-Porter and Moda Operandi, as well as rental, discount and reuse luxury sites such as eBay, Vestiaire Collective or luxTnT.com. Such sites can be connected through hyperlinks, a key feature of the web sphere (Schneider and Foot 2005). Indeed, on the World Wide Web (WWW), texts are hypertexts, that is texts which by virtue of being related to other texts through hyperlinks are always on the move, making of the web a fluid, borderless, a-centred space

(Landow 1997; Bolter 2001). The Vuitton website, for instance, opens onto a multitude of pages, which users can access by clicking on the site's Instagram, YouTube or Facebook icons, for instance, or on words such as 'here', as in a post 'celebrating Monogram' in the News section (10–20 October 2014).

However, hyperlinking is also a highly controlled and strategic practice (Hindman 2009), and not all hypertexts offer equal unbounded movement across the WWW. The Vuitton site principally links back onto itself, with limited opportunities to leave the site, except perhaps when linking to the brand's Instagram, Facebook and Twitter accounts. The movement of the user across its pages is largely contained within them, and the flow of texts largely a flow of Louis Vuitton texts. The posts in the 'celebrating Monogram' series, for instance, never link to the site of the artists involved in the celebration, a linking which would be common practice on fashion blogs, for instance.

Manuel Castells opposes the idea that the information age is placeless. He notes:

> The Internet Age has been hailed as the end of geography. In fact, the Internet has a geography of its own, a geography made of networks and nodes that process information flows generated and managed from places ... New territorial configurations emerge from simultaneous processes of spatial concentration, decentralization, and connection, relentlessly labored by the variable geometry of global information flows. (Castells 2001: 208)

This geography also includes that which covers the path of users across web pages and which companies engineer through their strategy of hyperlinking. Decentralisation may well occur on the WWW, allowing for a broader range of voices to be articulated, as can be the case, for instance, with the fashion blogosphere (Pham 2011; Rocamora 2011, 2012). But processes of re-centring and concentration also take place through hyperlinkings that are creative of specific configurations of flows and movements that enable companies to create a geography of their own, to paraphrase Castells. By controlling its site's architecture of hyperlinks, a company can control the digital trajectory of its users, directing them through a path that serves its interest. Thus, as Cavanagh puts it: 'Against the image of the internet as constantly in flux, a libertarian, anarchic space, we have the relentless accretion of channels which form and modulate discourse. Against the idea of the internet as a smooth space, we have a highly striated one' (2007: 56), an idea I return to later.

Hypertexts bring together a variety of signs and genres of signs:

words, sounds and images. On the Vuitton website, for instance, one finds live-streamed or archived videos of fashion shows, short films, images of the advertising campaigns, news on the latest Vuitton events. This variety and abundance of texts makes of websites rich and dynamic platforms for the interrogation of the ways companies represent themselves online. However, it is also a richness that, by virtue of being synonymous with a vast quantity of data, often transient, can quickly overcome the researcher. Web texts are 'temporal and malleable', features which, however, like their 'hyperlinked and multilevel nature', make them difficult to analyse (Schneider and Foot 2005: 159, 157).

To contain the flow of texts on the Vuitton website, and to capture its dynamic nature, between June and December 2014 I visited it weekly, often daily. By bookmarking sections and pages and taking screen grabs I built a record of its content. By taking notes on my trajectory through its pages, in the manner of ethnographic field notes (see, for instance, Kozinets 2010), I traced some of the paths the website offers, critically exploring one's possible journey through Louis Vuitton online.

Schneider and Foot (2005) make a distinction between three types of approaches to the web sphere: the first they call 'discursive or rhetorical' analysis. It focuses on the texts and images of websites. The second, a 'structural/feature' analysis, focuses 'on the structure of the site, such as the number of pages, hierarchical ordering of pages, etc.' The third concentrates on analysing 'multi-actor, cross-site action on the web' (Schneider and Foot 2005: 164–5). My approach for this chapter is an instance of the first approach, one which aims at unpacking the discursive construction or symbolic production of luxury according to Louis Vuitton.

Finally, various authors have commented on the limits of the distinction that is often made between on- and offline spaces, and where the latter are seen as more real than the former, an idea which the expression 'In Real Life' (IRL) captures, to contrast, presumably, with the fake or false life of virtual space. However, 'Life on the screen' (Turkle 1995) is no less or no more real than life off the screen. Rather, the two are complementary (see, for instance, Kendall 1999; Sudweeks and Simoff 1999), an approach that informed my engagement with the Vuitton website. Looking at this platform led me to look into various aspects of the company, and of luxury, offline, and vice versa, the better to reflect on the ways the digital and the bricks and mortar, to borrow an expression from the field of retail, complement each other. In that respect then, hypertexts are also texts in permanent dialogue with offline texts, both being caught up in a complex network of intertextuality that reaches across on- and offline spaces.

The Production of Louis Vuitton

The 'World of Louis Vuitton', in the site's navigation bar, invites users to find out more about 'La Maison', including its 'Brand protection' policy. The page devoted to this topic opens on to a close-up of (white) hands at work with a hammer on an LV-embossed trunk, suggesting that Louis Vuitton luggage is made by hand (Figure 10.1). It is not mass produced, in contrast, the site implies, to counterfeit goods such as 'a cheap bag [bought] on a street in a faraway city while on holiday', and which the brand warns against, stating that counterfeiting threatens the 'creativity and the rights of designers, artists and brands'. Both the image of the hands and the reference to 'artists' anchor the brand in the realms of craft and the arts, away from mass fashion. Indeed, references to the former abound on the website. The men's fall collection 2014, for instance, is described as 'a unique combination of cutting-edge innovation and traditional craftsmanship' (News section, 1 August). The text captioning the Majestueux tote PM states that it is 'the result of the finest craftsmanship', and a pendant designed after a trunk is said to have been 'recreated with thorough craftsmanship'.

However, when in 2010 Louis Vuitton ran a series of 'Savoir

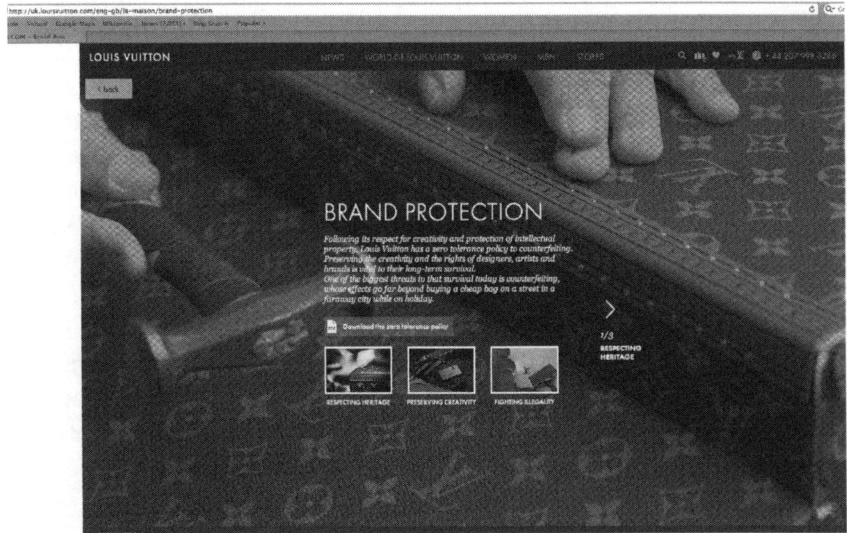

Figure 10.1 Representing Louis Vuitton luggage as handmade

Faire' (Know-how) advertisements depicting workers using artisanal techniques such as needle and thread, suggesting goods were hand-stitched, the Advertising Standards Authority ruled against the company on the grounds that not only did Vuitton also use sewing machines but they declined to reveal the proportion of work that is handmade (Hickman 2010). Thus, reporting on the Asnières-sur-Seine Vuitton workshop, Dana Thomas mentions the thousands of bags that are produced there every year. Some items are handmade but many others are machine-manufactured on assembly lines (Thomas 2007: 20).

An entry on the website is devoted to 'personalisation'. A video features (white) hands at work, once again reinforcing the idea of craftsmanship. The camera focuses on the hands embedding initials in a leather good, presumably those of its owner or future owner. The website specifies that the technique is called 'hot stamping' and the 'complementary service is a stamp of distinction and elegance'. Personalisation singles out objects and their owners, seemingly emphasising the uniqueness of both things and persons. However, as Jean Baudrillard (1996 [1968]: 142) reminds us, serially produced goods can only be modified at a superficial level. Their personalisation creates marginal differences only, a process which nevertheless enables the company to support the idea of uniqueness that its discourse on craftsmanship promotes.

Dallabona (2014: 218, 219) observes that luxury fashion brands are keen to emphasise craftsmanship as a means to add value to the objects they sell. This is a myth, however, that hides the fact that many fashion goods are mass manufactured through automated technologies. Thus in recent years Vuitton have equipped their ateliers – a word they seem to prefer to the less craft-like 'factory' – with advanced techniques of production in order to increase productivity and answer the growing demand coming from countries such as China (*L'Usine Nouvelle* 2012).

The automatisation of Vuitton manufacturing led the French magazine *L'Usine Nouvelle* (2012) to headline an article on the company 'Louis Vuitton, the industrialist'. For while the website is keen to associate the brand with the world of craftsmanship and handmade production, as Sicard (2010) observes, the luxury business, like any other business, is driven by the pursuit of profit and therefore mobilises all resources to that effect, including automatisation. Thomas puts it thus: 'Vuitton executives may crow about quality, but the company's focus is obviously on productivity' (2007: 194).

This is also why luxury companies, and French brands in

particular, are often eager to underplay business practices such as marketing, preferring instead to fashion themselves as involved in craft and the arts (Sicard 2005, 2010). Marion talks about luxury companies' 'staging of rarity' (2000: 306). Depicting Vuitton goods as made by hand contributes to this staging. Bruno Remaury cites the words of Veblen to insist on companies' desire to hide their mercantile nature: 'the marks of hand labour come to be honorific, and the goods which exhibit these marks take rank as of higher grade than the corresponding machine product' (Veblen 1994 [1899]: 97, cited in Remaury 2005: 380). Hands signify a 'veneration for the archaic', for a time which pre-dates the industrial era (Remaury 2005: 380, citing Veblen 1994 [1899]: 100), the very era during which, thanks to the concurrent transport revolution, the Louis Vuitton company was able to take off.

Regular references to the arts also help Vuitton to obscure the commercial dimension of their activities, thereby elevating their goods to the level of artworks as opposed to mere commodities. Bourdieu (1993a) has discussed the opposition between the field of art for art's sake and that of mass culture, with the former seen as nobler than the latter. This is why, he argues, fields that are lower in the hierarchy of culture mobilise references to the arts: it allows them to ennoble themselves. On the Vuitton website abundant references to the arts participate in the symbolic production of the brand as a luxury brand, as do the many art events the company organises. Where the website includes a section devoted to 'Art', the Paris flagship store, on the Champs Elysées, dedicates a whole floor to art installations and exhibitions – the 'Espace Culturel', which features on the website too. Both digital and bricks-and-mortar spaces fuel the idea of 'creative process' that the company repeatedly invokes on its website, such as in the section on 'Brand protection', for instance, where an entry is devoted to 'Preserving Creativity'.

The practice of discursively producing commodities is also what is called, in marketing terms, branding, capitalism's new take on commodity fetishism whereby layers of myths and symbols distance goods from the social relations involved in their production (Skoggard 1998: 58; Edensor and Kothari cited in Pike 2011: 16). The Vuitton website is key to this practice of imbuing goods with myths, the myth of craftsmanship and the arts, as mentioned earlier, but also the myth of 'made in France' and that of free movement across borders, as I discuss later. As Calefato argues, 'luxury has become "discourse" . . . replete with myths' (2014: 4).

The Vuitton website is a window; one, however, that is not made of a clear transparent pane allowing one to peer inside an enclosed space and see what is normally hidden from view, but a window similar to that of bricks-and-mortar shops, a highly polished and staged front that places a layer of stylised signs between the viewer and the commodity. Celia Lury (2004) has demonstrated the relevance of Erving Goffman's notion of the frame to branding to argue that a brand can be defined as a frame, that is, following Goffman, in terms of 'principles of organization which govern events – at least social ones – and our subjective involvement in them' (1986 [1974]: 10–11). A frame is both space and process; it is an interface and boundary in which the particular definition of a situation takes place (Lury 2004: 154). In that respect a website can be seen as a frame too, that is, a space or interface where a brand produces itself in a particular way – as a luxury brand, 'made in France', and by hand, in the case of Louis Vuitton.

The Goffmanian notion of region is also useful for conceptualising the role of websites in the construction of a brand's identity. Goffman (1990 [1959]: 45) argues that social interactions are set in two distinct regions: front and back. The former is a space of 'illusions' where 'idealized performances' take place aimed at impressing on 'the audience' a specific definition of an event or situation. It is where 'something that has been finished, polished, and packaged' is put on display (Goffman 1990 [1959]: 52). Back regions are where the 'dirty work', 'the long, tedious hours of lonely labour' unfold (Goffman 1990 [1959]: 52, 53). Mass production and automatisation are the dirty words, and work, of luxury, hidden from view so as to sustain the myth of handmade fashion. On the Vuitton website, a performance is staged, such as the one captured in the close-up of the hands working on a trunk, that aims at reinforcing the illusion that all luxury goods are the product of a timeless craft. This performance is supported by the 'Louis Vuitton Savoir Faire' videos posted on YouTube, where various Vuitton goods are shown made by hand. A caption reads:

> Seven crafts performed by hands outlined by daylight. They stitch the skin of a Speedy bag with beeswax-coated yarn, hollow a pea jacket at the waist, sheath the trunk case of a Wardrobe with a creaser . . . Gestures speak. Instruments confer . . . Bruno Aveillan brings his artist's eye to the House's know-how. (LV 2014a)

Where in high fashion the making of things, labour, is normally hidden from view, kept backstage, Vuitton move it front-stage on their website. It becomes visible labour as a type of labour that serves the interest of the brand in fashioning itself as precious and luxurious. In contrast, mass production is hidden labour.

However, not only do Vuitton draw a veil over processes of production such as automatisation, they also put a veil over the geography of production of goods. The 'World of Louis Vuitton' page, for instance, opens onto 'a legendary history' of the company. It tells 'how it all began' in 'a legendary workshop', the Asnières workshop. '[I]t is still where products are crafted today', the site states, neglecting to mention any other places and spaces where they are made. Significantly, this workshop is also a museum, a front region, like the atelier more generally, of the Louis Vuitton brand.

In contrast, the back regions of Vuitton's geography of production are hidden from view, for while much emphasis is placed on the brand's self-discursive construction in French workshops, and in particular the Asnières one, in reality the company's geography of production is much wider. The production of bags and wallets is dispersed throughout the world (Vulser 2014), with various components made in China and Romania and the bags then assembled in France and labelled 'made in France' (Perceval 2013).

The outsourcing of fashion to low-cost countries has been well documented, with many authors also pointing at the near impossibility of identifying the exact origin of a product in a context of accrued international division of labour (Skoggard 1998; Dickerson 1999: 172). When it comes to luxury brands, authors have found it a challenge to document this division. Thomas, for instance, who observes that one of the main ways luxury companies can 'trim' costs is by using cheap labour, notes how few luxury companies admit to having their goods made in China. A 'Made in China' label rarely appears on a bag, and when it does, it is carefully hidden (Thomas 2007: 203). When the journalist Frédéric Béghin (2011) asked Vuitton about their factories in India and Romania, the company replied: 'Let's talk instead about the twelfth French production site that will open in the Drôme in 2011.'

In the world of luxury 'made in France' is added-value, a discourse French luxury companies have been particularly apt at sustaining, not least in presenting luxury as a French invention, obliterating at the same time the many instances of the production of luxury in other countries and at other historical times (Sicard 2005). In the realm of fashion, France and, in particular, 'Paris' are highly loaded signs, synonymous with fashionability, elegance (see Rocamora 2009) and the 'good taste' which grants one the sense of distinction on which luxury thrives (Bourdieu 1984). Thus the Vuitton website repeatedly capitalises on the French identity of the brand, not least through recurring references to the French capital in both words and images. A promotional film for the Autumn–Winter 2014 shoe collection, for instance, opens onto a photograph of the Eiffel Tower. It is the cover of a look-book whose pages reveal different iconic Parisian places and buildings as backdrops for the staging of the shoes (LV 2014c). In 'The World of Louis Vuitton' section, Asnières, home of the 'legendary workshop', is not referred to as a suburb but as 'just Northeast of the center of Paris'.

Roger Caillois writes that 'Myth belongs by definition to that which is collective. It justifies, supports and inspires the existence and action of a community, of a people, of a profession or a secret society' (2002 [1938]: 154). The Paris myth supports the interest of the fashion profession (Rocamora 2009). Brands such as Louis Vuitton feed on and reproduce it the better to promote their commodities.

The Consumption of Louis Vuitton

Although Louis Vuitton established themselves as a trunk, luggage and handbag brand, in 1998 they opened a ready-to-wear line. It represents only a small percentage of total Vuitton sales but is key to generating media coverage, thereby supporting further sales of bags and luggage (Thomas 2007: 51; Koblin and Schneier 2014).

The website displays 'leather goods', 'ready-to-wear', 'shoes', 'jewellery & timepieces', but not all Vuitton goods are available online and many items can be found in the bricks-and-mortar shops only. This allows the company to maintain control of 'the selected distribution' which is key to the selling of luxury (Marion 2000: 307), and on which the LVMH website insists in a 'selective retailing section'.

The goods available online come in a range of prices albeit in a high bracket: a key pouch is £150; a 'monogram shawl' £335; the 'pégase 55' suitcase costs £2,610 and the men's 'Tambour Volez II' watch £20,800. In some instances, no mention is made of the price, as in the case of the high jewellery collection. Not all the goods can be ordered directly from the website. Instead the site visitor is invited to call a number 'for availability and information'. This is the case, for instance, with the £3,450 'Capucines handbag GM'. The mention of the word 'availability' conjures up the idea of the rarity luxury thrives on by virtue of suggesting that the demand for the good in question may be greater than its supply, for that which is rare but desired by many is key to the logic of luxury (Berry 1994: 32).

Hindman reminds us that 'gates and gatekeepers remain a critical part of the information landscape, even in the Internet age' (2009:

loc. 403). Contra celebratory discourses on the WWW as a land of democracy, a space open to all and a 'digital sublime' (Mosco 2004), gates and boundaries are re-embedded on digital platforms, allowing for the reproduction and maintenance of social hierarchies. In the case of Vuitton, both off- and online, price remains a crucial barrier, with the website reiterating the importance of economic capital in the consumption of luxury goods. Many Internet users may be able to access the site, but fewer will be able to progress past the screen to the goods themselves, in contrast with more affordable e-commerce sites such as Asos or John Lewis where 'add to bag', 'pay now' and 'check out' functions are the norm.

Moreover, in the same way that bricks-and-mortar Vuitton shops have doors that, in theory, are open to all passers-by but, in practice, are akin to barriers accessible to a few only – those confident enough not to self-exclude from the luxurious spaces they enclose and pass by the intimidating doormen that keep them – the Vuitton website too has doors akin to barriers. They are the virtual gates of the 'add to shopping bags' tab that feature next to hefty prices and that one cannot move beyond without a high economic capital. They are also the gates signalled by the 'for availability and information call +44 207 998 6286', a number users need to access if they want to go through with their shopping or simply to find out more about an object, as with the Capucine bag mentioned above. Jones notes that 'In the realm of what we might term "virtual estate", what we now find via the internet are "Gates-ed" communities, ones cordoned off in other ways, by interest and by access' (1999: 16). Similarly, in the realm of online luxury shopping one finds areas that are cordoned off, here by high prices, resulting in the establishment of what Jones calls 'limited-access "electronic communities"' (1999: 16), such as the community of the financially privileged whose high economic capital allows them to navigate freely through all the pages of a luxury website and pass through the price boundary towards check-out. It is a myth that by virtue of being accessible to a wide audience online platforms are democratising, for barriers are constantly reinstated that reaffirm status and distinction (see also Jones 1999). Among them are the economic barriers signalled in the high prices featured on a website such as Vuitton's, and which, as in bricks-and-mortar shops, feed on the logic of exclusion that supports luxury. In the first instance, access to these barriers presumes passage across the 'digital divide' itself, since access to the Internet at all is highly differentiated (see, for instance, Castells 2001; Green 2010).

Louis Vuitton started as a trunk company, and travel is a recurring theme on the website, with a section devoted to it in the 'World of Louis Vuitton'. As mentioned earlier, Berry (1994) singles out travel as 'a subset' of shelter, one of four categories of luxury goods. Similarly Calefato (2014) identifies 'leisure and travel' as luxuries. On the Vuitton website, travel clearly is a luxury. It is constructed as experiential, a 'journey' towards introspection and beauty. It 'is not a trip', as 'The Spirit of Travel' video states, 'It's a process. A discovery' of the self (LV 2014b). Lavish images of dreamlike landscapes, lit-up urban spaces, and individuals in a seemingly meditative spirit are shown interspersed with close-ups of LV-embossed luggage. The consumption of luxury commodities is placed on a higher plane of experience, as a noble, pleasurable and almost necessary pursuit.

However, all travel is not equal and, for many travellers, a journey across space is not a luxury. Indeed, there is, as Bauman notes, a 'global hierarchy of mobility' (1998: loc. 1095; see also Lash and Urry 1994); 'the freedom to move' is 'a scarce and unequally distributed commodity' and a 'stratifying factor' (Bauman 1998: loc. 60). Thus, Bauman makes a distinction between two types of travellers: the tourist and the vagabond. Where the tourist's movement is light, free and unencumbered, that of the vagabond takes place under constraints and the weight of political, economic and social tensions. The tourist, whether on holiday or business, moves freely across boundaries, and is extra-territorialised. The vagabond is under pressure to cross boundaries.

The idea of the disappearance of time and space is one of the myths of globalisation (Ferguson 1992: 74). For most of the population, 'forced territoriality' (Bauman 1998: loc. 393) is the norm. Freedom and ease of movement tend to be the preserve of a 'mobile elite', such as the owners of Vuitton luggage, whose economic capital and privileged social situation allow them to experience, in style, 'the new weightlessness of power' (Bauman 1998: loc. 313). In that respect the doormen at the Vuitton shops I mentioned earlier are also there to ensure that the desirable tourist is let in and the unwanted vagabond is kept out; they are there to enforce, but also to signify, distinction.

LV-signed luggage is both a mark of socio-economic privilege and a testament to the aesthetics of consumption, which, Bauman argues, guides tourism. What matters for the logoed tourist 'is the display of extravagant, even frivolous aesthetic taste' (Bauman 1998: loc. 1501). Witness a staple of celebrity gossip pages: photographs of stars arriving at an airport followed by a heap of LV-embossed luggage, often handled by airport staff. It is easier, it seems, to experience the 'weightlessness of power' (Bauman 1998) when labour is at hand, most likely local, territorialised or deterritorialised, to use

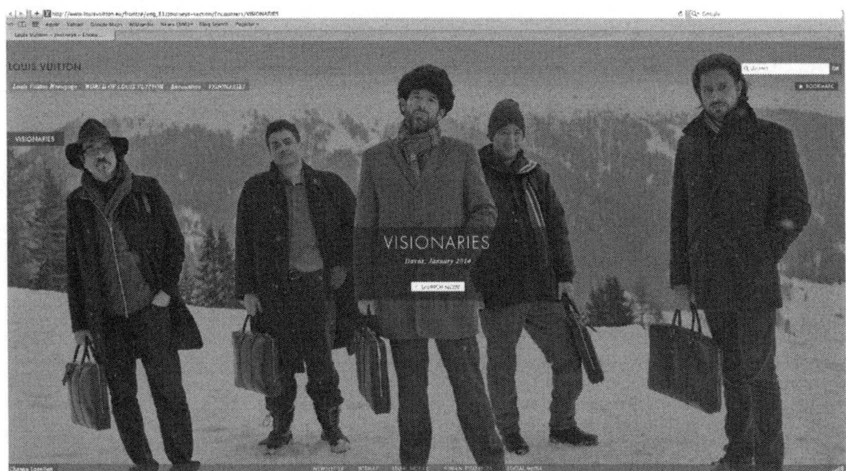

Figure 10.2 The 'Visionaries' as male global elite

Bauman's terminology, to carry the loads of what he calls the exterritorialised tourist. Thus, as Elliott and Urry observe, 'through styling and stylization' and the display of luxury brands such as Bentley, Louis Vuitton or Prada, the global elite 'has become an increasingly well-identified social figure'; 'mobile forms of life', such as the ability 'to be elsewhere', they argue, have become desirable and a key means of accruing prestige and symbolic power (2010: 80).

The mobile elite of Vuitton customers are the professionals the brand features, for instance, in a video entitled 'Visionaries' (LV 2014d). In the opening page five men are shown outdoors at the top of a mountain during the January 2014 Davos Summit (Figure 10.2). All carry a Vuitton porte-documents in an image captioned by 'the art of travel', 'dare to move frontiers' and 'spirit of elegance'. The visionaries are Tom Reiss, the site states, 'an American historian, author and journalist at the New York Times'; Atiq Rahimi, 'a French-Afghan author and movie director' and Prix Goncourt winner; Félix Marquardt, 'Former Director of Communications of the International Herald Tribune' and founder of 'the strategic communications firm Marquardt & Marquardt'; Lourenço Bustani, 'one of Brazil's star entrepreneurs'; and finally Gino Yu, 'Associate Professor and Director of Digital Entertainment and Game Development in the School of Design at PolyU', in Hong Kong. All are part of 'the professional-managerial classes of the advanced societies', which, as Lash and Urry observe, 'are the most footloose' (1994: 29).

In the video they are interviewed, their words reinforcing the myth that time and space have disappeared. The world they describe is free of frontiers, desirable as such or made up of connected individuals. It largely consists of tourists, in Bauman's sense of the term, and seems oblivious to the many for whom movement can only happen under constraints: Reiss argues that 'the books that are being written now ... connect human experiences ... throughout the word but also throughout time'; Marquardt that 'The frontiers of the nation state are disappearing slowly'; Rahimi that 'it's through these waves of immigration, globalization, etc., that little by little frontiers disappear'; Bustani that 'we're part of one global community'; and Yu that 'what entrepreneurship and innovation is really about ... stepping beyond your frontier'.

Significantly all the Vuitton visionaries are men, and most are white, which reproduces existing visions of elite travelling as masculine and gendered, and mostly directed at the 'new bourgeoisie of private sector executives', as Thurlow and Jaworski have shown in their research on airline companies (2006: 207). Thus, to quote Cavanagh again, 'Against the idea of the internet as a smooth space, we have a highly striated one' (2007: 56), striated, in the case of the Vuitton website, along the lines of gender, class and race. To this list can be added body shape and size as well as age, since young, white, tall and thin bodies dominate the brand's digital platform as they do the fashion media landscape more generally. As Heilbrunn reminds us, 'the luxury model derives from a hierarchical model of society and rests on the strength of authority and thus on the implicit idea of a certain form of power of one group over another' (2005: 355). On their website Vuitton do not part from this model. Quite to the contrary, they reproduce it the better to position their goods as luxury goods, excluding from their field of vision and representation figures that do not fit in with the fashion industry's normative gaze. Marion (2000: 300) notes that luxury feeds on exclusion, and this is a logic at play on the Vuitton website.

This is why one cannot but see the inclusion of a Chinese 'visionary' as a strategic move on the part of Louis Vuitton. Until the beginning of the 1980s China was one of the poorest countries in the world along with India, and it remains a very divided nation with a rich minority of very wealthy consumers and a large proportion of poor people (Das 2009). In recent years it has emerged as the leading luxury market. *The Economist* noted in 2014 that 'The number of luxury consumers has more than tripled in under 20 years, to around 330m people. Spending has risen at a similar rate, to an estimated €217 billion ($300 billion) in 2013. Around 130m of these consumers are in emerging markets, and 50m of those in China' (*Economist* 2014). Online media platforms have started documenting this rise, in the process representing China as a land of opportunities for luxury brands. *The Business of Fashion* (BoF), for instance, features a section entitled 'The China Edit', which, the platform states, 'is a weekly curation of the most important fashion business news and analysis from and about the world's largest luxury market'. In November 2014 it launched BoF China, in both English and Chinese. An email was sent to the site's subscribers announcing that 'Today, we are pleased to unveil BoF China, bringing our authoritative, analytical, award-winning journalism to the $300 billion Chinese fashion and apparel market.' Similarly, *China Internet Watch* (2014) headlined a November 2014 entry 'China the Biggest Luxury Goods Buyer Worldwide', while *Jing Daily* (2014), a site devoted to 'The Business of Luxury and Culture in China', tells the reader 'How to get China's Rich to Take up Skiing: Sell the Lifestyle'. Similarly numerous are the business books whose titles sell the idea of China as a nation to capitalise on: *Luxury China: Market Opportunities and Potential*, *Elite China: Luxury Consumer Behavior in China* and *Luxury Brand Marketing in China* are a just few of the many texts that present China as capitalism's new El Dorado.

In the same way that the inclusion of Gino Yu in the Vuitton 'Visionaries' video can be read as a sign of the company's interest in capitalising on the Chinese market, so can its occasional featuring of Chinese models on its website and social media platforms. On 24 November 2014, for instance, of the seventy-four pins included in the 'Louis Vuitton Friends' section of the brand's Pinterest platform, other than the fifty-one white Western friends (well-known models, actresses and other celebrities), one finds black American singer Pharrell Williams, Japanese actress Rinko Kikuchi, Japanese model Ai Tominaga, retired Japanese football player Hidetoshi Nakata, Japanese-Australian actress Shiori Kutsuna, model Lily Kwong, who is of Chinese, Irish and German origins, and Chinese actresses Fan Bing Bing and Sun Li. The brand's interest in both the Japanese and the Chinese markets is clearly articulated.

In July 2012 Vuitton opened their biggest shop in China in Shanghai, and the city features on a map the website shows of Vuitton stores across the world. On this map, the name of each city is taken over by the LV logo, as if the city's name was that of the luxury brand. Persson notes the importance, in digital spaces such as websites, of 'abstracted and highly symbolic objects, such as icons, menus and buttons' (2001: 44). As displayed on the Vuitton digital platform, the LV logo becomes an icon at the service of the company's branding of cities as Louis Vuitton cities (Figure 10.3), of travel destinations as places whose value resides in their quality

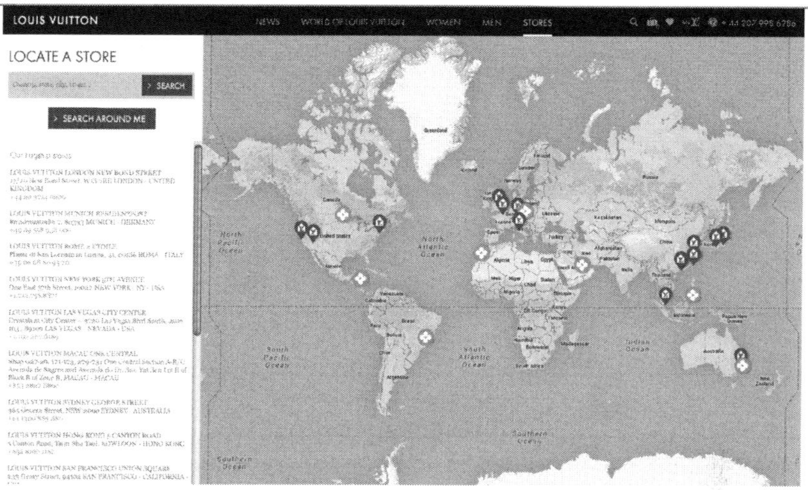

Figure 10.3 Louis Vuitton cities

as luxury shopping destinations, a dimension the brand also emphasises in their recently launched Shanghai travel guide, one of the
guides the brand devotes to cities across the world. There, as in
many tourist guides, shopping is placed alongside activities such
as visiting museums, in a process of commodification of tourism
many authors have documented (see, for instance, Urry 2002). The
promoting and selling of LV monogram luggage also participates in
this commodification.

The map also indicates that Louis Vuitton clusters around certain parts of the world only. The agglomeration of LV signs clearly
displays a centralised core of Louis Vuitton cities located in an axis
spanning North America, Western Europe and East Asia. Similarly,
the 'Choose your location' section of the website lists the following areas: Europe; Americas; Asia; Oceania; Middle East (English);
International (English).

Lash and Urry (1994: 28) make a distinction between core and
periphery whereby the core consists in 'the heavily networked more
or less global cities' and the periphery in 'isolated areas in the same
countries, in the former Eastern Europe or in the Third World'. The
core-periphery distinction reminds us that globalisation does not
follow a symmetrical pattern (Lash and Urry 1994: 28). Although
it has been argued that this distinction no longer holds true (see,
for instance, Das 2009), the geography of consumption of Vuitton
goods, as presented on their website map, intimates that urban hubs
still dominate the geography of luxury consumption, and that when
it comes to luxury goods globalisation certainly is not a symmetrical

process. There are, as Dicken argues, 'persistent peripheries': 'most of the continent of Africa, parts of Asia and parts of Latin America', where poverty and deprivation reigns (2011: 606). These peripheries have not been included in the trajectory of globalisation, with its 'progressive spatial segregation, separation and exclusion' (Bauman 1998: loc. 71), reminding us once again that 'Luxury divides' (Calefato 2014: 36), and it does so in terms of both social and geographical spaces.

Conclusion

The process of inclusion which informs luxury is concurrent with a process of exclusion, for 'the diffusion [of luxury goods] to the whole of the social body would abolish the very notion of luxury' (Marion 2000: 300). In this chapter, I have interrogated the role a brand's website plays in the articulation of the logic of exclusion that fuels luxury, to look at the ways luxury online can obscure dimensions of experience and of the social world that do not serve the interests of commerce and profit. In doing so, I have also drawn attention to some limits of theories of globalisation and digital culture. Internet technology is not inherently all welcoming and inclusive. The technological is social too and as such is only as democratising as its producers and users can allow it to be. David Harvey exhorts us to 'get behind the veil, the fetishism of the market and the commodity, in order to tell the full story of social reproduction' (1990: 423). This process includes paying attention to spaces of articulation of brand identities such as the web sphere, for, like print media, digital media are key to the building of collective imaginaries, to the 'ideoscapes' 'electronic capitalism' creates and feeds on (Appadurai 1998: 8), and in which the luxury industry has carved itself a place.

References

Appadurai, A. (1998), *Modernity at Large*, Minneapolis: University of Minnesota Press.
Barthes, R. (1990), *The Fashion System*, Berkeley: University of California Press.
Baudrillard, J. (1996 [1968]), *The System of Objects*, London: Verso.
Bauman, Z. (1998), *Globalization*, Cambridge: Polity. Kindle iPad edition.
Béghin, F. (2011), 'La fabrication se mondialise dans le plus grand secret'. Available at: http://www.capital.fr/enquetes/dossiers/l-argent-fou-de-

l-industrie-du-luxe-571431/la-fabrication-se-mondialise-dans-le-plus-grand-secret/(offset)/1 (accessed 29 September 2014).

Berry, C. J. (1994), *The Idea of Luxury*, Cambridge: Cambridge University Press.

Bolter, J. D. (2001), *Writing Space*, New York: Routledge.

Bourdieu, P. (1984), *Distinction*, London: Routledge.

Bourdieu, P. (1993a), *The Field of Cultural Production*, Cambridge: Polity.

Bourdieu, P. (1993b), 'Haute couture and haute culture', in *Sociology in Question*, London: Sage, pp. 132–8.

Caillois, R. (2002 [1938]), *Le Mythe et l'Homme*, Paris: Gallimard.

Calefato, P. (2014), *Luxury*, London: Bloomsbury.

Castells, M. (2001), *Internet Galaxy*, Oxford: Oxford University Press.

Cavanagh, A. (2007), *Sociology in the Age of the Internet*, Maidenhead: Open University Press.

Cavender, R. and Kincade, D. H. (2014), 'Leveraging designer creativity for impact in luxury brand management: an in-depth case study of designers in the Louis Vuitton Möet Hennessy (LVMH) brand portfolio', in J. H. Hancock II, V. Manlow, G. Muratovski and A. Person-Smith (eds), *Global Fashion Brands*, Bristol: Intellect, pp. 199–214.

Challenges (2014), 'Luxe: nouveau record de ventes pour LVMH en 2013'. Available at: http://www.challenges.fr/entreprise/20140130.CHA99 10/luxe-nouveau-record-de-ventes-pour-lvmh-en-2013.html (accessed 10 November 2014).

China Internet Watch (2014), 'China the biggest luxury goods buyer worldwide', 21 November. Available at: http://www.chinainternet-watch.com/10733/the-biggest-overseas-luxury-goods-buyer-worldwide (accessed 24 November 2014).

Currah, Andrew (2003), 'The virtual geography of retail display', *Journal of Consumer Culture*, 3 (1): 5–37.

Dallabona, A. (2014), 'Narratives of Italian craftsmanship and the luxury fashion industry: representations of Italianicity in discourses of production', in J. H. Hancock II, V. Manlow, G. Muratovski and A. Person-Smith (eds), *Global Fashion Brands*, Bristol: Intellect, pp. 215–28.

Das, D. K. (2009), *Two Faces of Globalization*, Cheltenham: Edward Elgar.

Dicken, P. (2011), *Global Shift*, 6th edn, London: Sage. Kindle iPad edition.

Dickerson, K. G. (1999), *Textiles and Apparel in the Global Economy*, Upper Saddle River, NJ: Prentice-Hall.

Economist, The (2014), 'Disillusioned hedonist shoppers'. Available at: http://www.economist.com/blogs/schumpeter/2014/02/luxury-goods-market?zid=319&ah=17af09b0281b01505c226b1e574f5cc1 (accessed 20 August 2014).

Elliott, A. and Urry, J. (2010), *Mobile Lives*, Abingdon: Routledge.

Ferguson, M. (1992), 'The mythology about globalization', *European Journal of Communication*, 7 (1): 69–93.

Goffman, E. (1986 [1974]), *Frame Analysis*, Lebanon, NH: Northeastern University Press.

Goffman, E. (1990 [1959]), *The Presentation of the Self in Everyday Life*, London: Penguin.

Green, L. (2010), *The Internet*, Oxford: Berg.

Harvey, D. (1990), 'Between space and time', *Annals of the Association of American Geographers*, 80 (3): 418–34.

Heilbrunn, B. (2005), 'Le Luxe est mort, vive le luxe! Le Marché du luxe a l'aune de la democratisation', in O. Assouly (ed.), *Le Luxe*, Paris: Regard, pp. 353–69.

Hickman, M. (2010), 'The hand-crafted Louis Vuitton bags made on sewing machines'. Available at: http://www.independent.co.uk/life-style/ fashion/news/the-handcrafted-louis-vuitton-bags-made-on-sewing-machines-1982968.html (accessed 2 September 2014).

Hindman, M. (2009), *The Myth of Digital Democracy*, Princeton: Princeton University Press, Kindle iPad edition.

Jing Daily (2014), 'How to get China's rich to take up skiing: sell the lifestyle', 24 November. Available at: http://jingdaily.com/how-to-get-chinas-rich-to-take-up-skiing-sell-the-lifestyle (accessed 24 November 2014).

Jones, S. (1999), 'Studying the Net', in S. Jones (ed.), *Doing Internet Research: Critical Issues and Methods for Examining the Net*, London: Sage, pp. 1–27.

Kendall, L. (1999), 'Recontextualising "cyberspace": methodological considerations for on-line research', in S. Jones (ed.), *Doing Internet Research: Critical Issues and Methods for Examining the Net*, London: Sage: pp. 29–55.

Koblin, J. and Schneier, M. (2014), 'At the end, a new start'. Available at: http://www.nytimes.com/2014/03/06/fashion/Nicolas-Ghesquire-Debuts-Louis-Vuitton-Collection-paris-fashion-week.html?_r=0 (accessed 30 July 2014).

Kozinets, R. V. (2010), *Netnography*, London: Sage.

Landow, G. P. (1997), *Hypertext 2.0*, Baltimore: Johns Hopkins University Press.

Lash, S. and Urry, J. (1994), *Economies of Signs and Space*, London: Sage.

Lipovetsky, G. (2003), 'Luxe eternel, luxe emotionnel', in G. Lipovetsky and E. Roux, *Le Luxe Eternel*, Paris: Gallimard, pp. 13–96.

Lury, C. (2004), *Brands*, Abingdon: Routledge.

L'Usine Nouvelle (2012), 'Louis Vuitton, l'industriel'. Available at: http:// www.usinenouvelle.com/article/louis-vuitton-l-industriel.N155197 (accessed 10 September 2014).

LV (2014a), 'Louis Vuitton savoir faire'. Available at: http://www.youtube. com/watch?v=SYcrN5YU3hQ (accessed 3 November 2014).

LV (2014b), 'The spirit of travel'. Available at: http://uk.louisvuitton.com/ eng-gb/travel/life-is-a-journey (accessed 1 September 2014).

LV (2014c), no title. Available at: http://uk.louisvuitton.com/eng-gb/stories/ women-shoes#/film (accessed 1 September 2014).

LV (2014d), 'Visionaries'. Available at: http://uk.louisvuitton.com/eng-gb/ travel/visionaries# (accessed 25 April 2014).

LVMH (2014), 'Key figures by business group'. Available at: http://www.lvmh.com/investor-relations/lvmh-at-a-glance/key-figures (accessed 12 November 2014).

Marion, G. (2000), 'Objets et marques de luxe', in O. Assouly (ed.), *Le Luxe*, Paris: Regard, pp. 293–317.

Michaud, Y. (2013), *Le Nouveau Luxe*, Paris: Stock.

Mosco, V. (2004), *The Digital Sublime*, Cambridge, MA: MIT Press.

Pasols, P.-G. (2005), *Louis Vuitton*, New York: Abrams.

Perceval (2013), 'Quand le luxe délocalise: la main dans le sac, Vuitton'. Available at: http://fortune.fdesouche.com/307551-quand-le-luxe-delocalise-la-main-dans-le-sac-vuitton (accessed 23 September 2014).

Persson, P. (2001), 'Cinema and computers: spatial practices within emergent visual technologies', in S. R. Munt (ed.), *Technospace*, London: Continuum, pp. 38–56.

Pham, M. T. (2011), 'Blog ambition: fashion, feeling, and the political economy of the digital raced body', *Camera Obscura*, 26 (76): 1–37.

Pike, A. (ed.) (2011), *Brands and Branding Geographies*, Northampton: Edward Elgar.

Remaury, B. (2005), 'L'Objet de Luxe à l'Ere de la reproductivité technique', in O. Assouly (ed.), *Le Luxe*, Paris: Regard, pp. 223–40.

Rocamora, A. (2009), *Fashioning the City*, London: I. B. Tauris.

Rocamora, A. (2011), 'Personal fashion blogs: screens and mirrors in digital self-portraits', *Fashion Theory*, 15 (4): 407–24.

Rocamora, A. (2012), 'Hypertextuality and remediation in the fashion media', *Journalism Practice*, 6 (1): 92–106.

Schneider, S. M. and Foot, A. Kirsten (2005), 'Web sphere analysis', in C. Hine (ed.), *Virtual Methods*, Oxford: Berg, pp. 157–70.

Sekora, J. (1977), *Luxury*, Baltimore: Johns Hopkins University Press.

Sicard, M.-C. (2005), 'Identités et relativisme du luxe', in O. Assouly (ed.), *Le Luxe*, Paris: Regard, pp. 319–37.

Sicard, M.-C. (2010), *Luxe, Mensonges et Marketing*, 3rd edn, Paris: Pearson. Kindle iPad edition.

Skoggard, I. (1998), 'Transnational commodity flows', in A. Brydon and S. Niessen (eds), *Consuming Fashion*, Oxford: Berg, pp. 57–70.

Sombart, W. (1967), *Luxury and Capitalism*, Ann Arbor: University of Michigan Press.

Sudweeks, F. and Simoff, S. J. (1999), 'Complementary explorative data analysis', in S. Jones (ed.), *Doing Internet Research*, London: Sage, pp. 29–55.

Thomas, D. (2007), *Deluxe*, London: Allen Lane.

Thurlow, C. and Jaworski, A. (2006), 'The alchemy of the upwardly mobile: symbolic capital and the stylization of elites in frequent-flyer programmes', *Discourse & Society*, 17 (1): 99–135.

Turkle, S. (1995), *Life on the Screen*, New York: Simon and Schuster.

Urry, J. (2002), *Consuming Places*, London: Routledge.

Veblen, T. (1994 [1899]), *The Theory of the Leisure Class*, London: Dover.
Vulser, N. (2014), 'Dans la maroquinerie de luxe, les délocalisations sont moins fréquentes'. Available at: http://www.lemonde.fr/economie/article/2014/04/08/dans-la-maroquinerie-de-luxe-les-delocalisations-sont-moins-frequentes_4397520_3234.html (accessed 3 September 2014).

Index

EU Authorised Representative:

Easy Access System Europe Mustamäe tee 50, 10621 Tallinn, Estonia

gpsr.requests@easproject.com

Printed and bound by CPI Group (UK) Ltd, Croydon, CR0 4YY

13/05/2025

01869399-0001